WARNING

Sophie Cunningham has worked variously as an editor, publisher and journalist since 1989. She was editor of *Meanjin* from 2008 to 2010 and until recently was Chair of the Literature Board of the Australia Council. She is the author of *Melbourne* (2010) and the novels *Geography* (2004) and *Bird* (2008).

SOPHIE CUNNINGHAM

WARNING

THE STORY OF CYCLONE TRACY

TEXT PUBLISHING MELBOURNE AUSTRALIA

textpublishing.com.au

The Text Publishing Company
Swann House
22 William Street
Melbourne Victoria 3000
Australia

First published in 2014 by The Text Publishing Company

Cover and page design by W. H. Chong
Typeset in Granjon 12/16 by J & M Typesetting
Map by Guy Holt
Index by Richard McGregor

Printed in Australia by Griffin Press, an Accredited ISO AS/NZS 14001:2004 Environmental Management System printer

Author: Cunningham, Sophie, 1963- author.
Title: Warning : Cyclone Tracy / by Sophie Cunningham.
ISBN: 9781922079367 (paperback)
9781921961526 (ebook)
Subjects: Cyclone Tracy, 1974.
Cyclone Tracy, 1974—Personal narratives.
Cyclones—Northern Territory—Darwin.
Natural disasters—Northern Territory—Darwin.
Darwin (N.T—History—1972-1975.
Dewey Number: 994.295

FSC
www.fsc.org
MIX
Paper from responsible sources
FSC® C009448

This book is printed on paper certified against the Forest Stewardship Council® Standards. Griffin Press holds FSC chain-of-custody certification SGS-COC-005088. FSC promotes environmentally responsible, socially beneficial and economically viable management of the world's forests.

This book is dedicated to all those who went through Cyclone Tracy and the wild times thereafter.

CONTENTS

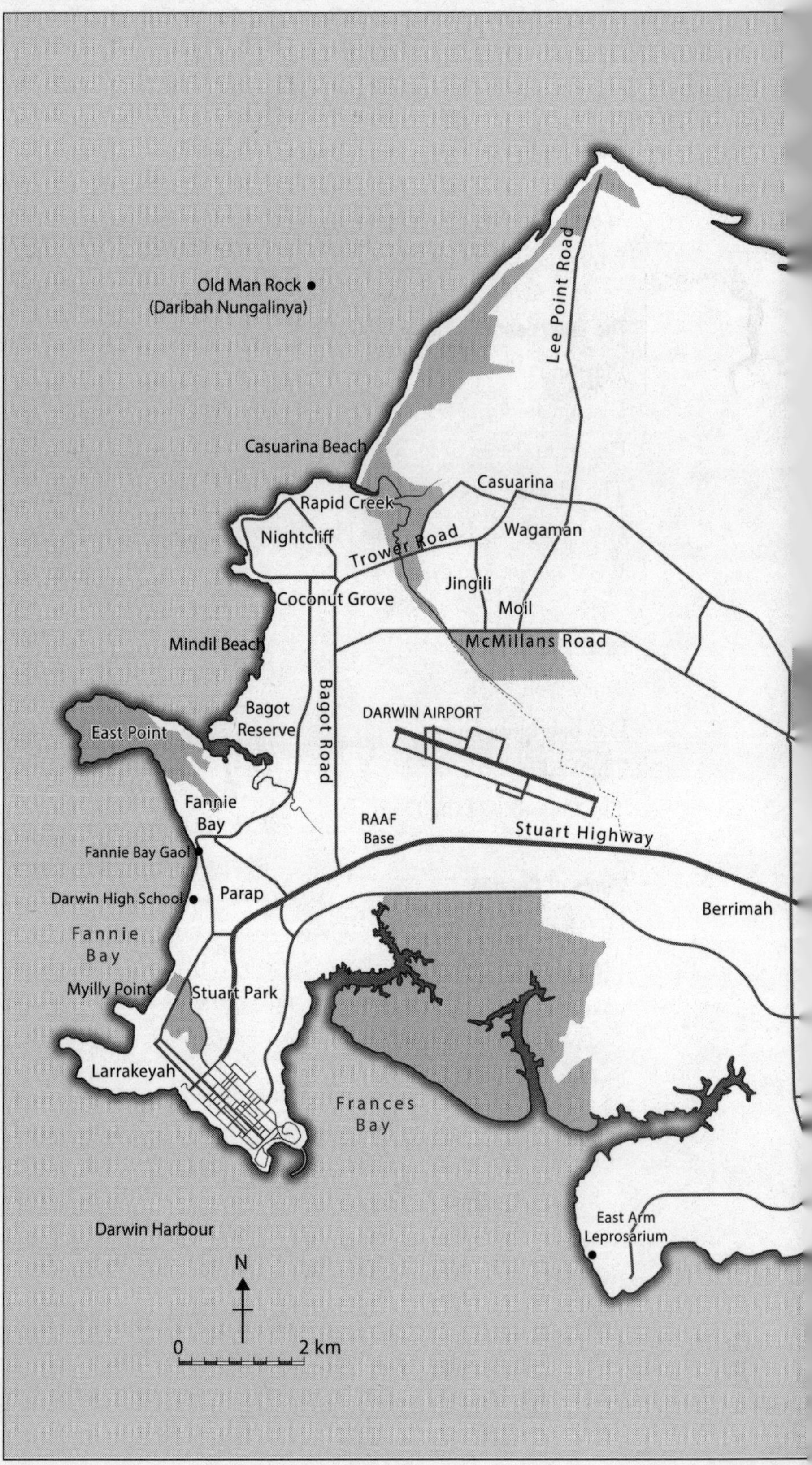
Old Man Rock
(Daribah Nungalinya)
Lee Point Road
Casuarina Beach
Casuarina
Rapid Creek
Nightcliff
Trower Road
Wagaman
Jingili
Moil
Coconut Grove
Mindil Beach
McMillans Road
Bagot Reserve
Bagot Road
DARWIN AIRPORT
East Point
Fannie Bay
RAAF Base
Stuart Highway
Fannie Bay Gaol
Darwin High School
Parap
Berrimah
Fannie Bay
Myilly Point
Stuart Park
Larrakeyah
Frances Bay
East Arm Leprosarium
Darwin Harbour
N
0
2 km

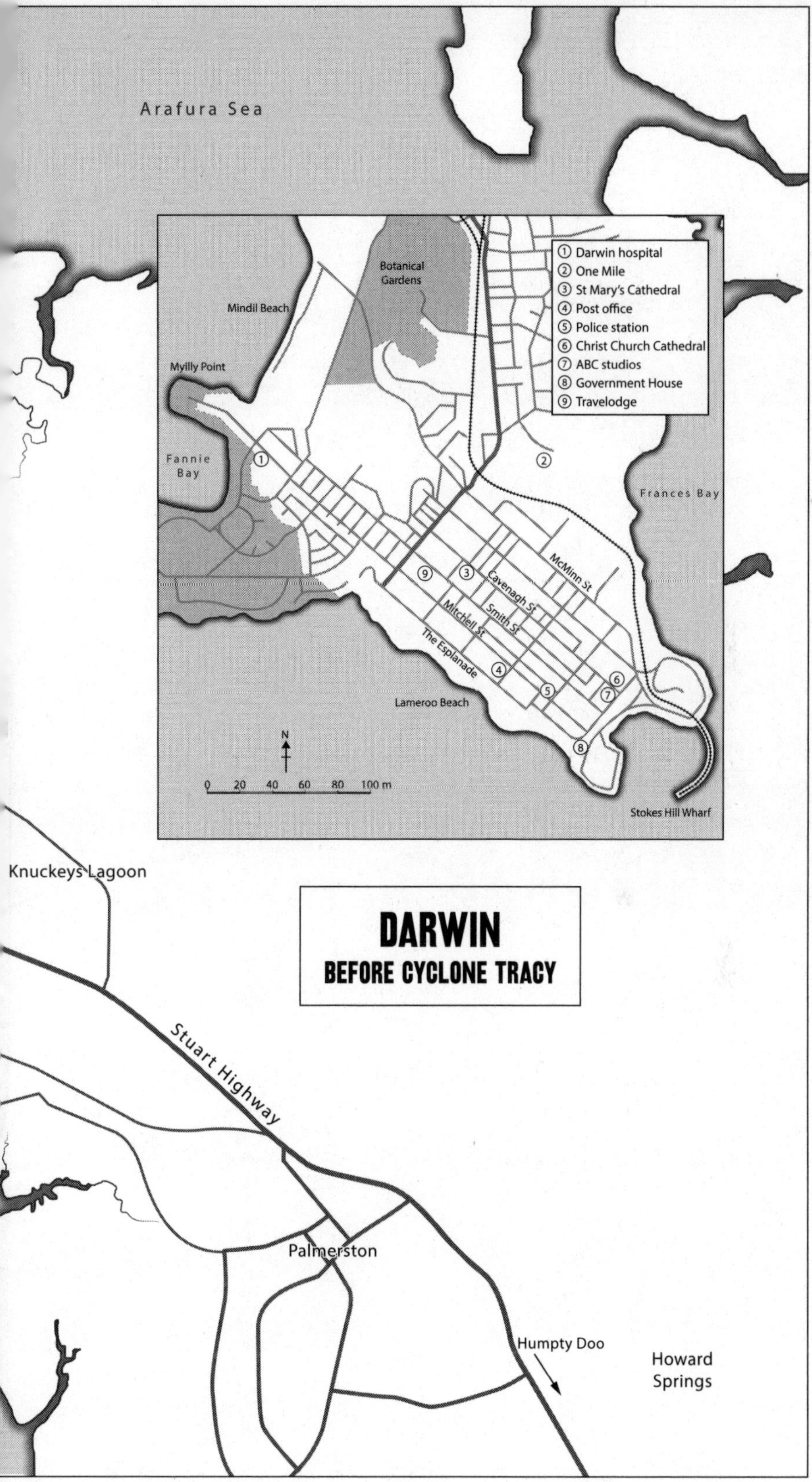

Arafura Sea
Botanical Gardens
Mindil Beach
Myilly Point
Fannie Bay
Frances Bay
① Darwin hospital
② One Mile
③ St Mary's Cathedral
④ Post office
⑤ Police station
⑥ Christ Church Cathedral
⑦ ABC studios
⑧ Government House
⑨ Travelodge
McMinn St
Cavenagh St
Smith St
Mitchell St
The Esplanade
Lameroo Beach
N
0 20 40 60 80 100 m
Stokes Hill Wharf
Knuckeys Lagoon
DARWIN
BEFORE CYCLONE TRACY
Stuart Highway
Palmerston
Humpty Doo
Howard Springs

WARNING

PROLOGUE

IT'S A steamy tropical night. The sky is glowing slightly, an eerie green. There is lightning all around and the wind is wild. Bernard Briec is only ten and has lived in Darwin for five years; Colleen D'Arcy is forty-three and has been in the Territory for thirty. They are singing together in the St Mary's Cathedral choir, to celebrate midnight mass on Christmas Eve.

This is a modern church, built in 1962 using white stone carved from local cliffs. It has the light-filled simplicity typical of tropical churches and there are louvres set high among the eaves. Bernard and Colleen find they are having to sing louder than usual this evening, straining to make their voices heard over the shriek of the wind, the pelting rain, the restless congregation.

Colleen nearly didn't make it into the church at all. The wind buffeting her VW Beetle made it almost impossible to open, then close, its doors once she arrived. Bernard was already there, standing at the back. Too small to see over the balcony, he could still tell things were amiss. Soon the power went out and the organ fell silent. There were gasps and murmurs, but the choir kept singing. Nuns moved quickly to fetch candles. The flickering flames were pretty, adding to the atmosphere, but the wind kept blowing them out. Then there was the crash of the high louvres exploding, the tinkle of glass falling to the ground. Bishop O'Loughlin, who'd become increasingly unsure about the wisdom of holding mass at all, rapidly wound things up. 'Go home,' he said, 'and look after yourselves.' Another priest, Ted Collins, left the church but was soon forced to take shelter in St John's College, where he made a recording of the wind, the wild scraping of corrugated iron. St Mary's survived the night (so did the tape), but its sister cathedral, Christ Church, was reduced to rubble less than an hour after midnight mass was called to a close. All that was left of that stone church, which dated from 1917, was a porch.

Getting home was no easy task. Colleen headed off in her Beetle, while Bernard, who was with family and friends, took off in a convoy of cars that headed for Myilly Point just down the road. This was where most senior public servants lived, high on the cliffs in houses on stilts that looked out over the Arafura Sea. The group stopped briefly, so a friend could nick into his house to grab a camera, but getting in and out of the house seemed to take him forever. It also took a very long time to drive the ten kilometres to the suburb of Moil because the rain was so heavy Bernard's dad couldn't see out the windscreen. He steered by hugging the gutter the whole way, hitting it lightly from time to time and allowing it to nudge him in the right direction.

It was very late when they got to the house where the party was. But they were celebrating Christmas in the European style, and Christmas Eve was the big night, so the kids ran around the house and everyone ate. The wind and rain got wilder all the while. When things became so loud that it seemed time to find cover, everyone headed for the bathroom: semi-regular cyclone warnings had emphasised that the smallest rooms were the strongest. When they opened the bathroom door, they saw a wall of the bathroom had vanished. Their host assured them that the garage he'd just built was safe, so that's where they tried next. They opened the door to the garage to find that, too, had blown away.

My childhood in Melbourne was defined, in part, by the build-up to Christmas Day and the long summers that followed it. But I can't remember much of what actually happened most Christmas Days and I certainly can't remember what I was doing on Christmas Eve 1974. I was the same age as Bernard Briec, which means a bit too old to want to catch Santa in the act, but young enough to feel the thrill of impending presents. I know my parents would have tried to get me to bed early to compensate somehow for the fact I'd be waking at dawn. I would have been in my bed for several hours by the time Bernard squeezed under a bed with four women and numerous children in an attempt to stay safe—unable to move at all because they were so tightly squeezed together that if he rolled, he'd squash the baby that was jammed up against him. The rain was coming in everywhere, then he heard men shouting, 'The roof is gone,' and one of the boys under the bed with him started yelling, 'We're all going to die.' The sound of the thunder was constant, the sky was roaring.

While my mum and dad were drinking a claret or three and wrapping our presents, Bernard's dad probably watched what Bernard reckons must have been half of Darwin flying overhead. But he doesn't know, he'll never know, because his father won't talk about it. For twenty years (it was twenty years later that Bernard told his tale) his father wouldn't speak of what happened that night. It was, Bernard said to Francis Good, the man who interviewed him in 1994, the longest night of his life.

It wasn't till dawn—around the time I was jumping on my parents to wake them up—that Bernard was allowed to crawl out from under the bed. When he saw what remained of Darwin it seemed as if a nuclear blast had hit the city. He thought everyone other than his family and friends must be dead. He thought his world had ended.

Now this I can remember, as clearly as if it were yesterday: on Boxing Day 1974, which was my eleventh birthday, I walked down the driveway of my suburban Melbourne home to pick up the paper. The *Age*, tightly rolled to get it in the mail slot, took a minute or so to open out. Once I'd managed it, I stood trying to make sense of the photo before me: an image, from almost four thousand kilometres to the north, of flattened piles of rubble and twisted pieces of corrugated iron.

That photo has haunted me to such an extent that here I am, writing this book, almost forty years later. I can't tell you why it shocked me so deeply, but it was to do with Cyclone Tracy hitting at Christmas—*Christmas*—and all those kids missing out on their toys. It was also to do with the realisation that a city could do what Darwin did. It could disappear overnight.

But despite the powerful effect that image had on me, when I returned to those newspapers—on microfiche, in Victoria's State Library—some thirty-eight years later, I found that my recollection was incorrect. The cover of the *Age* that Boxing Day was not a photo but an illustration of a map of Australia with a satellite photo laid over it, so we could see Cyclone Tracy's dense swirls hovering off Australia's northern coast. The photo that I remember was on the cover of the *Age* two days later, on Saturday 28 December 1974. Memory is a slippery thing.

These are the bare bones of it: around midnight on Christmas Eve, 1974, a cyclone hit Darwin. Around seventy-one people died, hundreds more were injured and seventy per cent of the homes of Darwin's 47,000 inhabitants were laid waste. That left only five hundred residences habitable out of some twelve thousand. Every single public building was destroyed or seriously damaged. While the loss of life was limited, the material damage was unparalleled. The population of Darwin endured winds that some believe reached three hundred kilometres per hour. In the week after Tracy, close to thirty thousand people were airlifted out of the ruined town in what remains Australia's biggest evacuation effort. Many of them never returned. The damage bill has been estimated at between 800 million and 1.3 billion dollars, which is the equivalent of 6.1 billion[1] today. This, set against the town's relatively small population means it still ranks as one of the world's most costly disasters.

The damage was contained, comprehensive and explicitly material: Tracy wiped out a city. Perhaps this is why it has become Australia's most iconic catastrophe, even if not its worst. When floodwaters swamped the Queensland town of Grantham on 10 January 2011, Tracy was the first point of reference. The late Paul Lockyer, the ABC journalist who arrived in the town the morning after the deluge hit, stood in the rain surrounded by swirling water and debris and said:

> My best parallel comparison would be Cyclone Tracy 1974. The houses here are better built than they were in Darwin but this wall of water that's come down from Toowoomba and lightning just striking over me now is, had caused, there's some thunder, has caused as much damage as Cyclone Tracy did to that community I can tell you...And a bit like Cyclone Tracy when day dawned on Christmas Day in 1975 [sic] we waited for the worst and that's what's going to happen here, I fear.[2]

*

I don't know exactly what I expected to find on the second floor of a fairly drab green brick building in Cavenagh Street, Darwin, when I arrived back in the dry season of 2011. That is where the Northern Territory Archives lived back then, and I was running late for my appointment with an archivist. Parking in the centre of Darwin was nightmarish but parking a long way away means you turn up for meetings red-faced and sweaty. Françoise Barr, the archivist who I was to meet, was elegance itself. A French woman who's lived in Darwin for some thirty-four years, she had the job of helping me trawl through all the listings and to figure out where I could start. She sat me down at the computer and off I went.

There were dozens of government reports, of personal collections of photos and clippings. Boxes piled high could have been (and were) brought to me on a trolley for weeks on end. There were hundreds of oral histories and I started ordering them up in impossible numbers. I read people like Richard Creswick, Hedley Beare, Bill Wilson and Curly Nixon, I met Colleen D'Arcy and Bernard Briec. These people, who now feel like friends, brought the cyclone and all that followed alive for me. Although I also interviewed many people myself, most of the interviews within these pages come from these archives. My debt to all the interview participants, and to the Northern Territory Archives, is immense.

It was towards the end of that first visit that Françoise suggested I look at the Commissioner of Police reports written by officers about their personal experiences. These reports had been commissioned in case there were questions about the ability of the police to do their work in the days and weeks that followed. And it was there, in the plain, blunt, unemotional language of men like Detective Sergeant Thomas Baker, that I really got a sense of what it might have been like for the people of Darwin. These reports, unadorned and uncrafted, had cyclonic force.

> On opening the bathroom door, I saw that the roof was off that part of the house and when I opened the door the ceiling of the room also disappeared; we then went to the toilet which was next door to the bathroom and as I opened the door, I saw the outside wall of the toilet disappear; I then went to the main bedroom of the house and saw that the outside wall had disappeared and that the side walls of the room were moving under the pressure of the wind...My wife and I attempted to hold the bathroom and toilet doors shut and we placed our two children between our bodies to protect them.[3]

And that, in short, is what happened. People confronted an unimaginable force of nature with only their bodies to protect themselves and their children. Everything else: roofs, furniture, walls, birds, trees, gardens, meaning.

All that disappeared.

Notions of apocalypse have nagged away at me for years, exacerbated, perhaps, by a three-month trip to Sri Lanka soon after the Southeast Asian tsunami of 2004. Sri Lanka's ancient cities Polonnaruwa and Anuradhapura have long given mute testimony that cities can indeed rise then disappear; and of course I was surrounded by more recent signs of devastation. There was much talk about the fact that people who lived by the beach but had only moved there recently hadn't known how to read the signs: hadn't known that the moment when the sea collapsed back in on itself, leaving beaches bare and sea life floundering, was when they should run. Instead, racing down the beach to gather up stranded fish, they ran into the mouth of the wave.

After the Black Saturday bushfires in Victoria back in 2009, these feelings became even harder to shake. I reread *Tracy*, a book by

Gary McKay published a few years ago. I found myself talking to the mother of a friend about how, at nineteen, she'd gone to Darwin for a holiday over Christmas in 1974 and ended up sheltering in the wine cellar of the Victoria Hotel with a group of strangers; her sense of bewilderment when she finally emerged. I sought out Neville Barwick for a conversation—Canberra sent him to Darwin shortly after Tracy—and he described to me the way the buildings rattled and rattled as the wind blew until they simply 'unzipped'. I read a series of articles written by Tony Clifton, essays that described Darwin as the broken-jaw capital of the world, a spoilt and rotten place. I read Adrian Hyland's *Kinglake-350*, a book about those disastrous 2009 bushfires, in which he also wrote of the findings of the 1939 commission into Black Friday. The way in which the lessons learned are forgotten once the trauma has passed:

> Sometimes, through sheer intelligence or perhaps because of the emotions generated in a jurist who has peered into the abyss, there are flashes of wisdom. Justice Leonard Stretton, who headed the 1939 Royal Commission, coined one such insight with the comment: 'They had not lived long enough.' He meant that his fellow Australians were living in an environment into which they had not had time to evolve...More miles on the clock we well may have, but our cultural awareness of the environment has not kept pace. Some would argue that it is slipping backwards.[4]

Quotes leap out at me as if highlighted whenever I read. 'We speak about the weather / because in truth it tells us what is within us,' Kevin Brophy told me, in a poem. Then, from Patrick White's *The Eye of the Storm*: 'If only you could describe your storm; but you could not. You can never convey in words the utmost in experience. Whatever is given you to live, you alone can live, and re-live, till it is gasped out of you.'[5]

In Alexis Wright's *Carpentaria* it is the dogs who bear witness to the ruination of human civilisation:

> He was met by the bony, hollow-ribbed, abandoned dogs of the town that had run to the hills and back again after the cyclone. Now, having appeared from nowhere, they roamed along streets that no longer existed, searching for their owners. They did not bark or howl. The shock of the cyclone had left them like this: speechless, dumbfounded, unable to crack a bark. Unable to emit a sound out of their wide-opened mouths.

But perhaps my biggest motivation is the fact that the human race is transforming the land, the seas and the weather. There are signs of that all around us, and in a country that already tended to extremes of drought, flood and bushfire we are now facing a world where there will be more calamities more often and larger numbers of us will be affected. There is a line in the Yolngu language of northeast Arnhem Land, *Wä ngam ngarra marrtji buma ngarra dhuwal*, which translates as: 'I create different places as I travel.' In another version, the line is: 'I make this place as I go' and it is true, we are doing this: we are making this place as we go. I want to understand somehow, what it is we are making.

THE EMERGENCY

WARNING

THE SKY at the Top End is big and the weather moves like a living thing. You can hear it in the cracking air when there is an electrical storm and as the thunder rolls around the sky. It's a kind of call and response cycle which brings to mind a story—that cyclones are crocodiles thrashing and fighting through the air: roiling storm clouds moving with intent. It's a dance of sorts, a constant movement between cold and hot air, between high and low pressure.

Cyclones need sea temperatures of 26.5 degrees Celsius or above to form, because that's the temperature at which water vapour turns to cloud. This means that cyclones tend to form towards the equator. Systems that form on the north side of the equator spin anticlockwise and are called hurricanes. Those that form on the south side spin clockwise and become cyclones. If the cyclone forms in the tropics it becomes known as a tropical cyclone. When a low-pressure system moves into this area it begins to warm, causing it to rise, pulling clouds into it as it lifts. The system becomes denser and denser with moisture. The faster the air heats, the quicker it rises and this creates an updraft. It is the air rushing in towards the middle, sucked in by the updraft, that forms the devastating winds of the cyclone and it's this central column that becomes the eye. The more extreme the temperatures—the hotter the high air, the colder the low—the more unstable the system: the higher the velocity of the winds, the wilder the rain, the greater the rotation of the clouds. The energy of the rising air produces enough momentum to move a weather system but how fast it might move, and what path it might take, are hard to foresee. This was certainly the case with Tracy. But of course sometimes a system loses momentum altogether and dissipates. All these elements make predicting cyclones a difficult art.

Tracy—unformed and unnamed—began her life in the northern hemisphere, which had had its coldest winter for a decade. Freezing air had massed low over Siberia in early December and then this low-pressure system had moved heavily, slowly, towards the equator. Some time on 19 December, northeast of Bathurst Island, above the warm Arafura Sea, the dance between temperature and pressure began in earnest.

By 21 December the low-pressure system was only 220 kilometres away from Darwin, but then it stopped moving and sat, heavy in the sky, brooding. It was officially powerful enough to be described as a cyclone and it had a name: Tracy. Early on Christmas Eve Tracy suddenly turned ninety degrees southeast, towards Darwin. This took some by surprise and led others to assume it would make another dramatic turn before it actually hit the town.

Judging a cyclone's movements was such an inexact science that early on Christmas Eve Ray Wilkie, who was thirty-nine years old and the Director of the Bureau of Meteorology, was worried he was making too much of things. 'I could see on the bunting on the service station, a little bit of wind just moving them. That's how gentle it was. And then this slight bit of high cloud coming in, just a bit of high cirrus.' Tracy was so small and slow moving 'you could have walked a quick walk and kept up with it'.[1] And it stayed small. At its height Tracy's eye was twelve kilometres wide and the winds spiralled out for about forty. In comparison, Hurricane Katrina was a massive 644 kilometres wide when it made landfall in 2005. But the fact Tracy was slow meant that once it hit, it stayed. And stayed. And stayed.

When people talk about their childhoods in 1970s Darwin, you get some idea of why it was a good place to grow up. Ten-year-old Bernard Briec had come with his family from Senegal, via France, arriving in Darwin in 1969. After school: 'I came home, took my shirt off, took my shoes and socks off and went running around the place barefoot. Used to go down to Rapid Creek on McMillans Road, and we used to go swimming in the waterholes there, in the creek there...Life was very good.'[2]

These days Julia Church is an artist who lives in Canberra but when she was a kid she too lived in Darwin. Her parents, immigrants from the UK, moved to Darwin in 1971 after a brief stint in Sydney. For her father, 'Darwin was a dream come true'[3] and his dream was of a 'working person's utopia'. Julia, eleven when they arrived, says that the whole family immediately felt at home.

> It was a very romantic place, an amazing place. It felt as if it was a new community we were building. Because it was small people managed to do a lot when they got there... Back then there was a lot more untouched bush. The bush was closer. Crocs helped maintain that feeling of the power of the natural world that might creep back in. The beautiful gardens were tropical and wild and misbehaved. In your

> garden you had wildlife from fruit bats to frill-neck lizards: It was rich and smelly, a cacophony of sound.

But there was a darker side to Darwin, as there had been since white settlement. In the 1970s it held the world record for per capita alcohol consumption. It was the 'hardest-drinking town in the world',[4] as ABC journalist Mike Hayes put it in a twenty-fifth anniversary special put together by ABC-TV's *7.30 Report*. Seventy per cent of the workforce were public servants, and many of them had been in Darwin for less than two years. They tended to be under thirty-five, and there were more men than women. People came and they went, but the recent election of the Whitlam Labor government after twenty-three years of Coalition rule meant there was an even higher turnover than usual. The exception, according to Ray McHenry, who was first assistant secretary in the Department of the Northern Territory, was 'a core population in Darwin of some 8000, who would truly be described as Darwinians. Persons of Aboriginal descent make up a large section of that core group.'[5] There were close to 2500 Indigenous people living in Darwin at that time. Some of them were Larrakia and some were from the stolen generation. The total population was about 47,000.

In 1974 ABC journalist Richard Creswick was twenty-seven and new to Darwin. Interviewed fourteen years after the cyclone, he was blunt about the advantages of his posting: 'It was a quick way—a two-year way—of getting a promotion that might take many more years in the older cities.'[6] Ken Frey, who'd worked for the Department of Works and Housing in the Territory for close to thirty years, put it this way:

> We lived in a younger community; there were very, very few old people here at all. All the older people from Darwin had been moved out during the war; not that many of them

> actually came back...Every two to three years there'd be a great dearth of many people in the public service—and privately—and there'd be a great inroad of new people coming in. And so you found it difficult, in many cases, to develop very close friendships, and things like this.[7]

Some ten thousand people got out of town for Christmas that year as they always did, and many of those remaining didn't really understand the damage a bad cyclone could do. Only a few had lived through the last big cyclone, which had blown through in 1937. Tom Baird, an Indigenous man who was born in 1923, had. It left him feeling that newcomers just didn't get it. 'Some of them said, "We'll go down the beach and watch the cyclone come in"...They didn't actually believe what the old timers used to say about how devastating the cyclones could be.' But he also acknowledges that no one really expected a cyclone as bad as this one. With gusts as high as 250–275 km/h, Tracy was a severe Category 4. Gusts over the Cox Peninsula may have been more than 325 km/h (that is, Category 5), while at Nightcliff and East Point, which were a few kilometres out of the centre of Darwin along the coast, the winds were more like 250–290 km/h. 'We had no idea ourselves that the cyclone would be as bad as Trace or anything like that.'[8]

Other than Indigenous people, it was mainly Darwin's Chinese population who could date their connection with the place back for any period of time—a century in some cases. They knew a bad wind when they felt it. Lily Ah Toy, who lived a couple of hundred kilometres down south in Pine Creek, felt the build-up from down there: 'The wind was jerky, this went on for days and my in-laws—my mother-in-law said, "Now, this wind is not good, it's no good at all it's been jerking for days."'[9]

Old-timer Curly Nixon, who'd lived in Darwin since 1949, was cautious also. While he hadn't weathered a major cyclone himself, some of his friends had. 'Old Snowy was living here…I took notice of him…and I put six-inch nails into my roof and tied everything down that I couldn't put under cover.' Jack Meaney had lived through five cyclones. 'You could almost feel it. If you've been through a cyclone, everything sort of dies before it comes along; the calm before the storm they call it.'[10]

Of course, some newcomers also had an understanding of what weather could do. Journalist Barbara James had grown up in tornado country in the States so she took the warnings seriously. So did fifty-four-year-old Charles Gurd, Darwin's Director of Health. He'd lived in Fiji and his wife had once been shipwrecked during a cyclone, so he knew exactly how bad things could get. Soon after he arrived in Darwin in 1972 he'd put a plan in place for Darwin hospital that assessed which buildings would be safest should a cyclone hit, and established procedures for handling mass casualties should they occur.

Some old-timers, on the other hand, maintained a carefree attitude based on the view that Bathurst and Melville Islands would protect them from cyclones. Historically there was some truth to this, but Cyclone Tracy was to break all the rules. Dentist Howard Truran had lived in Darwin for twenty years. 'They used to have a habit of coming around Bathurst and Melville Island and sort of being stationary, like Tracy was. And then they would sort of veer off down the west coast.'[11]

Ida Bishop, a woman in her late forties who'd been born in Darwin, worked for a shipping company called Northern Research. She had twelve prawning vessels to take care of, which meant she took cyclone warnings very seriously. She remembers discussing the possibility of the cyclone with her boss, Nao Nakamura. 'I said to him: "I don't like today…There's something dreadful going to happen."'[12] Nakamura called her fanciful but Bishop's concerns persisted. 'There was no sound of a bird. There was always "whoo-hoo" and things going on, but there was this ominous quiet. And the heat. And it just made me feel creepy. I thought: "There's something going to happen."'

Vicki Harris said as much to her friend Fay. 'I've got this funny feeling,' she said; she'd been saying something similar to her husband for weeks already: 'Something dreadful's going to happen, I can just feel something's going to happen'.[13] Harris was only twenty-two at the time but when she was interviewed almost thirty years later she remembered that the clouds were high and strange. The sky, as someone else put it, was 'purple and green and everything it shouldn't be'.

It was midday on Christmas Eve when Len Garton, a fifty-six-year-old insurance assessor who'd lived in the Territory since 1941, actually saw the thing. He was sitting in an office at Mudginberri Station, about 250 kilometres east of Darwin, and everything went dark. He walked outside and saw 'a black velvet cloud hanging down from twenty [or] thirty thousand feet to almost ground level'.[14] It was rolling, or pulsing, at the same time.

At the Bureau of Meteorology, Ray Wilkie began placing calls to let people know Tracy was on the way. Gurd got his call and the hospital staff began their preparations with some trepidation. They had 237 patients to look after that night, and several babies on the way. Cyclone warnings started appearing hourly on the ABC, the announcements recorded by broadcaster Don Sanders himself because he wanted to shake people up a bit, make sure they weren't just hearing the same old voice and therefore assuming it was business as usual. Sanders was fifty and had a classic ABC voice: rich and calming. He told people to check their transistors, batten down their houses, remove pictures from walls and ornaments from tables. He suggested sheltering under beds and tables, filling the bath with water.

He was right to be worried that these warnings would be ignored.

They usually were, partly because they were so frequent: every wet season there were around twelve warnings or so. Three weeks before Tracy there were warnings that the city would be hit by a cyclone called Selma, which petered out at the cost of a few trees and some minor injuries—Beth Harvey almost miscarried when Selma's sirens started up. This made it even more likely than usual that people wouldn't fuss much about this latest alert. As Kate Cairns, a woman who'd lived in Darwin for four years, put it, 'We'd been told to batten down so many times before and nothing had really happened and—you can't live in a battened-down situation.'[15] Others commented that there were so many cyclone warnings it was like 'crying wolf'. When Dr Ella Stack, who would become mayor within a few months of Tracy, spoke to the *7.30 Report*, she put it this way: 'In the ten years '64 to '74, there were twenty-five major cyclones in our area—twenty-five that were named. So it's not that you get blasé about it, but, you know, they so rarely strike that you're most surprised when they sort of hit you.'

Beth Harvey's husband Pete worked at the weather bureau so she was better informed than most. Earlier that day she'd got a call from him saying: 'Tell the ladies [at playgroup] they'd better get their cooking done today 'cause they won't have any power tomorrow... And by the way, Ray Wilkie's not going to any Christmas parties... he's not even going to have a beer, so it's serious.'[16] Beth had known people who'd gone through cyclones in Townsville, which added to her nervousness. She spent many hours trying to convince her friends not to shrug the warnings off.

The 1986 miniseries *Cyclone Tracy* depicted the citizens of Darwin as complacent (and Darwin's meteorologist as incompetent, though there is no suggestion that was, in fact, the case) and the story that tropical laissez faire was Darwin's main problem is a persistent one.

Surveys done after Cyclone Tracy suggest that about a third of those who heard the warnings did nothing at all.[17] Around ten per cent had, like the workers at the hospital, some kind of cyclone protocol to follow, about sixteen per cent made serious attempts to strengthen their houses. The rest did a few bits and pieces or nothing at all. So: despite the fact that cyclone warnings were going out over the radio every hour, some twenty-five warnings in all, most people did little more than make a few low-key allowances such as walking the dogs earlier than usual, cleaning up the yard and putting water in the bath.

The fact Cyclone Tracy hit on Christmas Eve made people even less responsive. 'It will not happen to me' syndrome, as it's called, joined, in a devastating fashion, with Christmas celebrations and the general sense that only good things happen at this time of year. Jim Bowditch, a former editor of the *Northern Territory News*, was a man described as 'a Character, though that should probably be written as CHARACTER. After a few drinks Bowditch was capable of firing the entire newsroom, without preamble or explanation'.[18] He was interviewed just a few months after the cyclone and he was refreshingly frank on the subject.

> I was pretty sloshed when Tracy was moving in on Darwin, because with some thousands of other Darwin people I was celebrating at a normal Darwin Christmas-eve party, which were always pretty boozy, and I was boozing with printers. Anyone who knows printers knows what that means...I, with a lot of others at the party, had listened to the warnings of the approach of Tracy and, as with most other people, I ignored them.[19]

In his book *The Furious Days*, published only a year or so after Tracy, Major-General Alan Stretton (appointed by Canberra to head the relief effort) made himself unpopular by describing Darwin authorities as lacking initiative and being 'completely unprepared'.[20]

Air Commodore David Hitchins, who became heavily involved in the evacuation effort, acknowledged, when he was interviewed in 1987, that 'there's an element of truth in what General Stretton says about the lack of a total coherent plan for coordination of civil relief in such a situation. Yes, I guess that's pretty right.'[21]

There was in fact a disaster plan in development; but in light of Darwin's catastrophe-strewn history the fact that such a thing did not already exist is hard to understand. As the ABC's Bill Bunbury has written, 'Darwin has had a long history of destruction and rebirth [that has] given the Top End's top town a special character.'[22] In 1875 about a quarter of the white population of Darwin was drowned, travelling on leave from a tour of duty in a ship sunk by a cyclone off the Queensland coast. The town was hit by destructive storms in 1878 and again in 1881. A massive cyclone that coincided with a high tide hit in January 1897 and destroyed most of the town's buildings, two-thirds of its pearling fleet and twenty-eight of its inhabitants. In 1915 three boats were sunk; in 1917 a cyclone drowned three people and buildings were extensively damaged; in 1919 two sailing vessels were sunk in the harbour and across the Beagle Gulf the Bathurst Island Catholic mission was wiped out. The cyclone that swept in from the northwest in March 1937 killed one person and caused widespread damage to most of the town's buildings.[23]

However Stretton's rhetoric did ignore the fact that the Northern Territory had just completed Australia's first emergency protocol procedures, procedures that were quickly enacted after the cyclone hit. Indeed, Stretton had helped institute them. Les Liddell of Tennant Creek was responsible for emergency services in the area and remembers being handed a disaster plan for Darwin that set out what they envisaged would happen if major storms or a cyclone were to hit the city over Christmas. '"Les, you're the only one left in town, you might need this." And off they went.'[24] Liddell went on to play an important role in assisting evacuees after Tracy.

A year before Tracy, in the wet season of 1973–4, the roads to Darwin had been cut off for almost three months. There had been major floods around Australia and in some parts of the country rainfalls had been the highest ever recorded. Almost every river in Queensland had been flooded, and in the northwest and the Gulf country, the flooding had been extensive and enduring. On Australia Day 1974 Brisbane flooded and sixteen people died. Ray McHenry knew there were indications that the Territory could expect a difficult wet season and he was attempting to prepare for it. It was during that time that McHenry approached the Natural Disasters Organisation in Canberra and 'obtained the services of a military officer to familiarise himself with the Territory's problems and to develop a comprehensive plan for disasters of both a Territory and a Regional nature'. According to McHenry that plan was developed with input from the federal government, local government, the private sector and representatives from all over the Territory. It was approved on 5 December 1974, twenty days before Tracy. Talks about the management of the wet season in Darwin were held in Canberra four days before Tracy struck. McHenry was also in the middle of preparing drafting instructions for the introduction of a disaster management bill to the fledgling Legislative Assembly of the Northern Territory. (Disaster plans were not backed by legislation in most states back then. Victoria didn't get an act until 1986 and Western Australia has only enacted such legislation in the last decade. The lag between planning and legislation continues to this day.)

Ray McHenry was to become an important and divisive figure in the story of Cyclone Tracy. Long-time Darwin resident Harry Giese, who for twenty years had been Director of Welfare, was one of his many critics. Giese's job had involved being a long-term member (1954–73) of the Northern Territory Legislative Council, which meant he had to introduce and defend bills on behalf of the federal government, and fight these into legislation. He had to rebut attacks both from those who thought he was too progressive, and from those who wanted a faster pace of change. It was a difficult position to be in. Then, said Giese, 'I got a call, on the morning after the announcement of the Whitlam victory, from McHenry, advising me that I no longer had a job in the Northern Territory and that he was taking the job as Director.'[25] His deputy, Ted Milliken, has commented that Giese's 'displacement…was one of the meanest things that I have ever seen done to anybody in my life'. McHenry was unpopular but he was also tough, canny, and extremely competent.

Malcolm McKenzie, who ran the Rapid Creek betting shop, described the people of Darwin as 'eternal optimists'[26] but it's not just the people of Darwin who tend to optimism. In his book *The Human Side of Disaster*, Thomas Drabek emphasises the fact that people, particularly men, often don't respond to warnings. They go into denial and have a tendency to minimise the risks. Jim McGowan, the deputy chairman of the Queensland State Disaster Management Group from 2007–11 says that despite three days' warning, Brisbane residents failed to take the appropriate action during floods in 2011. 'People knew that they were coming for three days and yet at the end of it people said they weren't warned. I think the new level of warning goes something like, "I want to know that the flood is going to come to the third rise of the back steps of my house."'[27] But some people I spoke to felt that this was inevitable and that uniformed emergency services had an unrealistic sense of what you could expect. Certainly people will only act on warnings when they are expressed in a way that is made meaningful to them. In the archival interviews several mentioned this—that the wording of some of the warnings regarding when and where Tracy might make landfall were technical and slightly incomprehensible. You also have to ask what responding to warnings would have achieved. People who filled up their baths and cleaned up their yards had their houses destroyed as completely as the next person; in fact filling the bath created a problem when they had to hide in the bathroom. The only thing that people really could have done to look after themselves was to leave town.

Members of the Bagot community stayed put like everybody else, despite being aware that something was coming. Aboriginal activist and welfare worker Vai Stanton told Kevin Gilbert that she had been 'very involved at that time [of Tracy] with the fringe-dwellers because we were trying to get them tarpaulins for the wet season because we were expecting a very wet "Wet", you know'.[28] And there were 'claims that a prominent Larrakea [sic] leader, Bobby Secretary, told "quite a few people" in Melbourne in September 1974 that "the spirit who watched over their land, had said that a very big cyclone was to come".'[29]

Beth Harvey expressed a fatalism that both black and white residents shared: 'There is no point panicking. If it's coming it's coming. You just have to be prepared.' Liz Foster, a thirty-four-year-old woman who'd lived in Darwin for two years, remembered that the wildness of the weather that Christmas Eve evoked 'a fear, but not really believing that you're going to get killed or anything. It's just this awe that you have about nature—this thing that is so much bigger than you and that nobody has any control over—wouldn't matter what you had—nothing could control that.'[30]

DISAPPEARED

DARWIN OLD-TIMER Edna Harmer was worried about the cyclone, but what can you do? She spent the evening repairing crochet that fringed a tablecloth so it would look nice for Christmas Day. Charles Gurd stayed back from work for the hospital's Christmas party but drove home relatively early in the evening because the weather was making him nervous. Richard Creswick spent much of Christmas Eve at a long lunch. He went back to the ABC to oversee the evening's television news before driving home through the pounding rain. Down at Humpty Doo, a few miles inland, Bob Collins—only twenty-eight but already a senator for the Northern Territory—spent most of the evening trying to save his stereo. Hedley Beare, who for the last two years had been the Northern Territory's Director of Education and who lived in a house on the Esplanade in the centre of town, became quite agitated. At about ten that night he put the kids' Christmas presents back in a cupboard and got the children out of bed to shelter in the hallway near the bathroom. He and his wife Lyn wheeled a steel-framed bed from one of their sons' rooms into the hall as an extra source of protection. They sat there for the next nine hours. Julia Church remembers: 'We started to open our presents then decided to wait till the morning—so we'd have a few presents left. It was a longstanding family tradition, not being able to wait till Christmas morning.' They all went to bed, but then rain started coming in through the louvres and the house became like a 'bowl filling up with water'.

Maria Donatelli, born in Italy, had quickly become a Darwin institution and in 1974 she owned the Capri, an Italian restaurant in Knuckey Street. Becoming concerned about the wild winds, she called her staff and told them to go home. They couldn't leave because the customers were refusing to go; soon after, though, they left the customers to it. Cypriot Savvas Christodoulou, owner of Savvas Motors and a Darwin resident since 1948, was holding his annual Christmas party at the garage. The winds were so strong by the end of the night that many of his guests didn't want to leave, but he managed to get rid of them by 11.30 pm. This was around the time that Toni Joyce, who was visiting Darwin to spend time with the ABC cameraman, Keith Bushnell, saw Bushnell's roof lift—then drop back into place. Bushnell looked at her and said, 'It's OK, kitten,' promising her she'd be 'safe as houses'. An unfortunate simile.

Janice Perrin had lived in Darwin her whole life and wasn't too fussed at all. She was trying out a new recipe—glazed and steamed ginger chicken—and watching a thriller on the telly when the power went. A little later some tendons in her husband's foot were sliced by flying glass; her memories after that become vague. She remembers that she was menstruating, and was dressed only in underpants and a nightie. As the night wore on this worried her, but there was no way she was going to be able to change. 'I remember being in the kitchen,

I remember the colours of the kitchen, I remember putting a mattress on the floor…'[1]

Over at the Fannie Bay Watch House the police on duty were dealing with a man who had 'turned himself in'. 'He was in a very drunken condition and continued to rave about his missing wife…He continually stated that he thought she had been murdered and said, "I don't think I would have done her any harm—but you never know after a bottle of whisky."'[2] Policeman Bill Wilson was not on duty that night. He was with his wife Patricia, a former policewoman—he'd met her on his first day on the job—and she 'spent a large part of the time with the cat tied in a towel and strapped to her'.[3] Dr Ella Stack was at the Darwin hospital when a nurse, Sister Anne Arthur, told Stack to go home to her family. In a spectacular case of bad timing, Sister Arthur happened to be going into labour at the time so Stack left, but somewhat reluctantly. When she got home she was seized by an 'intuition'. She dragged her sleeping husband out of their bed and a few minutes later a wooden beam speared it. Many people describe these moments of insight; moments that, in hindsight, saved lives.

Despite teasing Ida Bishop for her 'intuition', her boss had sent his prawn trawlers to sea to ride out the cyclone. During Cyclone Selma they'd moored them in the harbour but the moorings had snapped, so they were trying a different approach. Getting the ships out of the harbour with a Christmas skeleton staff was trickier than usual, but nonetheless they headed out around 7.30 pm. Soon the trawlers were battling ferocious seas and a wind velocity estimated at over 170 knots. Bob Hedditch of Northern Research's *Anson* said that by midnight things were really bad. 'The wind blew in our windows on the bridge and tore the back off.' By that stage he was measuring the winds as reaching 280 km/h.[4] Another trawler, the *Frigate Bird*, was taken out of the harbour at 11.30 pm in an attempt to stop it smashing into the wharf. At some point her engine failed and she capsized, then grounded on a reef. Captain Odawara of the Gollin Kyokuyo Fishing Company took the *Flood Bird* to sea around the same time. As the HMAS *Arrow* rode out, 'one of the ship's company remembers counting some seventeen vessels—prawn boats, two ferries and a schooner—anchored behind them in Darwin's inner harbour before the tropical cyclone struck.' Meanwhile, back at home in her house at Parap, Ida Bishop put on her nightie, then put the kids' Christmas bikes by the bed. She didn't want the cyclone to ruin Christmas.

Presents—the giving of them, the loss of them, the finding of them in the wreckage—would soon take on enormous symbolic power. By the next morning undelivered Christmas presents would sit among bodies at the Nightcliff post office; unopened ones would litter the ruins.

Charles Gurd sat in an armchair in his bungalow on Myilly Point with his dog on his lap and watched water stream down walls, thinking these were his final hours. Ken Frey and his wife had moved to the bathroom when the winds first got bad, but ended up going down to the storeroom because of concerns the bathroom wasn't safe. Pat Wright, who lived in Smith Street in the centre of town, found her husband, Arthur, being lifted up by the roof as he tried to stop it pulling free from the house. His shoulder was being badly wrenched. Pat convinced him to give up on the roof and hide in a downstairs toilet in the dark. They sat there and listened to the house being destroyed around them and became increasingly concerned that a nearby water tower would come down on top of them. 'You could hear the nails coming out of the timber and everything else.'[5] At Savvas Motors the garage began to break up so Christodoulou ran around bracing it with timber. 'I couldn't find the hammer that night, to nail the nails, and the only thing we found—the chopper. I hit the nails with the opposite end of the chopper. I never even hit my fingers once. We nailed about two thousand nails.'[6] A nun at the East Arm Leprosarium describes 'a rush of wind, a sudden crashing noise, and the whole panel of glass louvres above my bed splintered…[there was a] terrible grind as the entire roof was lifted off.'[7] At Bagot community some people broke into the shop because it was safer in there. Eight-year-old Stephanie Nganjmirra Thompson hid under the kitchen table with her mother and three siblings. It was very noisy, particularly once the roof soared into the sky. Her mother was a big woman and she protected her children with her body. She promised them that she'd stop drinking if they survived. (Stephanie's mother went on to become a president of Bagot Reserve.)

By one in the morning the winds had really got going. Ida Bishop, who had a great eye for an image, said 'it was like a giant running his hands down the side of the house going *vvrrrrrrrr* like this, and you could feel the shudder of the wind going along'. Ray Wilkie spent the night under his office desk, on the phone while he still had a line, trying to keep track of the situation. His last call before the phones went was to Don Sanders. 'Well, if I sound a bit panicky, Don,' he said, 'it's because I am.'[8] People hid under their beds, often finding that their animals had beaten them to it. A woman saw her dogs flung through the sky on their chains but by some kind of miracle, they made it back to the house. The Church family ran for their lives. Julia was totally naked, her sister was in a nightie, her dad was in his shorts and her mum wasn't wearing much either. As the roof began lifting off a vacuum was created. 'We ran down the corridor toward the lounge. The door was buckling inward; my father grabbed it instinctively and we formed a chain down the corridor.' The door went and they ran into the bathroom. The walls went there as well and they made a dash for it, downstairs to the unlocked car. Julia was desperate for a wee and at some point used an ice cream container she found in the car. The piano blew out of the house, narrowly missing them. Julia wasn't actually frightened. None of them were. 'The human spirit,' she tells me, 'is amazing.' Plaster flew around them, white and flaking. Julia imagined they were in a snow dome.

It was about now that some people were whisked out of their houses. Ken Frey describes a colleague's experience:

> One of our architects, who had three children, went into the bathroom, and the two youngest they put into the bath itself, thinking that it was fairly safe. And the mother, I think, was against one wall with the husband. And one of the children was hanging onto the hand basin when the wall went out; the bath went with the wall, and so did the hand basin. So all three children went out and the two parents were left in there…

Shirley Gwynne was sucked out of the house in Wagaman that she'd lived in for six years, then flung on the ground and hit by flying chunks of concrete. She described it as like being caught in a giant washing machine. She then managed to crawl towards their storeroom with her baby Damian in her arms, but as she was doing this the family pool collapsed, releasing forty thousand litres of water and washing her son from her arms. 'I thought I had lost him forever…' Gwynne crawled around in the dark, searching for him. Miraculously, she found him caught under the tyre of her Mazda. The car lurched and threatened to crush them both but she somehow found the strength, in winds of more than two hundred kilometres an hour, to lift the car off herself and her child. Her husband was screaming at her to crawl into a car trailer.[9]

Soon after the 'hard blow' at around 2 am, the crew member from HMAS *Arrow* who'd counted seventeen vessels in the harbour looked around to see none left. 'All had presumably sunk.' Soon after that, the *Arrow* hit the Stokes Hill Wharf in the harbour and there was a series of explosions as the ammunition on board went off. Some of the men managed to get onto the wharf before the boat sank. They held on to whatever they could in wind and rain so fierce it ripped off their clothes. The boat's skipper, Bob Dagworthy, got to a life raft. Out on the *Anson* Bob Hedditch recalls: 'By 2 am we had no lights, no steering and only the main engine to keep us going...We lost both our anchors and I didn't have a clue where we were.'

Bishop Mason sat drinking beer with Bishop O'Loughlin, both men feeling regret at having held midnight masses. The Wilsons decided their house was no longer safe and were forced to put the cats and dogs into the car and leave them to it while they staggered towards the roadway. Bill put Patricia's arms around a street sign but then 'her feet lifted off the ground, the wind was that strong. It's like those cartoon things you see with people hanging onto a sign, almost horizontal.' No one, and I mean no one, was adequately dressed for the occasion. Elizabeth Carroll wore her new long nightie, one pretty enough to wear as an evening dress, into the toilet. She stood there, alongside three adults and five children, for the entire night. The independent member for Nightcliff, Dawn Lawrie, escaped her collapsing house with nothing but her kids, a dog, the puppy and its puppy food.

> Well, there were already seven people in the car. So with my husband, myself, our three kids and the two dogs, we somehow piled on top of these. And out of the gloom staggered a drunk, and we said: 'Quickly mate, hop in [and] we'll get you to the college.' And he said: 'No, she's right. I'm looking for a party.' I said, 'You crazy man, the whole town's blown away.'...That was the last we ever saw of him [*laughter*]. Presumably, he was blown to Timor.[10]

When she got to the cyclone shelter she put her kids in an industrial fridge for safety.

Wendy James, a much-loved figure in Darwin, had moved there in 1937 when she was a small child. When her sister-in-law Barbara James warned her about the cyclone she'd sent two of her four sons to her mother Pearl's house in Rapid Creek, so they could keep an eye on her. Quite a few people weathered the cyclone at Pearl's. That house stood strong while Wendy's collapsed around her and her family after a tree crashed through the roof. She, her husband Earl and their two younger boys went downstairs to hide in the shed. Only when the door had slammed behind them did they realise that the pool chemicals kept there had exploded through the tiny room. They tried to get out but something had blown across the door and they were locked in.[11]

Constable Terence David Barry lived on Trower Road in one of the newer northern suburbs. At two in the morning his house, like many, started to disintegrate.

> I placed two mattresses on the floor of the hall [and] the three eldest children lay down on them. I was just about to fetch the baby, when I heard a crash from the baby's bedroom. I rushed in and saw that the whole ceiling had fallen onto the cot that the baby was in. Had the infant been on the bed, he would surely have perished. I picked up the child, who was laughing, and went into the bathroom, where the wife had placed the other three children. I placed a mattress in the tub and placed the children in there. The violent shudders of the house were coming at the rate of about 30. Sec. each. I opened the bathroom door to see what was going on. I saw that we had no roof what so ever. Then the ceiling of the bathroom fell in on us. My wife and I supported the ceiling for about ten minutes. I then opened the door to have another look, I saw that the master bedroom at the end of the house and the lounge at the other end had almost completely disintegrated. At this stage I had no idea of the

> time, but I would guess that it would be about 0130 to 2000 hrs. on the 25th. I then called out to the wife and children that we had better get out of the house and try and get the car. I took the three eldest children and my wife took the infant, we went down the hallway over all the rubble to the back door. I kicked it open and we went down the stairs, I shelterd [sic] the three eldest kids behind the laundry wall, I then gave assistance to my wife with the infant, we went down the hallway over all the rubble to the back door. I kicked it open and we went down the stairs, I shelterd [sic] the three eldest kids behind the laundry wall, I then gave assistance to my wife with the infant to get down the stairs. I thought we were all behind the wall, when I noticed that the three-year-old boy, Kevin was missing. I thought all sorts of terrible things had happened to him, then I looked around the corner and saw him hanging on for grim death to the door handle of the car.[12]

It's at this time the cyclone rates a mention in the Fannie Bay Watch House diaries, where it was noted that at 2.05 am blankets were taken to the front counter to keep members of the public warm.

Barmaid Paula Dos Santos had lived in Darwin for more than twenty years. She was huddling with her grandchildren in the corridor of her house in Rapid Creek when:

> someone opened the top of a can, and the whole roof went. And where the manhole was—that had gone—and we were looking up at the stars—there was no rain. And we could hear the noise going away. I went out the back and there was already a great deal of debris in the backyard, and I could see this big black ribbon like a tornado, going down towards Nightcliff. I glanced over here and I saw another one.[13]

Dos Santos was not the only person who lived around Rapid Creek who reported seeing tornados and, while tornados within a cyclone are unusual, they're not impossible. More surprising was Curly Nixon's description of tornados south of Humpty Doo, twenty miles or so from the coast.

> Well, I think the missus hit it on the head, and Snowy seemed to half agree with her; but he, being a seaman, I don't think he wanted to. She reckoned it consisted of a lot of cockeyed bobs—it wasn't a cyclone as a cyclone was—it was more a corkscrew and then little corkscrews around the outside of it and if you got hit with one of them little corkscrews it was 'goodnight nurse'.

Some have surmised that it was the fact that tornados formed within the cyclone that meant the wind speeds were, at some moments, excessively high—estimated to be three hundred kilometres an hour or more—and why the destructiveness of Tracy was not predicted. In other words the town was not just struck by a cyclone, but by dozens of small tornados as well.

At 2.40 am the windows of the Fannie Bay Watch House blew in. By three the phone had gone down. Grant Tambling, a member of the Territory's first Legislative Assembly, remembers being 'amazed by how far glass could bend before it would break'. Sister Arthur was now in the final stages of labour. 'They couldn't give me anything for the pain because they had run out of injections...Our son, Barry, was born at 3.23. Shortly afterwards, the plate glass window in the Nursery began to bow dangerously.' Then the lights went out. 'A big tree fell on the maternity ward, then the toilet block (which collapsed), hit Ward 2 and then hurled back into Ward 5.'[14] It was 3.30 am and Darwin was in the cyclone's eye.

*

'It was just like coming in to land—when your ears pop. It was very strong pressure in the ears, nausea, and then all of a sudden the wind dropped. Deathly silence.'[15] This is how Peter Spillett describes the pressure drop that accompanied the eye's arrival. Stars could be seen and sheet lightning moved around the cyclone's walls. Liz Foster: 'There was this utter, utter silence, stillness, and there was like a glow in the air.' Harry Giese described the eye of the cyclone as the most frightening period.

> It was one of the most eerie experiences that I think you can have. At one instant there was this horrific wind and rain lashing everything, and you could hear the trees, branches, breaking off and crackling, and the next moment there was an absolute dead silence. And you wondered then whether it was the end of the world had come, or that you were the only remaining inhabitants.

Architect Peter Dermoudy, who was hunkered down in the gun battlements of East Point, watched the strange green glow of this otherworldly sky as the eye moved over the town. Lightning flashed, brilliant and bright: so bright he could read the newspaper by it. Wilkie had glimpses of a ruined Smith Street as if under a strobe light, and began to get a sense of the damage that was being done.

The eye took about thirty minutes to pass if it was directly overhead, less if you were on the edge of it. At the Harveys' place in Nightcliff there was a lull, and an eerie feeling, but they were two streets away from the edge of the eye itself. At the Tamblings' house in Larrakeyah there was no eye at all, just a bit of a lull before the wind changed direction. This was a dangerous moment in that long night, because people didn't know how long they had. People stepped outside their houses trying to figure out if it was safe to move. Voices inaudible only moments before carried through the streets. Chemist Roy Barden was one of many who walked over to check on his neighbours. They were okay and said to each other, 'Oh well it won't be any worse going out.'[16] Shirley Gwynne's husband Laurie heard a neighbour call and, despite the fact that their suburb didn't get a proper lull, he managed to get to the house, where he found a man and his child half-crushed under their bed. He freed them but as he ran back to his family he was cleaned up by a piece of corrugated iron that knocked him over, swept him up and flung him forty metres. His feet were badly smashed up. A friend of Beth Harvey's was found dead alongside her daughter under their storeroom wall. The husband tried to resuscitate his daughter, to no avail. He couldn't find his wife and had lost his glasses. It was neighbours who finally came to his aid and found his wife's body. Bishop Ted Collins knew a bloke who was lying in his house after his louvres had blown in thinking he had some spares and could fix them in the morning. 'The rain's coming in on top of him and he's covering himself up and then the eye of the cyclone came and a man came and shone a torch on him. And he said, "What are you doing in my house?" and the fella said, "What house, mate?"' It was Bishop Collins who had the foresight to make a tape recording of the cyclone—a recording you can hear if you stand in the sound room at the now-permanent Cyclone Tracy exhibition at the Northern Territory Gallery and Museum.

Janice Perrin and her husband tried to drive away from the ruins of their house, only to find themselves jammed up against a fence with water up around the car doors and starting to come in. Janice was vomiting with fear. The Jameses had managed to escape their toxic shed and were huddled under their landing when the eye arrived. Concerned that Pearl and their older two sons were dead, they headed for their car intending to drive the three kilometres to Rapid Creek to find them. Before they got there, flexing power poles heralded the cyclone's return. They stopped the car then ran to a building that turned out to be an empty school and sheltered there for the rest of the night. Bob Collins' roof had blown off so he gave up on his stereo, and he and his wife headed for the CSIRO labs at Berrimah. There was so much debris being hurled around that 'bits of Berrimah were basically passing over our heads'.[17] The amount of rubbish that got caught under their car had Collins worried they weren't going to make it. 'We got there by the skin of our teeth, when it was basically back to full fury.' He found some seventy-odd people sheltering at the labs, including a few who'd been so drunk when the cyclone hit that family members had had to carry them there. 'They had gone to sleep in a lounge chair in their house, and woke up jammed in with seventy or eighty other people, in a laboratory in Berrimah. Their complete disorientation was, even at that stage, I have to say, fairly amusing to the rest of us.'

Roy Barden returned from his neighbour's just in time.

> As soon as the eye was over well then we came back and we said alright everybody button up. Now we've got to wait and find out where the wind comes from and instead of the wind coming from the north-east it suddenly came from the south and so well it was blowing pretty hard for a while and it was gradually getting a bit worse and so another chap [Con] and myself we both put our backs up against the door to hold the door which was in two parts and then all of a sudden we heard a roar that was like about twenty planes taking off, all at the same time, about twenty jets roaring away and then all of a sudden it hit us and within a matter of seconds well he [Con] was blown across the room and I'd been pushing hard against my door and it collapsed and I fell out onto the verandah and by the time that I'd—I got onto my hands and knees to look round over my shoulder,

> the roof, the ceiling and everything was just disappearing up into the sky.

Barden grabbed hold of the railing to try and right himself, but every time he tried to get up could feel himself being lifted up again so he gave up and lay on his verandah. He was there for three hours but can't remember much more because he 'kept getting knocked out'. Kim Clough, who was a child at the time, remembers that her entire family was out in the open, being pelted with debris. Her mother was killed. Her brother, Perry, was badly injured. She remembers her father, Colin, screaming as he was hit by flying tin and the metal sank deep into his back.

When it came to the details, many of which slipped into a vague blur over the days, indeed years, after Tracy hit, there was one thing the survivors never forgot. The noise. The sound of the cyclone returning after the eye had passed was described variously as hundreds of petrol tankers heading up the street, the scream of a banshee, a jet plane in your garden, forty thousand trains, and 'rather like an express train going through a tunnel' but one that went on for hours and hours. Beth Harvey used an analogy people also use with bushfires: 'I've never been hit by a steam train, but that was the sense of power it had.' Ted D'Ambrosio, the deputy lord mayor, said, 'The noise was so great and the wind was so devastating, and there was the screaming of people and so forth, that it was just something out of a horror movie.'[18] Government architect Cedric Patterson comments, 'The thing about the noises that you could hear, and I couldn't—you can't really identify what was making these noises. There was screeching, ripping, tearing sound but the important thing was, that there were no echoes. There were no after-sounds. Whatever sound there was, it was sharp, defined and that was it—bang! Nothing else—no reverberation or that sort of business.'[19] Kate Cairns put it this way: 'When I first heard the roar of the cyclone coming back [after the eye had passed]—and it was a roar—I remember thinking: "Why are there jets taking off? It's too dangerous."' Kate Cairns remained terrified of the noise of wind for years to come. A friend of hers had a tape of the noise, and brought it around some time after the cyclone.

> We didn't have a tape [player]. It was one of the things that we hadn't replaced at that time. And he said: 'Well I can play it on my recorder in the car.' So we went out onto the street and he put it in, and played the noise of Cyclone Tracy, and there was no way I could listen to it. I just couldn't—I went cold all over.

The sound of a Category 4 cyclone can, and did in the case of Tracy, lead to psychological damage, much as the massive roar of a bushfire can, or shells on a battlefield, or bombs over a city. Thirty years later Bill Wilson returned to this memory, the memory of the sounds of the cyclone, several times during his extensive interviews with the Northern Territory Archives.

> The noise stays with me. The noise is in the back of my mind all the time when there's a cyclone. It comes back to me and I remember that squealing, screeching, howling noise...You wanted to scream because of this noise. The wind howling, the tin screeching as it's dragging along the road, the branches cracking and whipping off, the rain pounding. You put all of that together, and that noise is, to me, a cyclone, and that sticks in my memory loud and clear.

No one was—nor perhaps could they be—prepared for the ferocity of the returning winds. Winds that hadn't built up over several hours as the first half of the cyclone had, but hit, *bang*, at over two hundred kilometres an hour. The wind measure at the airport blew away as the wind speed reached 217 km/h. Peter Spillett, who had survived the bombing of London and the Burma campaign, described Tracy as 'the most traumatic experience' he'd ever had. Paula Dos Santos, who'd lived through the bombing of Darwin in 1942, found the experience comparable. It was perhaps even worse for those who had nothing to compare it to.

It was now, when the wind returned, that things tipped. Things to that point had been bad, they'd been indescribable, but it was now that everyone was untethered from the world they knew. The Harveys' house lifted from its moorings and dropped again. Rattled buildings, buildings that had been shaken for hours, exploded into the night, evaporated into the air. Darwin slipped through the looking glass into a new kind of reality. A young policeman, Robin Bullock, actually says this—that he felt his sense of reality shift as the cyclone went on for what 'seemed like a lifetime'.[20] Sections of the roof at the Fannie Bay Watch House were blown off and prisoners were moved from block one to block three. Ted D'Ambrosio's brother was out at the Darwin Golf Club and tied himself to a pillar to stop himself flying away. His son drove home in a small Mazda and when he, somewhat miraculously, made it home, told his dad he'd seen caravans flying through the air over the Stuart Highway. Cedric Patterson's archival interview reads like a dreamscape as he talks of his house slowly falling apart and the stars coming in. He saw 'a piece of asbestos cement about the size of a dinner plate and it was just floating in the passageway. And I can remember brushing it out of the way with my hand and thinking: "That's strange."' He talks of hiding under the drawer and feeling dazed, of walls collapsing. Walls are described as 'melting' and one man describes being sucked out of his roofless house as if he were riding a magic carpet. Shards of broken glass swirled around rooms as if in a giant blender. Everyone started making deals with God, even the atheists. Some people couldn't breathe, the wind was so ferocious. Elspeth Harvey, stuck in her car with her family and a menagerie, was so desperate for a piss she held on to the car door handle and 'had the fastest pee in the world', but while the door was open her cat escaped.[21] Petrol was sucked out of petrol tanks and air out of car tyres. Houses rocked like boats at sea. People sheltering in cars were picked up into the air, blown a few hundred metres and then dumped down again. Bead curtains, all the rage in the early seventies, whipped through the air like stock whips. One woman was blown out of the house with her five-month-old son in her arms. They landed uninjured but the baby was dangerously cold and instinct drove the mother to lick him, much as a cat would, in an effort to keep him warm.[22] Another mother remembers being blown three blocks from her home with her young daughter in her arms, the two of them spinning like feathers through the air. Housing girders twisted themselves into forms of abstract beauty. Thousands of sheets of corrugated iron scraped and scratched along the ground, sounding like millions of fingernails running down a blackboard. Ordinary household objects became lethal. Sergeant C. Simpson: 'I was struck on the left shin by a china mug and the handle became embedded in my leg…'[23] A refrigerator wedged itself in the high water tank near the airport.

At the Wrights' house things actually became less ferocious after the eye because everything had already been torn down. Arthur hugged Pat until dawn saying, 'It's all right love, don't worry, just stay here with me.' Twenty-eight-year-old barrister Tom Pauling, lover of theatre and already sporting the flamboyant moustache that would survive Tracy and many decades beyond into his term as Administrator of the Northern Territory, played to type by taking to the Courvoisier VSOP cognac. David McCann, the city's magistrate, sat in the YMCA with a mattress pulled over his head. Richard Creswick sat in the bath with three cats, a dozen tinnies and a bottle of something strong and taught his housemate Eric (who was sitting under the hand basin) the words to 'Waltzing Matilda'. At some point Creswick began to crawl towards his bedroom to grab his duffel coat, only for a lightning flash to reveal the bedroom had been blown away. Over in Nightcliff, Howard Truran narrowly missed being impaled by a thirty-foot piece of timber with a pointy end like a javelin that was flying through the air. It went through the ceiling above him, then stopped four feet from where he and his wife were lying. Truran believed his wife's crucifix had protected them from being speared. The palm in the Botanical Gardens that was about to flower for the first time in a hundred years that Christmas Day was destroyed.

As well as these ferocious winds there was 255 mm of rain that night. The wind chill factor of all that rain and wind meant that, for some, hypothermia set in. And almost everyone rode out the night wondering why they had been subjected to such terror, assuming that other people, in other houses, weren't having such a bad time. Constable Stephenson expressed what many felt when he said, 'I thought it was only my house and kept thinking "why us".'[24]

All this: the fear, the destruction, and the noise, finally finished at, as Charles Gurd put it, 'the first uncertain light of dawn'.[25] When Tracy was finally done with Darwin it headed, slowly, southeast across Arnhem Land. A week later the cyclone petered out over the gulf country of Queensland.

UNCERTAIN LIGHT OF DAWN

'IT WAS like going to sleep in England and waking up in Alaska,' was how Ida Bishop described the shock of stepping outside her house into Christmas Day. Savvas Christodoulou took in what he saw—his garage survived but his house didn't—and decided he needed to take an entire two days off work. Edna Harmer found she hadn't just lost her crochet, she'd lost everything she'd ever owned. Jack Meaney went out to look at the damage then came back in and said to his mother, 'The whole bloody town's gone.'[1] Don Sanders, who'd weathered the storm at the ABC studios, describes emerging to 'a most unneerie [sic] sort of sky and cloud formation. It was the utter silence. It was, as I can well imagine Hiroshima was two hours after the big "egg" went off; just nothing.' Bernard Briec, looking around at the devastation and wondering if a nuclear bomb had hit, thought: 'Everyone's dead and we're the only people who survived.' Cedric Patterson wiggled out of the wreckage, 'And when we saw the scene ahead of us, it looked like a view or a picture of the Great Western Front, over the trenches.' Charles Gurd said, 'Well, it was like a moonscape, you know. By this time [dawn] it was raining quite hard and blowing horizontally, and it was still pretty near dark, sort of half light, it was a very weird kind of feeling. It felt like wartime. It felt like a scene from the war more than anything else.' Hedley Beare says it was 'a world I could never have conceived of. It was almost like stepping into another planet'. He and his youngest son Martin went for a walk. 'We walked in silence. When we got about opposite the Catholic cathedral, or thereabouts, Martin just turned to me, buried his head in my tummy, and said: "Oh Dad, this is terrible."'[2]

Robin Bullock had arrived in Darwin with his family not long before Tracy. He had weathered the night with them as well as his mother and step-father, who'd come up to celebrate Christmas with him. When he walked out of what was left of his house he found that an explosion he'd heard in the night had been caused by the roof from the block of flats across the road. It had sailed across and was sitting on his Toyota Land Cruiser. 'It was very nice we didn't decide to hide in the car, because there was a piece of six-by-four straight through the roof and into the driver's seat. That would've been a bit ordinary.' He ventured out further, but what he saw was almost impossible to comprehend. 'You were looking at a place you'd never seen…It was incredible. And just people walking around, as they do. Like some of the footage after September 11th, after it had settled a bit and people just wandering around aimlessly.'

Bill Wilson: 'It was like soldiers coming out of battle, having listened to shell-fire for hours and hours and hours and trying to make sensible decisions…' This issue—of the incapacitating effect of trauma—was a source of some contention in days to come.

The war analogy spoke to many. On 19 February 1942 Darwin had been subjected to Japanese air raids amounting to the largest attacks ever mounted by a foreign power against Australia. They were the first of almost a hundred air raids over the next two years. Howard Truran first moved to Darwin in the early fifties, when the city was still rebuilding. On Christmas Day 1974 his garden was so stripped he could see the Travelodge Hotel, standing seven miles away in the centre of town. 'We're right back where we started from,' he thought.

There was a storm surge of about four metres at Casuarina Beach, but it was not nearly as bad as it could have been. If the cyclone had struck during high tide much more of Darwin would have been submerged and, according to Ray McHenry, 'the bulk of the population would have been washed into the sea'. It is true the damage would have been even worse.

The view was so clear that Beth Harvey suddenly realised how close her house was to the water and became nervous about tidal waves. Peter Spillett looked out at the sea and saw a sheet of water all the way through East Point.

> It was yellow. The whole area was misty—it was raining—a very yellow mist. It was an awful looking colour...No sounds at all—no birds, no frogs, nothing, I think that was one of the things that hit us more than anything else, was that there was not a sound of anything which you would normally associate with the wet season, like cicadas or birds or frogs—nothing, absolutely nothing.

Keith Cole's 'ten-acre block was covered with the soaked, dead bodies of numbers of lorikeets that used to nest in our trees'. Animals ran up and down the streets howling and crying.

Wendy James headed to her mother Pearl's house, to find the house intact and her mother asleep. When Pearl woke she said, 'I told you to come here.' And she was right. Out of six family homes lived in by the various members of the James family, only Pearl's had survived. To Wendy's distress it turned out her seventeen-year-old son, Alan, had walked through the tail end of the cyclone in search of her and was now nowhere to be found. They were eventually reunited, but Alan didn't talk to her for a year about what happened as he searched for his parents. Apparently a car had hailed him in the hope he could help them—the driver's child's legs had been amputated; Alan could not help. When he finally made it home the neighbours told him that his folks had disappeared during the eye and offered to put him up if they couldn't be found. Wendy had spent the night convinced her son was dead and now Alan was fearing the worst for her. It was, to say the least, a stressful time.

The first thing the Wilsons did when the cyclone calmed was to go back to the car where they had put their pets. The animals had survived and had 'obviously come to a truce, because the cat was still in the front and the dogs in the back'. Then they had a scotch for breakfast: a Christmas Day ritual they continued for some twenty years. When Roy Barden came to, he 'thought I was the only person left alive in Darwin'. He'd lost a lot of blood from multiple cuts he'd received when peppered with debris. There was something draped across his leg that he was worried might be the body of a member of his family, though he soon realised it wasn't. His hip was so badly injured it took him twenty minutes to walk down the stairs to see if anyone had been blown over the side of the house. He started to limp off to the police station for help when he came to his senses and realised his family might be alive and in need of him, so he staggered back up the stairs and knocked on his door. His son Douglas called out, 'Is that you Dad?' Barden remembers it as 'the best cheer squad I'd ever had in my life'. He went into the bathroom and his wife Doris threw her arms around him. Another son, Arthur, was under a quilt in the bath with their corgi, though the only sign of the dog was its nose.

Maria Donatelli went to the Capri to find that her bar had been drunk dry by the customers trapped there through the night. Colin Clough and his three children, including his twelve-year-old daughter Kim, still shocked and stunned by the death of their wife and mother, simply lay there.

Kate Cairns found one of her cats dead. 'I cried for the cat, not for the devastation and the fact that we didn't have anything dry to put on or—[*laughter*] we'd lost our house—none of that…I think that was a good thing that came out of that cyclone. I think you get your values back.' She couldn't find her dog Zac because he was hidden in a caravan over the road. Her relief was great when her neighbour walked across the road to her, wading through the water with the dog in his arms, saying, 'Look what I've got, look what I've got.' Later that day, as she sorted through her freezer, she made sure to put some meat aside for her own and other animals to eat.

Everyone checked on their neighbours. Tom Pauling ended up walking up the street with a neighbour, a man he'd fought with constantly in the past, but that morning they were 'almost arm in arm'.[3] They found people sheltering in their cars and took them to the remains of Pauling's roofless brick house. Then he headed to friends', and on the way saw a man:

> standing in what remained of his lounge room which was just the floor. In the middle of the lounge room was this artificial Christmas tree complete with decorations that for some unknown reason hadn't blown away. While we were there, he looked at us, picked up the tree and said, Happy f— Christmas, and hurled the tree down onto the ground.

When Ken Frey visited his neighbours one lot didn't answer and, to his shame, he walked off. He found out later they were in a wardrobe that had fallen over, door first, and they'd had to break their way out the back of it. The claustrophobia doesn't bear thinking about. Frey's colleague, the architect whose children had gone flying out of the house, found his kids: 'The two boys had somehow or other got across the road, and they got behind a fence across the road and they dug into the flowerbed.' That family was one of the families who chose never to return after they were evacuated. The Wrights were stuck in the toilet because so much debris was thrown against the door. Someone called out to them, then responded when they shouted back. They went to a neighbour's and used swimming-pool water to make a cup of coffee. According to Pat 'it was the sweetest cup of coffee I'd had in a long time...' Hot beverages were in demand as people recovered from the cold. One old woman waited three days, pinned under the wreckage, before she was found, and the first thing she did when she was rescued was ask for a cup of tea.

Charles Gurd walked to the hospital at dawn. 'It felt like High Noon. There was no one around...Darwin as a city had ceased to exist.' When he got to the hospital the floors were awash with water that was red with blood. There was no power or electricity—but nor was there much structural damage. The hospital's anaesthetist had been killed by flying corrugated iron while at home. Casualties had already begun to arrive and over the course of Christmas Day there were 128 formal admissions to the hospital—that is, people who were seriously injured. More than five hundred outpatients were treated. Most of the harm had been caused by flying objects and glass, and ranged from minor lacerations to extremely serious injuries. Roy Edwards, who'd lost a lot of blood after being gashed by flying louvres, told Ella Stack, 'I was bemoaning my fate a little bit and I happened to turn my head to one side and on the...bed next to me was a young lady without a foot. So I didn't feel sorry for myself any longer.' One of those patients was Ted D'Ambrosio's wife, who had an injured arm. D'Ambrosio had

had to cut his car free of fallen trees with a chainsaw to get her there. A bloke in a VW turned up and took Roy Barden to the hospital. 'He went through the water just like an amphibious vehicle.' It turned out they were among the first people there but then people began arriving in their hundreds. 'There was this mass of people descending on the hospital with wounds and cuts…' Barden had the glass pulled out of him, was given twenty stitches and then put to bed with plastic over his feet to keep the rain off, because the hospital's windows no longer had any glass.

Ray McHenry picked himself up off his bathroom floor, looked around and said, 'Oh my God.' He, like almost everyone else, had thought that it was only his house that had been blown away. He solicited his neighbour's help to rescue one of his eight children, who'd become trapped under a cupboard. McHenry ended up taking a carload of people to the hospital, including a pregnant woman he'd rescued from the ruins of her house. What was usually a fifteen-minute journey took him three hours.

Having managed to save his own life, his family's and indeed his neighbour's, Laurie Gwynne 'sat on a heap of rubble and cried'[4] before organising to get the family to the hospital. The children were covered in bruises inflicted by debris, but also by Shirley, who'd kept pinching them through the night to make sure they were still alive. All Laurie's toes were broken. At dawn Janice Perrin got out of her car nearly naked and walked until a car picked her up and took her to a nearby fire station, which had become an evacuation centre. That was where she found her mother, who'd been blown away along with her house and was badly injured. Perrin was given clothes to cover herself up and then went for a long drawn-out search for tampons or sanitary napkins. In the end she had to make do with Chux.

The *Northern Territory News*, when it returned on 31 December, made light of these private dilemmas, and took to running a series of stories on how the women left in Darwin were pining for sunglasses and cosmetics under headlines like 'A Lift for the Girls'. The issues were more fundamental and Charles Gurd remembers that 'things like women's sanitary things, you know, no one had them, and we didn't normally stock them, but we had to fly them in'. After Perrin was sorted out she went to the hospital with both her mother and her husband, Warren. 'Well the hospital was an absolute mess, there was no power of course and there were a million people everywhere.' She stayed and organised tea for people, Warren got his foot stitched up and it was decided her mother needed to be evacuated.

Bernard Briec remembers that a story went around about a guy who'd booked himself into the Mandorah Hotel across the harbour, slept through the entire event, then woke demanding room service. The lord mayor, Tiger Brennan, was a former miner who'd once lived in a caravan on the Nightcliff foreshore. Aided by a cocktail of rum, antihistamines and painkillers, he'd slept through the entire night and woken to a house that either lost its roof or didn't, depending on who you believe. Either way it was a heroic sleep. 'When I woke up at seven in the morning I looked out and saw this house over here had disappeared in which the lady who used to do my laundry used to live. I threw on a singlet, a pair of shorts, and my brothel brogues, and tore round to see what I could do with it, but she was gone from there.'[5] After Ted D'Ambrosio had taken his wife to hospital he went to see how Brennan had fared. He found the mayor staggering around asking, 'What's happened to my town?' They broke his fridge open and had a beer. After that Brennan dropped by Harry Giese's up on Myilly Point with his usual hat on, and:

> He was dressed in an old pair of shorts which looked as though they'd been used pretty substantially in removing

> debris and materials...Tiger had come up to see what the situation at the hospital was...It's difficult to explain the feeling that you have, that you're probably among very few people who would have survived this sort of blow. Indeed, before Tiger came along, you had almost the feeling that you might have been alone. There was a euphoria that you felt, that at least you'd been spared the sort of situation where you were beside people who were killed or badly injured...I could feel for those people, many in the northern suburbs... it must have been traumatic in the extreme.

Senator Collins, who was a volunteer for St John Ambulance, grabbed a CSIRO vehicle and drove the fourteen kilometres from Berrimah into Darwin to see what was happening. He was lucky he could drive—most cars weren't starting and those that did soon had their tyres shredded by debris. And there was this: the task of finding the car keys. Some found them in a few hours, some after a few months, and many never found them at all. The damage Collins saw on that drive was so extensive he claims he wouldn't have been surprised to find out that ten thousand had died. 'The closer I got to Darwin, the more bizarre the sights became...I mean huge pieces of H-iron steel were twisted like liquorice.' Knowing that what lay ahead of him was likely to bring on an asthma attack, he stepped into a chemist and nicked some Ventolin. 'I walked over to the chemist shop, which was smashed to pieces, and just walked inside.' Even this, the collapse of normal etiquette, was disorientating. 'I felt really weird...I actually expected to feel a hand on my shoulder at any stage, saying, "You're under arrest for stealing Ventolin."' Collins arrived at the ambulance station to find it had suffered fairly significant damage. Nonetheless casualties had been quick to turn up. 'There were thousands of—in today's terms—quite serious foot injuries from broken glass.' Collins himself headed out on the road, and was amazed to find that, despite the early hour, earthmoving equipment had already started to clear the streets. 'They had graded tracks down Bagot Road, through all of this debris.' He went on to work for three days straight. 'There were no reserves, we all had to do it...In those three days and nights we would have seen more trauma, physical and mental...than most ambulance officers would have seen in an entire lifetime...' After that intensive stint many of the ambos were evacuated out due to exhaustion. It was quite a few days later before Collins managed to return home. To his surprise his stereo equipment had survived.

Richard Creswick staggered into work for his 10.30 am shift at the ABC to find that staff were gathering. 'There's no doubt we were all shell-shocked although I think at the time we didn't realise it... We—none of us had any enthusiasm for work, although I think we all realised that we were all in the midst of probably the biggest story of our lives.' Keith Bushnell knew it was, that's for sure, and he'd got out of the cupboard that he and his friend Toni were hiding in, found his camera still intact, and headed out to take footage. 'He and Mike Hayes went out together,' recalls Creswick, 'and Mike did a voice piece about the devastation in which I think he used the line that: "It was the end [of] a bloody good town". Keith convinced a pilot to take that footage south for him and that ended up being the film of the devastation that got out.' The footage is easily found these days, and it's still shocking to watch Hayes report from a ruined Darwin, head bowed:

> Like a lot of the people who've left I'm just wondering about the new Darwin...It wasn't a very pretty place [but] it was a place of people with a unique way of life. This is Mike Hayes from ABC news, in the wreckage of what was a bloody good place to live.

Hayes became emotional again in 1999 when talking about it on the *7.30 Report*.

> I was much more frightened after the cyclone than I was during. And I think a large part of that is, you know, shooting news…I might have exposed myself to some pretty frightening scenes and I was also well aware that this was Darwin, a couple thousand miles from the cavalry, and the wet season could well have cut some roads between here and there and I feared for what might develop in the next weeks.

Danny Thomas, the assistant general manager at Northern Research, had gone down to the wharf to find that only one boat of twelve was left, though some began to arrive home over the next few hours. Ida Bishop had gone into work as soon as she could to see what had happened to her colleagues.

> I went in and saw the men all standing around the corner, all very quietly not saying anything. So I went up, and I said, 'Is everything okay?' And Danny Thomas said: 'No.' And I said: 'Who?' And he just said names, and I said: 'Oh' and I walked away.

Bishop coped by going home and holding onto familiar things. 'Barbara had won a turkey on the chocolate wheel in town earlier in the afternoon of Christmas Eve. And so, as I said, there's nothing else to do but to continue in routine…'

Thomas, as it turned out, had spent the morning searching the beaches. He'd found the drowned body of Koji Yoshanda, Bishop's former boss and the operations manager of Northern as well as Don Hoff who had been on the *NR Kendall* with Yoshanda. An engineer who'd managed to escape from that boat scaled the cliffs at Larrakeyah and got himself home. Thomas also found the bodies of people who weren't colleagues. In all, Northern Research lost two boats with six badly damaged, from a total of eighteen. The Gollin Kyokuyo company suffered even worse material losses, losing seven men and three of six steel-hulled trawlers. The official number of deaths at sea now sits at twenty-two.

The families of the Japanese men who worked on these trawlers often didn't speak English so their experience of the cyclone was particularly extreme. It's hard to imagine the isolation of the women and children after they found out their husbands and fathers were dead. Ella Stack remembers taking in one woman whose husband had died. 'There was nothing the Japanese company could do to take them anywhere. They were living in cars themselves. They had nowhere, no accommodation, so they just stayed in one room with us. And we managed with our little bit of English.' The barge *Alanna Fay* returned to harbour to find 'all the boats floating upside down'. Five boats from around fifty were left in Darwin Harbour and only one patrol boat, the *Assail*, was in good enough shape to conduct search and rescue duties on Boxing Day.

People familiar with Darwin will know the glorious Nightcliff pool, which sits on a cliff overlooking the usually calm seas, its lawns spotted with a few palm trees. I go there most mornings I'm in Darwin and swim laps before the water heats up beyond reason. The pool was there in '74, but come Christmas morning there was a body in it. Nonetheless, it served as drinking water over the next few days. When the health department were told about the body, they suggested boiling any water taken from the pool for twenty minutes. So that's what people did.

Half-prepared Christmas food was salvaged before the heat ruined it, and camp stoves were used to finish the job. People sorted through freezers trying to figure out what would go off the quickest. All manner of things were eaten over the next few days, from tins with the labels washed off. A meal might be a salad fashioned from beetroot and marmalade.

Over the course of the night the entire Church family had got banged and knocked about. The worst injury was a deep cut to Julia's dad's foot, which soon enough developed into an ulcer. That morning Julia found a small towel, which she wrapped around herself as a gesture to modesty before the family headed for Casuarina High. It was on that walk that they realised that it hadn't just been them. 'The entire suburb had been reduced to a series of platforms—the "dance floors"—all that was left after the walls and roofs had gone. They looked like oil rigs in the sea. Usually around there was frangipani and bougainvillea, a riot of colour—but the colour had blown away.'

Julia witnessed several pretty crazy scenes at relief centres and remembers it now as a kind of microcosm of a society under stress. Some people were good organisers—guys with army reserve experience took over—while others were good at taking instructions. Some people sought out injured people and Julia's mum was one who used her windowless car to drive people around. Julia helped dig deep trenches for latrines. But other folks went feral. People built strange fortresses out of cushions and rugs. Agreements were made to pool the food and share buckets of water—but then some women would drop used nappies into the buckets. Fridges were set on their sides with doors open to form a vessel for water, but someone broke glass into that to ruin the water supply. The basest human reactions were on display. Forty-eight-year-old Irene Cormick, who'd run a tourist park that had been destroyed overnight, headed into town to help and saw something similar at the centre set up at the Wagaman School.

> I saw things in humans that I would never ever wish to see again. I saw the panic. The people that you thought were strong, were weak; and the ones you thought were weak were strong. It was the grabbing...But you would not believe that people could change, from people into such horrible creatures.[6]

Some people simply got in their car and drove out of town. People started arriving in Alice Springs from Darwin around four-thirty or five on Christmas afternoon, which means they'd headed out through the rubble and ruined streets first thing in the morning. Their cars were pretty battered. Alan Hawkins, head of Alice Springs Apex, said, 'I think it was just instinct that they got in the car and got out as quickly as they could.' People were shell-shocked and:

> basically arrived in the clothes they had on their backs. They had no money, no food. Some of them had the presence of mind to take water, or bring water with them, but they just arrived. They were worn out physically, and I think just mentally they didn't know what was going on. They had no idea what was going on.[7]

The wife of one such couple, he recalls, had cradled her dead baby all the way down from Darwin. One thousand battered cars arrived in Alice Springs over the next three days, then were stranded because of the need to get a roadworthy before going further south. At Tennant Creek, where food was scarce because the wet season had cut supplies, Indigenous people went and harvested watermelons and rockmelons and brought them into town to give to people who were driving through. 'There you are,' they said, 'you need food for the people, here it is.'[8]

Without any landmarks to orientate them people could not find their way to their houses, or the houses of friends and family. According to Ray Wilkie, 'The whole geography of the area had completely changed—the topography nearly had changed—so you got lost.' People talk of this time and time again, their intense disorientation when their town was no longer recognisable to them. 'Everything looked so different, there wasn't a bloody leaf on a tree. You know, there was absolutely nothing, which meant you could see for miles and miles and miles, something you could never do before.' There wasn't much of anything else, either: no sewerage, water, electricity or phones.

It wasn't just buildings that fell to pieces, it was people. As journalist Gay Alcorn put it, 'The cyclone destroyed not only lives, houses, furniture, photographs and pets but a way of living and thinking.'[9] A friend of mine expressed it to me more bluntly. 'The cyclone made people psychotic. Not the night itself, but the fact it destroyed everything.' Teacher Ruary Bucknall, who was in Alice Springs when the cyclone hit, returned to Darwin on Boxing Day, on the same flight as the acting prime minister, Jim Cairns. When he got to Wagaman and saw the damage to his home he sat down at the house and 'bawled my eyes out for about—I don't know—ten minutes or so. Just couldn't get over the shock of the whole thing...the complete state of devastation. I don't think it's anything that a normal person can comprehend.'[10] When Alan Hawkins got himself to Darwin an entire ten days later he decided to walk from the airport. 'I got halfway into town, and I just stopped and looked at the devastation. I reckon I just sat there and cried for about twenty minutes; I just couldn't take it all in, it was just too much for me.'

When Dr Slim Bauer, the first director of the ANU's North Australia Research Unit, heard news of Tracy he went to Brisbane, bought a caravan, loaded it with food, tools and materials, then drove north to Darwin. He got there four days after the cyclone and, despite having been warned how bad things were, was extremely shocked. 'The thing which struck us—the first thing which struck us really forcibly was that when we topped the rise at Yarrawonga, we could look straight across to Darwin town, to the downtown area and the Stokes Hill, and of course you never had been able to do that before.'[11]

In this strange new world, everyone's sense of time began to shift.

Chronology frayed. People remember the devastation they awoke to, but after that things blur. Ella Stack wrote: 'The days had lost their names: it was no longer Monday, Tuesday or Wednesday.' Beth Harvey describes that first day, and many thereafter, as like 'a dream'. Harry Giese was concerned that age was getting to him though his memory was no worse than many much younger than him. 'I've got, I must admit a very confused memory, whether this is a result of the shock at that time, or whether it's a case of old age affecting memory, I wouldn't like to hazard a guess.' Liz Foster can't remember how many days after Tracy it was that she thought she saw a ruby sparkling in the rubble and went to pick it up—only to find that yes, it was a ruby ring, but there was still a finger in it. The way in which people spoke of what they endured had a liturgical quality. Elizabeth Carroll: 'I honestly don't remember what we did, how we did it. I remember just these specific things: the rubbish bins, washing my hair. I remember the fear.'[12] Colleen D'Arcy described it as 'strange—a time out of your life that you can't really explain'. Several men interviewed struggled to remember when their family was evacuated, and when they got to see them again. Often they ended up confessing to Francis Good, or whoever interviewed them, that they simply had no idea. Even General Stretton, who didn't arrive until late that first night, wrote that he quickly 'lost all track of time'. By 27 December, 'It seemed months ago since I had left my family sitting down to Christmas dinner at home in Canberra.'

When Law is sung in Indigenous songs it becomes a way of structuring and interpreting knowledge as well as communicating it. Boundaries between the past and the present are fluid and while references will be made to establish a rough time period—'That horse and buggy time'[13]—chronology is less relevant than remembering events in a way that emphasises their meaning. An extension of this is what Deborah

Rose has described as 'Year Zero':[14] the moment that something irrevocable shifts in a culture. For Indigenous people, 'Year Zero' is white settlement.

A version of this approach to story seems to have been taken up by survivors to Tracy. Those interviewed about the cyclone, white and black, talk about pre- and post-Cyclone Tracy. Neroli Withnall described it to the *7.30 Report* this way: 'It was such a cataclysmic event that everything was dated according to whether it was "before" or "after". It was like BC and AD.' Her now-former husband, John Withnall added, 'My own feeling is it's as if a line was drawn across our previous life. It's a strange feeling.' He said, 'I felt just a little while back talking to you as if we were almost talking about some other family, some other place, some other time.'

When we experience—or learn of—traumatic events the brain can capture this moment as if it's a photograph or a series of photographs. These vivid recollections are described as 'flashbulb memories'. The intensity of these flashes should not be confused with accuracy, as I learned that day when I found that the image of the cyclone I'd carried with me for thirty years belonged to the wrong day. It is now accepted that accuracy diminishes with time, even if the intensity of the feeling does not. So, for example, three years after 9/11 people tended to be right about the details of what happened to them, including how they felt, only fifty per cent of the time but their confidence in that memory remained high.[15]

People quoted in this book were interviewed as early as the day itself by journalists on the ground, or as recently as 2013, by me. The interviews conducted for the Northern Territory Archives—often, but not always, by archivist Francis Good—went on from the early eighties until into the early 2000s. For some, time had made the events of Christmas Eve 1974 more vivid, for some, less. More crucially though, there was the slippage caused by the shock of the night itself, and more was caused by what was to come. Constable G. Townsend: 'I was placed in the armory section at the station and was also the pet destroyer…My hours of duty are not possible to calculate.'[16] Many people, after that first sleepless night, were to go another night, or even five nights, without sleep. Oral historian Alessandro Portelli has observed that chronology is more likely to get blurry if events are endured as one continuous occurrence rather than a series of discrete episodes.[17]

Given this, some might question the point of even recounting people's memories of events, but I'm with oral historian Studs Terkel, who has argued that the impact of time and memory on personal narratives is not a flaw, but rather one of the things that make them interesting: 'The Memory manipulates facts and chronology to various symbolic and psychological ends. This can be as telling as shifting the truth to better fit in with a person's desired version of events. These gaps help us, in fact, to identify what is important.' Not all historians find this fluidity of oral history productive. Patrick O'Farrell wrote in 1979 that oral history was moving into a 'world of image, selective memory, later overlays and utter subjectivity…And where will it lead us? Not into history, but into myth.'[18]

After Hurricane Sandy in 2012, journalist Steve Fraser wrote that 'a mythic memory of communal suffering, self-sacrifice, and mutual aid' emerges after disaster. 'These are not fables, but moving accounts drawn from real life. They offer a kind of hope in disaster and, consoling as they are meant to be, linger on, sometimes forever. Meanwhile, interred and resting in peace are often the disaster's darker doings…'[19]

And it's true that myths play a large part in the story of Tracy; but, as with all myths, there is a kernel of truth at their heart. Hedley Beare's version of this myth is a moving one, and indeed, speaks to real experience.

> I understand that when a cyclone or a tragedy occurs, you normally check your immediate family, the extended family, your neighbours, and you go out into concentric circles. Since there weren't those extended families in Darwin everybody started checking on their friends. And one of the reasons why the place rehabilitated the way it did, in my view, is that it was—community emerged; people were caring about others. There were some enormous acts of altruism and kindness that erupted in that week following the cyclone.

I have no doubt that some of the people quoted here have misremembered what happened to them. Exaggerated or underestimated their trauma. Embroidered details. I let that stand. This book is testimony to their understanding of their experiences as well as to the facts, which were, it is certain, cold and hard.

THE MISSING AND THE DEAD

EXTRAORDINARILY, OUT of a police force of 208, only six failed to arrive at work on Christmas Day, rostered on or not—despite injury to themselves and family, the loss of their homes and, in some cases, their clothes (one bloke turned up in his speedos). Several were so badly injured they were unable to work and had to be evacuated. It must be said that there were officers who reported for duty under some duress, with one officer taking a while to come in after having had to take 'refuge in a cupboard in the bedroom on the non-approach side, remaining there until the cyclone ended'.[1] But come midday on Christmas Day there were sixty prisoners in the Fannie Bay Watch House and only three officers in attendance. Everyone was needed.

Robin Bullock was thirty, but he'd only graduated as a policeman that December. He can't remember what time he went to work, but it must have been early, and when he arrived he was put in charge of the morgue that was set up at the Casuarina post office and left there, unassisted, for some twelve hours. He'd never seen a body before, but by day's end the count was at thirty-three. Many of them were children. People came and went, identifying the dead who lay on the floor and tables and benches. Most of the bodies had suffered extreme compression—that is, things had fallen on them and suffocated or crushed them. Some people had also been severely cut, even sliced, by corrugated iron. Bullock described his experiences to Francis Good in 2002. 'I probably couldn't name them all but I could tell you exactly what they looked like…There was one little girl I remember in particular, who was a twin for my daughter. Her name was Geraldine Brown.' At this point in telling his story Bullock hesitates for some time and then the tape is turned off. After the tape is turned on again, Good gives Bullock the chance to talk about something else, but he doesn't take it. Instead he chooses to elaborate on how he felt. 'I thought I was over that,' he said, 'but I'm not.'

In an interview with the ABC in 1999 Kay Brown remembered how her daughter Geraldine died.

> The roof fell in on top of us and then, of course, we were trapped and they couldn't find us, obviously. Of course, they [rescuers] were walking on top of us and we're trying to yell out, 'We're underneath you.' Anyhow, they eventually got us out and that's when Geraldine died. Geraldine was really frightened and she crawled onto my back and then the roof caved in and the weight of it and all the debris crushed her.

Notes in the exercise book that Bullock kept tell us that Geraldine was found by Constable Stephenson who'd arrived at a house on the corner of Bradford Terrace and Trower Road, to be told by the girl's father that there was a 'girl underneath the house dead'.[2] Constable Stephenson himself had spent much of the night lying over his wife and child—first on a bed, and then in the bath—to protect them from falling debris after his roof had blown off. Once he reported for duty he 'spent the morning freeing trapped persons and conveying deceased persons to the temporary Morgue at the Casuarina Post Office' then took 'control of the Casuarina Shopping Complex with seven Probationary Constables to secure and issue essential clothing and food'. He 'continued this duty until we were relieved by the Commonwealth Police five days later, I think, as we had lost track of the time and days'. Stephenson only got to see his family once in the three days before they were evacuated.

Irene Cormick describes the 'terrible torment, those men, with those children that were left behind...In the police station, where they had the bodies of the lassies. They were identifying children. There was a couple of policemen there, and they worked—oh I think they didn't come out of that room for five or six days. And they were just walking like zombies.'

Many of the police who have written or been interviewed about what happened to them, or what they saw, reveal a real distress and a guilt—shared by non-police personnel as well—that they had survived when others did not. Constable Dane Smith: 'I...was directed to the body of Peter Brian Daffey, 6 yrs. killed when bed under which he sought refuge collapsed over him. Body taken to Casuarina Post Office. I failed to identify the body with the result it remained unidentified for several days.'

Bullock again: 'Another terribly sad one I remember was a fellow from the naval base—his wife and two young children. I remember him being there identifying them, and he was just—God, the effect it had on him, he was just a shattered man...' Bullock is referring to Geoffrey William Stephenson of HMAS *Coonawarra*, who arrived at the morgue to identify his wife, Cherry Leona[3] Rose Stephenson, twenty-two, his three-year-old stepson, Kenneth James Scott Wheatley, and his six-month-old daughter, Kylie Jane Stephenson.

Stephenson had been stuck on the *Coonawarra* for the duration of the cyclone and then had been looking in the harbour for bodies. He'd managed to retrieve a few. As soon as he got to shore he left the boat, and went to his house to look for his family. At first he was relieved when he didn't find them and assumed they'd got themselves to safety but after he left the house he had a bad feeling and returned to it. That was when he lifted the bed and found his family crushed underneath.

Bullock's handwritten notes sit in the archives in a file 'relating to the identification of deceased persons after Cyclone Tracy'. Reading these notes, looking at the fragile, spidery handwriting, feels strangely intimate, as if one were witnessing, almost forty years hence, the most private and vulnerable of moments. In the lie of bodies, in the clothes worn, the delicate details of life and death reside. Bullock tells us that Cherry was dressed in a purple cotton sundress, wearing a diamond engagement ring and wedding ring on her left hand, and a gold friendship ring on her right. Kenneth was wearing blue shorty pyjamas with a toy pattern. Like his mother, he'd been asphyxiated. Little Kylie was wearing a white cotton vest, a nappy and blue plastic pants. Her skull was fractured.

Darwin, originally known as Palmerston, came into existence in 1869. It was established because British administrators believed a defence outpost was needed against French and Dutch ships in the region. Its situation was precarious from the beginning, and previous settlements in the area had been 'defeated by starvation, lack of water, termites, disease and hostility from the Indigenous locals'. During this period, military diaries noted 'hurricanes'—not to mention the odd earthquake—as yet other trials to be endured. Only the Chinese seemed to be able to get any economic traction in such a fraught environment, a fact that—according to Tess Lea, the author of the recent book *Darwin*—'so alarmed the whiskered white men in power down south that the White Australia Policy was crafted'.[4]

The settlement became known as Darwin when the Commonwealth took control of the Territory in 1911. From the beginning it was a frontier town of outliers, pioneers—of men. It was a town that people in the rest of Australia, particularly southerners, didn't—don't—really understand and the place wears its outsider status with pride. This is one of the reasons that during the writing of this book I found myself having conversations like the one I had when I headed down the track (aka Stuart Highway) to the Katherine Writers Festival in 2011.

That night Drags Aloud were performing on an outdoor stage in the market yards. It was a warm and star-filled night. They did a satirical version of *Wizard of Oz*, a version that included a drag interpretation of Dorothy uttering the immortal line: 'We're not in Kansas anymore.' I found myself thinking, the Northern Territory is a bit like that. Things are different. If you're from down south you're out of your comfort zone. As we stood around and had a beer, a friend cautioned me that some Darwin locals (both white and black) might not like me writing about Tracy, they might feel I was stealing their story. She didn't mean that I had to follow formal protocols, though that might have been part of it. What she meant was that outsiders tend to come in, stay a few weeks, do their piece—and get things wrong. No doubt I have got some things wrong.

There's something about this proprietorial attitude that makes it hard to know what really happened up there. Many of the rumours that swept in like so many small tornados after Tracy spun themselves out. Others, less founded, still flourish today.

One persistent rumour was that there were thousands of bodies under the wreckage of the northern suburbs and that, as a consequence, mass graves were dug and bodies dumped in them. Richard Creswick knew of a journalist who'd been in Darwin:

> who travelled the Rotary circuit in Victoria for some time dining out on his cyclone experiences which included helping to personally load two hundred bodies on the back of truck at Katherine—or to go to Katherine—or something, and that story came back to us via the ABC in Victoria for us to confirm some months after the event. As I say, I don't believe it.

Senator Collins described rumours of mass graves as 'bullshit' though he understood why people were sceptical the official death toll was so low. 'I mean, it was a small town in those days and most people knew someone that had died, or knew the family that had had someone killed.' And post-Tracy Darwin certainly provided plenty of fuel for fantastic visions and stories of horror. Collins describes one…

> …extremely unpleasant scene, with a room with bodies on the floor, and coffins stacked all over the place, and we were there with this deceased person in a body bag on a stretcher…In the middle of this, suddenly, up popped a person out of the coffin that was in the room! And frightened the daylights out of both of us.

It turned out to be a worker grabbing a nap.

You could dismiss talk of a cover-up as paranoid, but conspiracy theory has a rich history in Darwin, where many also believe that the Australian government was evasive about the number of people who died during the bombings of 1942. As Tess Lea has documented in *Darwin*, the media and the government colluded to suggest the attack was launched from Papua New Guinea and that Japan 'did not have the capacity to wage an aerial war from sea'. Motivations were in part racist—no one wanted to acknowledge such a sophisticated approach to warfare from a non-white race, or the failure of the British to protect them. There was also the related concern that if the full extent of the attacks was known, people would panic.[5]

Prime Minister Curtin was upfront about the fact that many died: he gave the Lowe Commission a figure of 240 people killed. (This was reported, although there was also media coverage that downplayed the casualties.) But while the official death toll ended up sitting on 243, the figure some believe closer to the truth is one thousand. Certainly more Americans than Australians died during the raids and many of them lie in unmarked graves at sea. (Tess Lea has drawn a direct line from this 'blood debt' to modern Darwin's increasing role as an American military base.) In 2001 Paul Toohey spoke to Rex Ruwoldt who was stationed in Darwin at the time and knew people who dug graves for hundreds of bodies. They remembered a figure of three hundred for one grave and countless others in a second. Another solder interviewed by Toohey claimed: 'At Mindil Beach, there was over 300 buried in a bomb crater, who were possibly later moved and reburied in official graves…In those days, Darwin had a terrible lot of illegal people.'[6] It's been said that the bodies that washed to shore were buried in a mass grave around Mindil Beach, before being exhumed and moved to graves further inland. In 2012 author Roland Perry asserted that 'as many as 1100 people may have died in the bombing—and were buried in mass graves at Mindil Beach'.[7]

Historian Mickey Dewar says stories of the cover-up after the bombings have increased in credibility over the years, 'If only because old men have little reason to lie.'[8] Military historian Tom Lewis disagrees and attributes an inflated death toll to the kind of psychological processes that might well have led to the rumours after Tracy as well: 'Seeing death on a widespread scale, with hundreds more wounded, does cause psychological trauma. Bodies were indeed buried at Mindil Beach and in other places, records show—and then exhumed later to be taken to places such as Adelaide River War Cemetery.'[9] No one who had witnessed these burials and retrievals of decomposing bodies was ever going to forget them and, whatever the truth, we can see the similarities between these stories and those that sprang up after Tracy. Stories take on a life of their own. They change shape and move through time, telling and retelling themselves as needed.

There is a not-so-noble tradition of fudging disaster tolls, too. After San Francisco was ravaged in the 1906 earthquake the official death toll was 375. Steve Fraser writes: 'For a savage firestorm coursing through the most densely packed of neighbourhoods, that low figure surprised people and left some wondering. The answer turned out to be this: the city fathers were determined to cite a low number so as not to discourage San Francisco's rebuilding and the outside investments that would require.' The number of dead in San Francisco was probably ten times higher than the official figure. Ben Wisner has written about the fate of illegal immigrants working in the twin towers on 9/11, whose families could neither register their deaths nor claim any assistance. After Hurricane Katrina the death toll was estimated at 1836 (1464 within New Orleans itself) but hundreds remained unidentified. The organisation charged with contacting relatives and identifying bodies ran out of money in 2006. The death rate for those who had lived through the hurricane continued to rise for some months to come. Anecdotally, that seems to have been the case after Tracy as well.

Certainly the more you read of the devastation Cyclone Tracy wrought, the harder it is to believe that only seventy-one died that night (though there are still a hundred and sixty people listed as missing) so it's no surprise that the figure is persistently disputed. When I wondered out loud about this figure while visiting the NT archives, Françoise Barr told me that the morgue photos were held there: I could look at them if I wanted. Then she hesitated, 'but I wouldn't recommend it'. It was Françoise who first told me that photos had been taken to allow identification because the bodies themselves had to be buried quickly. I eventually had a brief look at the photos—or tried to. I found it easier to focus on the carefully set out exercise books filled out by men like Bullock, detailing who was found dead, what they were wearing and who they were identified by. When interviewed in 1987, coroner and magistrate David McCann explained that police had:

> quickly set up a system for identifying all the people who died and had details of description, photographs, what they were wearing, rings and ornaments and all those sorts of things, and then had ticks for whether they'd been identified for relatives or not...If they weren't identified before they were buried, they'd taken photographs and taken details of things so they had the information.

But the system was inevitably chaotic, as McCann himself acknowledged.

It's possible that the rumours of mass graves originated in the trenches that were dug as a short-term solution for the bodies that were on the official death list. It was David McCann, acting as coroner, who first called attention to the problem of storing bodies, given that there was no refrigeration. 'I told them or they asked me, but anyway I said, "Look, there's no way we can keep the bodies just lying as they are. They have to be buried smartly and there are all sorts of reasons, including public health problems if you don't."' Police Commissioner Bill McLaren says,

> I think from recollection I would say it was probably the twenty-eighth of December, twenty-eighth or twenty-ninth...several bodies were taken—were out at the cemetery at the same time, but each and every body was put in a separate grave. It's marked, recorded, and there's definitely

> no chance whatever of there being a mass burial, and every person that was buried had a burial service...[10]

Later on, a number of those bodies were exhumed for cremation or reburial.

This story differs slightly from truck driver Peter Talbot's, which, while it supports McLaren's views that the grave digging was for people on the official death list, suggests the procedures weren't as respectful as you'd hope.

> The Sunday I didn't go to work, my gang in the council—there's 3 of us on the truck—go and putting all the street signs up, repairing kerbing and making driveways and all that, doing stone pitching, they were called into the burial party. Because my mate, he was one of them, he was in the burial party. When he went out to the cemetery, there was the police—they just piled them on like sardines, you know, you know them vans, they had them stacked up like that with a tag on their foot, but this is what [name removed] was telling me, the policeman took—standing—having to pull the body out, had big rubber gloves. They were buried in the clothes they wore the night they got killed. Pull them out, just drop them into the grave and there was another policeman there, he took the number of the grave on the headstone. As they kept bringing the bodies in for burial, old [name removed] seen a couple of friends of his, and that upset him; upset him that much; like Billy Muir and a few other blokes. See on that job we was doing we seen a lot of people he knew. So it upset him and made him crook. He told the doctor what happened, he was upset, probably shocked too, I supposed.[11]

This was on Saturday 28 December and certainly Billy Muir was on the official list of the dead. An Indigenous man, well known around the town, he'd died during the course of the night, having protected his wife Hilda 'using his big, strong body as a roof,' as she later put it.[12] Talbot is Indigenous, as was the man who broke down. This story overlaps with a statement made by Police Commissioner McLaren that one man who dug trenches for the bodies had a breakdown. Such scenes are shocking for anyone, but possibly more so for Indigenous people, who have strict protocol around treatment of the dead. That aside, is easy to see how such a traumatic incident might have morphed into a tale of trenches and hidden deaths.

There were also those who were never a part of the official death toll but whose deaths could be traced back to the cyclone. Echo Cole remembers that a lot of people died in the years following Tracy and suggests that they should have been included in various fatality figures because there were so many heart attacks after the event. On 8 January the *Northern Territory News* reported that twelve people had died 'natural deaths' since the cyclone—which seems like quite a few given that only two weeks had passed. It was suggested by McLaren that these deaths were 'probably the reason for rumours of many more cyclone deaths than the actual confirmed figure'.[13] Edna Harmer's husband, Bill, was dead within six months. 'He fretted himself to death…I reckon the cyclone more or less finished him off.'[14]

Among the uncounted, the hippies loom large, though the definition of 'hippy' was a free for all. In the seventies, Darwin was on the counter-culture trail that linked Australia with Southeast Asia, India and the Middle East. Lameroo Beach, near the centre of town, was nicknamed 'Twelve Star Hotel' when it became a commune of sorts for those passing through. 'To get a feel for ancient Darwin,' writes Tony Clifton,

> you need to go back to Lameroo Beach. When I paid it a nostalgic visit the trees still swept down to the water's edge, the sun still set blood red, the trees were clean of human habitation and a handful of Aboriginal people were sitting and talking on the sand under the branches. The smoke of their fires drifted through the thick leaves as I walked back up to the neat park at the top.[15]

That was in 2005. When I visited in 2013 I was struck both by the place's beauty, and by how little actual beach there was. I assumed the beach had eroded but when I asked a friend who camped out there in the seventies he remembered that it had always been precarious, and that he'd had to sleep back from the beach on a narrow ledge. It's hard to imagine where any number of people could have slept, though tree houses are one answer to that question. Back in the late sixties and early seventies, 'the hippies smoked the local weed and played guitars in their tree-houses, perched in the overhanging branches of the casuarinas, which ran down a steep slope to the shoreline behind what is now the main tourist drag of Mitchell Street'.

What happened to these people when the cyclone hit? It's known that the beach itself was ravaged beyond recognition, but both Mayor Tiger Brennan and soon-to-be-Mayor Ella Stack have said that the area had been 'cleaned up' a month or so before the cyclone. Where, then, did everyone go? Did they simply move to another beach, and if so, how safe was that?

After the cyclone Paula Dos Santos was concerned for the fate of 'about two hundred men, women and children who were living across the creek at Casuarina Beach. They were in tents and makeshift shelters, mostly backpackers and drifters who had been removed from Lameroo Beach.' The day before the cyclone, she gave four of them a lift from town.

> I was shocked to see so many living like that, I said: 'Don't you know we are expecting a cyclone? You people will be blown away. You should go to a school or somewhere until it's over.' But they all said: 'We'll be right! Don't worry about us.' But I did worry, and the next afternoon I drove down to the beach and looked across the creek and it was bare—not a soul there. I still wonder how they coped or what happened to them.

Similar questions surround the long grassers, the Indigenous people who camped in the parks in and around Darwin. A 2011 report on Indigenous people and Cyclone Tracy quotes one respondent as saying:

> I mean we know a lot of people that lived in the bush and surrounding areas as they do today and we reckon there was a lot more people out there unaccounted for that they just didn't. They weren't able to count them. And so when you saw the devastation, and those 60 odd people, there's no way that only 60 odd people would have died in that. I mean there would have been a couple of hundred people living in the long grass, you know.[16]

It was often said that the Aboriginal people got out of town because they noticed that the green ants had disappeared along with the birds. Echo Cole: 'Because of my Aboriginal identity [I knew]—that something was going to happen to Darwin city at the time…Everything just went dead. There was no bird life; no movement; even the trees were still.'[17] A creature known as the Mandorah Monster (thought to be a giant manta ray) was spotted in Darwin Harbour in the build-up to the cyclone. This happened on the Rainbow Serpent dreaming track that stretched from Casuarina Beach to Mandorah and was seen, in retrospect, as a warning.

But Cole himself didn't leave town and I found no particular evidence that Indigenous people responded very differently from non-Indigenous people. That is, some were concerned and did their best to be prepared, and others ignored the whole thing. Some—Indigenous people included—make the distinction in the knowledge held by those living traditional lives, who did know something was up and got out of town, and those who were more urbanised.

In emphasising some kind of innate knowledge, there's a danger of slipping into a romantic myth, one that conveniently covers up the lack of attention paid to some Aboriginal communities around Darwin before and after the cyclone. There were around twenty-three Aboriginal camps around Darwin—five of them had had permanent residents for decades. Many of these communities had no radio and wouldn't have been in a position to hear the ABC's hourly warnings. Anthropologist Bill Day has recalled that during previous emergencies he'd had to relay warnings to various camps, otherwise messages were unlikely to reach them. He was not around to do that when Tracy hit. 'I know that a lot of the traditional mob they actually left because they were reading the weather signs and the warnings from the animals and things like that. But I do know a lot of people died because they were never given the warning. Or they couldn't understand.'[18]

In the wake of the cyclone it was also hard to get exact figures on the number of deaths at sea. According to harbourmaster Carl Allridge's report dated 4 January 1975, 'At least 29 vessels were sunk or wrecked, several were driven ashore and later refloated and at least twenty persons were lost.' On 7 January thirteen ships were still missing and twenty people still unaccounted for in Darwin Harbour. William Woodyatt, engineer, and Robert Wade, cadet fisherman on the *Frigate Bird*, both died. But the skipper of the *Bird*, Bob Joss, and cadet fisherman Bob Dowman were rescued a day and a half after the cyclone from an air pocket in a life raft in which they'd been trapped for nearly thirty hours. The skipper of the *Arrow*, Bob Dagworthy, was found alive, floating in his life raft, some thirteen hours after he took to sea in it. Two lives were lost on the *Mandorah Queen*. That ferry was found in 1981. A second ferry, the *Darwin Princess*, was not located until 2004.

As the fate of these ferries suggests, it was years, and in some cases decades, before all the boats were salvaged. The *Flood Bird* was located in May 1975 but it wasn't dragged ashore until 1977. Human bones were found in the wreck. The body of one crew member, Dennis Holten, was found soon after the cyclone, but three of the other four—Captain Odawara, George Roewer and David Fealy—were listed as missing until the vessel was recovered. A fourth crewman, Robert Swann, was not positively identified until 1989. Those wrecks still remaining in the harbour have joined those from World War Two, and several Vietnamese refugee boats, to become scuba diving sites.

Those not known to be dead were 'missing': by its very nature a category that's hard to pin down. Initially, to avoid vagueness, a ruling went out by telex on 13 January 1975. 'The only persons who are considered to be missing persons in the true sense of the word are the persons believed to be missing from the various boats sunk in the Darwin harbour and whose bodies have not been found.' At some point this must have been revised: the current official missing list is a hundred and sixty people. Seven years after the cyclone those still missing at sea were declared dead, but of course they were no less 'missing' after that.

When the *Booya* was discovered in 22 October 2003, intact and lying on its side, the bodies of the five people who'd been known to be on board were not found. 'It is not so much a grave but a living memorial,' said Rick Weisse, one of the divers who found the *Booya*. 'You look inside and it is crystal clear water and you can see inside the steering compartment.' One of the five was Ruth Vincent, a twenty-four-year-old barmaid and mother of three. She'd gone to the wharf for a party after her Christmas Eve shift at the Victoria Hotel. When the *Booya* was finally found Ruth's sister, Naomi Senge, was still hoping police divers would find her sister's remains. 'You have thoughts,' she said. 'Maybe, just maybe, she's still alive.'

Instead, following the 1975 coronial inquest that formally declared Ruth dead, she had to make do with some small items salvaged from the wreck. 'Cos you can see her with the ring on, you know, see her with the purse. Cos they were definitely Ruth's.'[19]

DOES ANYBODY KNOW THIS HAS HAPPENED TO US?

WHEN ELIZABETH Carroll stepped outside her house on Christmas morning she saw a plane flying overhead. 'The feeling I do remember having was: "Does anybody know this has happened to us?"' It was a good question and Carroll wasn't alone in her fears. A *Northern Territory News* feature, published twenty years after the cyclone, quotes one woman: 'We thought no one knew. Here we were in the catastrophe and they didn't know,' she said. 'There was this incredible sense of isolation...That we had been abandoned.'[1]

The extremity of the isolation the people of Darwin experienced is hard to imagine today. In early February 2011 I got up at three in the morning to read the tweets of one Carl Butcher, known as 'Cyclones Update', to see how Cairns was weathering Tropical Cyclone Yasi. After the Christchurch earthquake on 22 February 2011 people managed to use their phones to let rescuers know they were still alive and where they were. (This was still no guarantee of survival, though it may well have made those in peril feel less alone.) During the Brisbane floods of 2011 Twitter and Facebook helped spread information about where floodwaters were expected to be at their worst, and were also crucial in the coordination of the clean-up. At the time, writer and journalist John Birmingham described how, as 'an intense low-pressure system appeared over the city as a multi-coloured pixel swarm on thousands of smartphones and desktop computers, the #qldfloods tag on Twitter started to spike.'[2] According to Associate Professor Axel Bruns and Dr Jean Burgess from the Queensland University of Technology, 'In the first place people were passing on the raw footage, the images, the videos from Toowoomba, and the Lockyer Valley when the flash flooding happened there.' Professor Bruns says, 'But the focus shifts to Brisbane and preparing for and responding to the floods as they were happening. It was no longer a news event that people were passing on but they were providing practical information on how to flood-proof your house or after the flood had happened how to clean up.'[3]

It's not all good news. If events are moving quickly, reading a tweet that is an hour old can mean you're getting out-of-date information, much like hearing an expired radio warning. But there is no doubt that social media has been a game-changer and, according to the 2013 World Disasters Report, the widespread use of technology,[4] particularly mobile phone texting, played a role in preventing a large loss of life when Cyclone Phailin hit the state of Odisha in India. A cyclone in this region in 1999 killed ten thousand. In 2013, after Phailin, only fourteen are reported to have died.

But right up to the present day, laying blame when communications collapse has been a recurring theme in most disasters. Quite apart from any physical damage to the infrastructure, panicked friends and relatives trying to reach each other in the build-up to, as well as during and after, an extreme event quickly jam the phone lines. In the aftermath of Tracy a national registration and inquiry system was set up by the Natural Disasters Organisation and operated by Red Cross, but systems always find a way to crash. In 2009, for example, the Bushfires Royal Commission into Black Saturday interrogated multiple breakdowns in the Country Fire Authority's emergency warning and telecommunications systems.[5]

But back to 1974. Hedley Beare describes how it felt to be disconnected so suddenly: 'When you're without telephone, post office and all of those things, you're actually standing alone in the universe.' Or, as RAAF commander Air Commodore David Hitchins mused thirteen years later, 'Amazing how we are dependent on a telephone. You want to do something, you put your hands out for the phone and all you get is a hissing noise.' Hitchins had been out of Darwin at Smith Point in Kakadu (not then a national park) on Christmas Eve, and when he tried to tune in to the radio at first light all he heard was static. 'We didn't really know what had gone on and then late in the morning, out of the black clouds, appeared one of my old DC3s from Darwin...That particular aeroplane and that crew had been evacuated from Darwin.' He went to board the plane with his family but was told that his wife and daughter should stay where they were because there was nothing to go back to. So they stayed, and as he flew back over his own collapsed house he saw there was another DC3 wrecked in his back garden. The RAAF, with the airport next to it, is the largest single piece of real estate in Darwin. It was home to fifty or so light planes, the civilian airport facilities and hundreds of people. When Hitchins got there he found hangars built in World War Two had simply crumpled, aeroplanes were lying on their backs, helicopters were crushed. 'The whole place was just like one vast rubbish dump.' The control tower and the communications at the army base were wrecked. The emergency back-up in Berry Springs (shared with the ABC) had also been flattened.

Curly Nixon remembers that at around two on Christmas morning 'the ABC fellow that was on the air, he said: "Well the roof looks like it's going and I'm going." That was the last time we heard from the ABC.' The ABC fellow was Sally Roberts' husband. He'd driven in at midnight when it became clear how bad the cyclone was going to be, because he didn't want things left in the hands of an inexperienced announcer.[6] Sally was upset because she thought he should be with her, not worrying about the news. It was seven in the morning before someone who'd been rostered on for 5 am staggered into the studios and said that the northern suburbs were 'destroyed'. By that stage, there was no way that information could be shared. Don Sanders remembers that the ABC's communications were 'all part of a weird setup' that had been put together 'at the time of the Indonesian confrontation and put up down at the 32 mile, inland...Responsibility for the transmitter was shared between ABC, Telecom and Defence Department thus it all got a bit messy as to who was responsible for getting it up and running again.'

Don Sanders managed to get a radio message out of Darwin early in the morning by using a ship's radio, though he doesn't specify a time. 'All I said was, "Darwin devastated by cyclone. All transmissions stopped. Anticipated up to 35,000 evacuees." I wanted to let them know that in my estimation that they should be starting to do something...I just wanted to let them know that something bloody serious had happened up there.' Charles Gurd remembers finding a policeman—a Sergeant Kettle—who was in charge of communicating with ambulances and asking him to help get a message out. 'Who to?' Kettle asked. 'The outside world,' was Gurd's reply. That message, sent out via the Postmaster-General at Mount Isa, from where a message was sent to Canberra, was received just before 11 am. By that time other messages had already made it through.

Major-General Alan Stretton, a military man who'd served in

World War Two, Korea, Malaya and Vietnam, was the newly appointed and founding Director-General of the Natural Disasters Organisation. His new job was about to become very interesting, very quickly. It was 6.20 am Canberra time (4.50 am in Darwin) when Stretton got a call from the Cyclone Tropical Warning Centre in Perth saying that a cyclone had hit Darwin. That was around the time his kids were getting out of bed demanding their presents. 'This call started the longest week of my life.'

Stretton then called the Darwin police station to see what was going on and spoke to a sergeant on duty named Taylor. The cyclone was still going, it was dark, and Taylor couldn't judge, as yet, how bad things were. Ever the optimist, he told Stretton that the hospital had not reported any casualties. Of course at that time people were still battling the winds and couldn't have made it to the hospital if they wanted to. Stretton's call to Taylor was one of the last to get through for many hours. From that point there was no direct official communication with Darwin until about ten, when the Western Australian ship M.V. *Nyanda* entered Darwin Harbour, and managed to establish a tenuous Morse link. At 10.30 am a weather officer in Darwin spoke to a weather officer in Perth and reported that it looked as if the place had been bombed. A message was sent by the secretary of the Northern Territory at around the same time, via Adelaide. That message was addressed to both Jim Cairns and Stretton. 'Darwin completely devastated by cyclone last night...'

There was the issue of communicating with the outside world, but there was also the issue of communicating within Darwin itself. How do you make a series of practical decisions when the people on the ground have no way of speaking to each other unless they are standing face to face? Your first impulse would be to get in your car and drive but, on that first day at least, the rubble was so thick on the roads that cars couldn't make it through and the people driving them couldn't keep up with the number of flat tyres. Those who got anywhere generally did so on their rims. Cedric Patterson remembers:

> One of the other little things that occurred was that, as you went about your business during the day or such like, you would see somebody. For instance, I can remember seeing Babe Damaso and I waved to him and he waved back. Now when I saw somebody, I'd say: 'Well I saw Babe Damaso today, he's all right.' And Babe would say: 'I saw Cedric Patterson today, he's all right,' and that was the way the information got around.

In the hours and days after Cyclone Tracy this organic unfolding of events that took place as a series of autonomous actions led to what Bill Wilson called 'independent fiefdoms'. There was a lot of this happening: senior figures taking direct action without consultation, because consultation was not possible. It was necessary to make clear decisions at top speed but some decisions inevitably caused later controversy. The relationships, hierarchical and otherwise, between these senior men were to become increasingly tricky over the next few days because of the lack of clarity around areas of authority. Who had it and who didn't? Who cared?

David McCann's position as magistrate meant he was thrown into the thick of it. He describes the scene at Darwin police station: 'Officers said, "Look we've got a lot of prisoners here and Fannie Bay has been virtually destroyed."' Arrangements were made to send longer-term prisoners to Alice Springs, which meant that twenty-nine prisoners were put on a bus at around 4 pm that day. But there were other prisoners serving short sentences, or who had only been picked up the night before. Like most of the people of Darwin, they no longer had a roof over their heads whether they were in prison or

Cars in the pool of the Darwin Travelodge

RICK STEVENS / *SMH* FAIRFAX

THE AGE

Thursday, December 26, 1974 250 Spencer St., Melbourne 60 0421 (Classified 60 0611) 121st Year 16 Pages 9c

Death toll could rise as rescuers search rubble of buildings

Darwin cyclone kills 44

'It just ripped houses away'

By ROSS WARNEKE

"Darwin looks like a bombed city — it will be years before it's back to normal," Canadian Jack Wallace said last night.

Mr. Wallace, a builder, who has lived there for 10 years, said most of the city's buildings were "smashed to pieces. There is nowhere left for people to live".

Mr. Wallace fled to Katherine, 200 miles away, with his wife and 11-year-old daughter after his timber house was flattened at 3 a.m. yesterday.

"The cyclone hit us at about two o'clock," he said last night. "It was the roughest thing I've ever been through. It just ripped the houses off their concrete foundations.

"I'd say none of the 2000 houses in the northern suburbs would be liveable after this morning. There is no power or water.

"When we left town at midday everyone was sheltering in schools. They are about the only solid places around."

Mr. Wallace said Darwin knew the cyclone was coming. "The ABC radio station kept on the air after midnight to issue warnings, but everything went dead at two o'clock.

"No one was taking any notice anyway. We had a cyclone warning a few weeks ago and it turned out to sea before it reached us.

'Too cocky'

"I suppose this time we were too cocky."

Mr. Wallace said not even concrete structures were safe from the cyclone. A block of flats near his house collapsed, trapping several people beneath concrete pylons.

"After we thought the cyclone had passed, all the neighbors formed a group to check every house for injured people.

"But I guess we misjudged because the edge of the cyclone came back about four o'clock and kept blowing until about 5.30.

"I made my wife and daughter lie face down on the concrete slab our house was built on. It's the only reason they survived."

Mr. Wallace said the roads out of Darwin were like obstacle courses. "Hundreds of steel power poles were bent down to the ground. There was timber and glass and iron all over the place.

"When I drove through the central business area, some of the buildings were buckled. The roof had been blown off the hospital."

Mr. Wallace said he had lived through two cyclones, a hurricane and a tornado before he came to Australia. "I think this one was stronger than the four of them put together.

Mr. Wallace said the noise of the cyclone was "deafening".

"It was an unbelievable roar. When our place started to disintegrate it was even worse. There was nothing we could do.

"I was too scared to stand up to see what was happening."

Huge winds leave 25,000 homeless

At least 44 people were killed by a cyclone which wrecked Darwin yesterday. Hundreds more are missing or injured.

Most of the city was flattened by the killer wind, which ripped buildings apart.

Up to 25,000 people are reported homeless in the Christmas Day tragedy.

The Federal Government has mounted a massive relief operation. A complete evacuation of Darwin's 48,000 population is being considered.

Rescue teams fear the final death toll could be more than 100.

An army report received late last night put the number of known dead at 44.

The report describes Darwin as looking "like it has been hit by an atom bomb." Nearly every building has been destroyed.

Darwin was without power last night and food was running out. There was no fresh water and the sewerage system was threatened with breakdown.

Early this morning the Natural Disasters Organisation headquarters in Canberra received an urgent call from Darwin for water purification tablets and dried milk.

All aircraft in Darwin when the cyclone hit were destroyed.

Cyclone Tracy tore roofs from buildings, shattered windows and brought down power lines. Cars were overturned and trees ripped from the ground. Residential areas were flooded.

The cyclone hit Darwin at 2 a.m. yesterday. The city was lashed by winds up to 200 kmh until about 5.30 a.m.

Last night the cyclone was moving at about 10 kmh east-south-east over Arnhem land.

The Royal Australian Navy has ordered the aircraft carrier **Melbourne**, equipped with helicopters, to prepare to sail for Darwin at midnight tonight.

The destroyers **Stuart** and **Brisbane** were also ordered to prepare to sail tonight. **Stalwart, Supply, Vendetta and Hobart** are to sail at midnight tomorrow.

The director-general of the Federal Government's Natural Disasters Organisation (Major-General A. B. Stretton) said the Darwin disaster was potentially the worst in Australia's history.

The Acting Prime Minister (Dr. Cairns) is expected to fly to Darwin this morning. Last night he described the situation as "a national disaster".

A naval patrol boat, **HMAS Arrow,** capsized and sank in Darwin harbor when the cyclone struck. One man drowned and another is missing, but the other 16 crew survived.

Another patrol boat, **HMAS Attack,** was blown ashore but there were no casualties.

Other vessels known to have run aground are the **Mutual Enterprise,** the trawler **N. R. Harris,** the oil rig support boat **Bluff Creek** and the fishing vessel **Cat Bird.**

The roof was torn off Darwin hospital but patients had already been shifted to another building.

The Minister for Defence (Mr. Barnard) yesterday offered the full resources of the defence forces to help with relief work.

A VIP aircraft left Canberra yesterday afternoon with a surgical team and medical stores. Major-General Stretton was also on board.

An RAAF Hercules transport plane left Richmond (NSW) air base with a medical team and equipment.

The armed services and the Red Cross have been asked to assemble blankets, lightweight clothing and general welfare stores as soon as possible.

The army was assembling relief stores to be moved by the RAAF.

Buildings at Darwin airport were reported last night to be wrecked.

Naval shore installations, including naval headquarters in Darwin and an oil installation, were badly damaged.

Two walls of the Weather Bureau building fell away, forcing staff to evacuate.

Major-General Stretton said: "It is a scene of devastation. Cars have been piled up, telephone boxes smashed, the roofs of buildings have been lifted off, and one eight-storey building literally did the tango".

The Minister for the Northern Territory (Dr. Patterson) joined the VIP aircraft, a BAC-111, at Mackay.

Late last night, the proprietor of the Pine Tree Motel at Katherine, Mrs. Davis, said the town had received reports that the cyclone reached Pine Creek, about 60 miles from Katherine.

It the cyclone continued on its course in a straight line from Pine Creek it was likely it could hit Katherine, she said.

Four tons of baby food donated by the Heinz Company, as well as blankets, clothing and food, were flown out of Melbourne under the direction of the Red Cross yesterday.

Continued — 2.
• History of disaster — 2.

This is the fearsome eye of Tracy

CYCLONE
DARWIN
ALICE SPRINGS
BRISBANE
SYDNEY
PERTH
MELBOURNE

This satellite picture shows cyclone Tracy soon after it struck Darwin. The picture was taken by the American weather station, Essa-8, orbiting at an altitude of about 1000 kilometres.

Tracy could strike again, Weather Bureau officials warned yesterday.

The cyclone could "recurve" once it hit the Gulf of Carpentaria, they said.

The cyclone could gain strength at sea and career south on to the northern coastline of Australia a second time.

Cyclone Tracy developed in the Timor Sea north of Bathurst Island on Monday, and closed in on Darwin, taking a south-easterly course at about 10 kilometres an hour.

"The anemometer at the airport registered 140 knots before it was apparently blown away," a forecaster at the Perth Weather Bureau said last night.

Two walls of the Darwin bureau had been blown down.

The Perth bureau replaced its Darwin counterpart yesterday in monitoring Tracy's movements.

The Perth bureau said Tracy was heading in an east-south-easterly direction across Arnhem Land.

Like an atomic bomb: Army

This dramatic account of Cyclone Tracy was radioed from Darwin late last night by the Army.

It was sent from the duty officer at Larrakeyah army barracks, Darwin to the 103 Signal Unit, based at Townsville. The message said:

"Winds in tropical Cyclone Tracy have now been assessed as at least 170 kmh.

"Those who experienced Cyclone Althea in Townsville state that cyclone Tracy was much worse.

"The situation through Darwin is serious. There are 44 known dead.

"Almost all buildings are damaged.

"Casuarina High School is housing 3500 homeless refugees.

"The Department of the Northern Territory is requesting air evacuation of up to 25,000 refugees.

"No fresh water available, therefore sewerage is in jeopardy.

"Director of Housing and Installation states that there is not one electrical circuit in Darwin. All circuits will need to be rebuilt which will be a lengthy process.

"Darwin Hospital extensively damaged. However, Department of Housing is carrying out repairs.

"Darwin at present looks as though it has been hit by an atomic bomb.

"Regrettably historical buildings—Christ Church Cathedral, Naval Headquarters and the Administrator's residence, Flagstaff House — have all been destroyed.

"All commercial light aircraft destroyed. RAAF DC-3 destroyed."

NEWS SUMMARY

Housing approvals look up

New building approval statistics show the first improvement in approvals for housing since May. —PAGE 2.

Cairns warns on GMH

General Motors-Holden's workers would be wise to realise there is a chance of retrenchment, the Acting Prime Minister (Dr. Cairns) warns. —PAGE 2

Gair's remarks start storm

Liberals and the Democratic Labor Party bitterly attack remarks made in Dublin by the DLP's former leader, Mr. Vince Gair. —PAGE 4

$21m wanted to beat floods

Seven councils apply for a $21 million Federal Government grant to widen stormwater drains as a flood prevention measure. —PAGE 4

'Spy chief' resigns

The man named in newspaper reports as head of alleged illegal domestic spying by the Central Intelligence Agency resigns as head of counter-intelligence operations. —PAGE 5

Britain's poll on Market

Irish and British sources are believed to have told the Prime Minister (Mr. Whitlam) that Britain's Common Market referendum may be held in June. —PAGE 5.

● *ODD SPOT*

British undertakers have been warned that a new type of plastic-trimmed coffin could explode in the crematorium. The Cremation Society of Great Britain said coffins made with plastic beading and other synthetic mouldings are a hazard to staff.

INDEX TO PAGES

WEATHER TODAY

CITY: Few showers. Chance of a thunderstorm. Expected top temperature 17. (Yesterday 17).

Details — 4

Stonehouse in court today

Missing MP wants to stay here

By JOHN RENTSCH

Mr. John Stonehouse, the missing British Labor MP found in Melbourne on Christmas Eve, wants to stay in Australia.

His application to stay will depend on the outcome of his appearance in Melbourne Magistrates Court this morning.

Mr. Stonehouse, 49, a Privy Councillor and former Cabinet Minister, was detained as a suspected prohibited immigrant about 11.15 a.m. on Tuesday.

Immigration laws require that anyone detained for 48 hours be brought before a court to either face a charge, be remanded, or be discharged.

Commonwealth police guarded him at a Maribyrnong detention centre yesterday as he had a "better than average Christmas lunch".

Mr. Stonehouse's detention has ended an international search for him since he disappeared while going to a beach at Miami, USA, for a swim on November 20.

It also appears to have ended his political and international business careers.

Mr. Stonehouse has telegrammed an apology to the British Prime Minister (Mr. Wilson) but his disappearance has ruined his seven-year plan to make himself wealthy enough to bid for Labor Party leadership.

In his telegram to Mr. Wilson Mr. Stonehouse said: "My wish was to release myself from the incredible pressures being put on me, particularly in my business activities and various attempts at blackmail."

He said he supposed his disappearance could be summed up as "a brainstorm, or a mental breakdown".

His mother, Mrs. Rosina Stonehouse, 80, a former Labor activist, said yesterday: "I feel I'm in seventh heaven. The day of miracles has not passed."

She described some reports and rumors about her son, published since he disappeared, as "absolutely libellous".

They included reports that Mr. Stonehouse was a communist spy, an American CIA spy and a failing businessman.

Other reports described Mr. Stonehouse as a James Bond type character, wealthy and elegant.

Mr. Wilson denied the spy allegations after Mr. Stonehouse disappeared.

He told the House of Commons there was no truth at all in Press reports which had been published "in the form of alleged fact".

Mr. Stonehouse, the member for Walsall North in the Midlands, is a former parliamentary secretary, Minister for Technology, Postmaster-General and Minister for Posts and Telecommunications.

Pressures

Melbourne police, who detained him after "a couple of weeks of investigation", say Mr. Stonehouse told them he disappeared because he had been worried that "pressures" were becoming too much for him.

He said he wanted to shed his past and start afresh in Australia.

Melbourne police were not sure at first if he was Mr. Stonehouse or another missing Englishman, Lord Lucan.

Scotland Yard has been searching for Lord Lucan since he disappeared after his children's nanny was found murdered.

Mr. Stonehouse has lived in a $35-a-week flat at the Centre City Club, in Flinders Street, since arriving in Melbourne.

• Stonehouse MP detained — 3
Ebenezer column—2.

Mr. Stonehouse leaves Commonwealth police headquarters in Melbourne yesterday.

The *Age*'s Boxing Day headlines...

...as they appeared, 26 December 1974

FAIRFAX

THE AGE

Saturday, December 28, 1974 250 Spencer St., Melbourne 60 0421 (Classified 60 0611) 121st Year 40 Pages 9c*

It's a $500 million mess

Typhoid, looters strike Darwin

From DAVID ENGLISH

DARWIN. — Typhoid fever has broken out in cyclone-stricken Darwin. Health authorities fear a large-scale outbreak.

At least one case has been confirmed in an overcrowded refugee centre in North Darwin.

Police say shots have been fired at looters.

Large quantities of typhoid and cholera vaccine were airlifted into the smashed city yesterday. A mass vaccination programme has started.

There are already widespread outbreaks of dysentery caused by the breakdown of the water supply and sewerage system.

Darwin has been placed under strict police control and an extra 150 police have been flown in from southern States.

Police armed with shotguns and .38 revolvers are patrolling the city. Weapons are openly displayed.

Police have confirmed that looters have been fired on. Unconfirmed reports say five people have been shot at during looting sprees.

More police — probably another 50 from Victoria — are expected today.

Water crisis

Entry into Darwin has been virtually stopped because of the worsening water shortage. Natural Disasters Organisation officials have rationed people to one bucket of water each for washing.

Drinking water is extremely short and large supplies of beer and soft drink will be flown in today.

Medical items being sent to Darwin include four million diarrhoea tablets, 200,000 water purification tablets, 20,000 tetanus shots, 20,000 penicillin tablets, 24,000 penicillin capsules, 5000 sets of operating theatre clothing, and X-ray equipment.

Other supplies include 30,000 blankets, 20,000 one-day ration packs (equivalent to 30,000 meals), four tons of powdered milk, 350,000 disposable napkins and three semi-trailer loads of lavatory paper.

The massive airlift of refugees from Darwin went on yesterday. More than 2500 people, mostly women and children, were flown out on RAAF and commercial planes.

Lack of aircraft prevented the evacuation of another 500 who were scheduled to leave.

The director-general of the Natural Disasters Organisation (Major General Stretton) has called for extra aircraft today.

Armed guards were placed beside evacuation aircraft yesterday after cyclone victims rushed a plane.

Continued — 2.

Where do you start to clean up a mess like this? The bill is likely to top $500 million, say Darwin officials.

PM arrives today

From STAFF REPORTERS

The Prime Minister (Mr. Whitlam) will arrive in Darwin today for an on-the-spot assessment of relief work needed following the devastating Christmas Day cyclone.

Mr. Whitlam cut short his trip to Europe on Thursday night. He has called an emergency Cabinet meeting in Sydney on Monday to decide on Government action.

But the people of Darwin seem apathetic. Some are openly hostile to his visit.

One resident said: "We don't need politicians, we need help".

People, who were not willing to be named, said they thought the visit by a stream of politicians was not needed.

So far, the Acting Prime Minister (Dr. Cairns), Senator Douglas McClelland, the Opposition Leader (Mr. Snedden), the Attorney-General (Senator Murphy) and others have flown in to view the damage.

The Minister for Northern Development (Dr. Patterson) said in Darwin yesterday it would cost $500 million to rebuild.

This estimate had been worked out by his department, he said.

Last night Senator Murphy said the Federal Government fully intended to rebuild Darwin.

Mr. Whitlam said on arrival in Perth last night he had been appalled by the reports of loss of life and damage in Darwin.

He flew immediately to Alice Springs where he spent last night.

As Darwin slowly recovered yesterday from its ordeal, the extent of Cyclone Tracy's destruction became clearer:

- The death toll rose to 45. More than 400 are injured and at least 100 people are still missing. (Casualty list—page 4.)
- The RAAF was still searching for 13 small ships missing after the cyclone. One wreck was found 200 yards inland.
- At least 10,000 homes were completely wrecked. Construction authorities said the rebuilding would take years.
- Water supply and sewerage systems have been destroyed.

The massive airlift continued yesterday to evacuate up to 20,000 people from the city.

More than 3000 — mostly women and children — have already been flown out.

A further 5000 are expected to be evacuated today when giant Qantas 747 jumbo jets are swung into the rescue operation.

A navy task force of nine ships — including the aircraft carrier HMAS Melbourne — is steaming at top speed for Darwin with helicopters, power generators, building materials, water producing equipment and other relief supplies.

The first of the ships will not arrive until Tuesday.

The PM and the WA Premier (Sir Charles Court) in Perth

The death toll mounted yesterday as rescue workers began sifting through the tons of rubble of the wrecked houses, shops and offices.

Three more bodies were found, bringing to 45 the known dead.

The toll could go even higher.

Yesterday afternoon more than 2000 people milled around at Darwin Airport waiting to get on any aircraft going south.

Special measures have been taken to ensure that those evacuated have at least some money.

Mr. Whitlam said all Darwin evacuees would receive amounts equivalent to two weeks special benefit — $31 a week for adults plus $5.50 for each child.

DARWIN DISASTER

Victoria police have telephone numbers for inquiries about Darwin people.

The numbers are 663 4212, 663 4213, 663 4214 and 663 4215.

Police yesterday urged people to keep their inquiries brief.

They said people should first give the surname of the Darwin person they were inquiring about, then his Christian names and his Darwin address.

Darwin fund mounts

Australians gave hundreds of thousands of dollars yesterday to Darwin relief appeals.

"The Age" is acting as a collection agency for the Red Cross Darwin appeal. It has given $3000.

Donations can be delivered or posted to "The Age" offices at 250 Spencer Street, or 239 Collins Street.

Cheques and money orders should be made out to the Darwin Red Cross appeal.

NEWS SUMMARY

Stonehouse plea

British MP John Stonehouse has written to the Labor and Immigration Minister (Mr. Cameron) asking to be allowed to stay in Australia.

—PAGE 2

Child murderer

Sydney police continue their search for escaped child murderer Rhonda Hoffman and four other girl prisoners who escaped yesterday from Parramatta training centre.

—PAGE 2

Farmers' record

Wimmera and Mallee wheat growers are reaping record crops, a Grain Elevators' Board member says.

—PAGE 4

Baby drug danger

Many mothers are giving their babies analgesics and sedatives unnecessarily, according to doctors at the Royal Children's Hospital.

—PAGE 4

Jack Benny dies

Jack Benny is dead. The 80-year-old comedian, who kept the world laughing for 50 years, died of cancer.

—PAGE 6

AUS accused

Singapore Government officials claim Asian students are being groomed in Australia as political activists to oppose their own non-communist Governments when they return home.

—PAGE 6

ODD SPOT

Christmas Day was anything but a peaceful time in Johannesburg's African township of Soweto. Four hundred blacks were admitted with stab wounds out of the 600,000 population — all apparently from isolated incidents.

WEATHER TODAY

CITY: Local showers. Cool winds. Expected top temperature 22 (Yesterday 32).

Details — 13

...as remembered, 28 December 1974

FAIRFAX

Two days after the cyclone, the strain shows on the face of this woman as she carries her two children at Darwin Airport. 27 December 1974

VIC SUMNER / *SMH* FAIRFAX

out of it. McCann couldn't track down Jock Nelson, the Territory's administrator, to get permission for his preferred solution, so he took it upon himself to write 'released' against the names of prisoners who had less than three or six months left of their term (he can't remember which) and 'they all raced out of the police cells' at around three in the afternoon. Eight prisoners remained at Fannie Bay Gaol, and another four were picked up over the course of the day. Bill Wilson recalls seeing one prisoner, a man he'd arrested a few months before, wandering down the Stuart Highway. He gave him a lift. Quite a few prisoners ended helping out with the general clean-up, or on cooking duty at the various relief centres which were being set up in high schools around the town.

Over at the RAAF, Hitchins decided to spray the pesticide malathion as a protection against disease. He had 'spoken to the Department of Health and got nowhere. Bugger them all,' he thought, 'we'll do it ourselves.' His planes spent 'the next three or four days beating up and down the main streets of Darwin at about 100 feet and I think they used to possibly drink a little bit of beer in the evenings and Darwin got sprayed and we didn't have a health hazard. I do believe that the action I took was possibly a little high-handed.' High-handed it was, but no one objected and crop dusters fogged on and off over the next few weeks. While there are still questions asked about using chemicals like this, Darwin mists against mosquitos using malathion to this day.

There was no shortage of leaders, though they were not always the most obvious or most senior men around. As Ray McHenry put it:

> Born leaders came out of the rubble...Nobody really needed to tell Ben Hammond to have a look at what had happened with a power break-down...but he was at the power station at about 6.30 on Christmas morning assessing the damage. Bob Prickett, the man in charge of the Darwin water supply arrangement was in fact down at Darwin River Dam at

> 7 o'clock…Harold Bradford was at the bus depot about 7 o'clock assessing the situation of buses…Tom Abbot, the then town clerk, was another man who had council machinery and trucks with drivers available very early on Christmas morning, starting on a street-clearing operation.

McHenry himself had the seniority and the temperament to emerge as one such leader. This inevitably set him against the leader that the Commonwealth were flying in: Major-General Stretton. Stretton's understanding was that he was in 'supreme command' of Darwin during the days of the emergency and indeed, that is the authority Jim Cairns had given him. However, men like McHenry had already taken charge and remained unconvinced of the legitimacy of Stretton's certainty that he was in complete charge. Questions abound, one of which was whether a military figure should have such power, another being whether locals were in any shape to sort out the situation. Not surprisingly, the two men give conflicting accounts of what decisions were made in the hours after the cyclone, and who was responsible for making them, a situation which makes the truth hard to get to.

Stretton's version of events reads as self-aggrandising (which doesn't mean it is untrue, simply that he was immodest). He did not arrive in Darwin until eleven on Christmas night by which stage, according to the key players anyway, some major decisions such as the evacuation of Darwin had already been made. Certainly the first thing Stretton did when he arrived was to ask for the immediate establishment of a communications net 'between the police, army, RAAF and the MV *Nyanda*'. This became the responsibility of his chief of staff, Colonel Frank E. Thorogood, who worked closely with (and for) Stretton over the next six days.

It was forty hours before the radio returned, around lunchtime on Boxing Day. The song that accompanied this momentous event was the theme song to *Rush*, a historical TV drama set on the Ballarat gold diggings. People commented on the lightness of that moment; how the jaunty tune lifted their spirits. Twenty-nine-year-old Kate Cairns was interviewed thirteen years after the cyclone and she vividly remembered:

> the best thing of all that happened was when the wireless came back—well, the radio was back on…I could have cried…See, we didn't know. There was no communication. We didn't know what was happening, and then all of a sudden someone said…'Have you got a wireless that works, or a tranny?'…Anyhow we pulled it out and sure as eggs it—'Hello Darwin, we hope you're okay.'…Oh it was just wonderful. It was sort of a real communication thing, you know, it was fantastic.

Richard Creswick remembers that the ABC's return to air was accompanied by an 'influx of southern journalists'. As the first plane-load of journalists—there were some twenty of them—flew over Roma in western Queensland they were told to put their watches back an hour and a half—and twenty years. (Although given the state Darwin was in they probably should have suggested thirty years—back to 1944.) Those journalists played a crucial role in letting people around Australia know just how bad things were, but some locals were shocked by the media's insensitivity. You get a visceral sense of this watching some of the old news footage in which evacuees are doorstopped in a surprisingly blunt fashion. I watched as one badly injured man was asked what had happened to his wife. The man gulped and looked very distressed before saying, 'My wife was killed.' And I realised with a terrible start that this was Colin Clough and that I'd heard an interview his daughter Kim did for the *7.30 Report* twenty-five years later.

> You could hear this piece of tin, you could hear it coming, crashing and rolling over with the wind and the next minute Dad went 'Ahh!' and he screamed out really loud and I thought, 'Oh, God, no'. It had dug right into his back and he passed out on me and I'm lying there and I'm just thinking, 'Oh, God, what's going on?'...I screamed at [Dad], I said, 'Let's go to the car, let's go to the car.' He said 'We can't take Mummy.' And I said, 'I know.'...I remember looking at her and she only had one tiny little cut on her leg and I kept thinking, 'There's nothing wrong with you, you're not hurt.' And she was dead.

Stretton understood the power of communication and as soon as the radio was up he took to making regular broadcasts. Frank Thorogood believed that it was his way with radio that was 'one of the success stories. He has a natural ability to talk to people, an engaging personality that comes so easily. He was able to give the people the confidence that, you know things were actually happening.'[7] After Stretton died in late October 2012, his obituary in the *Sydney Morning Herald* described his time in Darwin as 'a refreshing change to the obsessive secrecy of governments in crisis long endured by Australians. Disarmingly open, he held two daily press conferences, [and] was honest.'[8]

Howard Truran remembers both his sense of isolation before the radio was restored and relief when Stretton took to the airwaves. Ten years after the event, in fact, he wrote to Stretton and thanked him. 'There was no radio; you had no contact with anybody outside your street. You never saw any of your friends, 'cause you couldn't get around, so you never contacted anybody. You just started to clean up yourself and then different words started to get around.'

Truran is referring here to the rumours that were ricocheting around the place, including the one about the numbers of the dead.

Another was that the cyclone was going to double back and hit Darwin for a second time. Later there were the stories of the apocryphal Greek men who dressed up as women so they could be evacuated on the first planes out. Anxieties about looters spread like wildfire. Police were rumoured to be shooting people's dogs out of car windows, as they drove around town. Some of these events, of course, turned out to be verifiable. But, Truran says, Stretton:

> came on the air, at night, and that was the best thing that he ever did with people, was that he talked to people at night, in his quiet voice. We used to lay in bed at night in the dark, with just the hurricane lamp, and he used to tell the people of Darwin—speaking to the people of Darwin—what had happened during the day, and what he was doing. And he says: 'Don't worry. Don't panic.' He said: 'We will get you all out.'

WE WILL GET YOU ALL OUT

THE DISASTER plan that was still in development when the cyclone struck had decreed a meeting point in the event of such an emergency. First thing on Christmas morning that point was six feet under water. Not a promising beginning. People then gravitated towards the Darwin police station and Hedley Beare recalls stumbling into a makeshift morgue along the way to the first informal meeting that took place.

> I went through, down a passageway that was dark, because there were no electric lights, and the water was dripping through the ceiling—this is the police station! When we came to the corner and turned there was a very darkened room, and all the corpses were lined up, one by one, on the floor.

Some planning committee members had been injured, and some were on leave, but others stepped into the breach.

David Hitchins remembers:

> Mr O'Brien being there with a can of beer in his hand. He was definitely not in full possession of his faculties and I do believe he was shocked and I was told that his house—he was married with several youngish children and I do remember being told that his house was torn asunder around his head and that may well account for the fact he was in a shocked condition.

According to Jim Bowditch, O'Brien had not long before been dug out from under his house by Fannie Bay prisoners.

Despite their various difficulties this group of men, including Charles Gurd, David McCann, Tiger Brennan, Alan O'Brien, Jim Gallacher, Grant Tambling and others, came together. One can imagine the unlit room in the police station that had only recently been built on the corner of Mitchell and Bennett streets. The temperature is starting to rise again, which means the humidity is too. There's filthy water and broken glass on the floor. A shocked and possibly hungover Brennan, his pith hat on as always, is filling the room (as always) with cigar smoke. Poor O'Brien is standing there with a beer in his hand. Beare is reeling from his slalom through the corpses, but he's hoisted a cheeky grin back onto his face because he's such a positive man. At forty-two, he wears his greying brown hair in an acceptably minor comb-over. His expressive dark eyes, in contrast to the smile, are sad. Gurd is imposing, tall and balding. Tambling has dark hair, longish by politicians' standards (it is the seventies after all) and a heavy-set brow. Ray McHenry is forty-one, a handsome man with a dimpled chin and the compulsory sideburns. It's a crowded, close room for a group of big blokes who have all survived the hardest night of their lives and are about to begin their longest week.

According to McHenry:

> The first meeting of the Emergency Services Group took place at 2 pm on Christmas Day. In the meantime those who had roles in the disaster situation as Heads of the various Committees had already swung into action...There was a distinct calm amongst those who had a role, yet I suspect many felt the enormity of the task at hand because, for the first time [we] were able to put together some basic appreciation of what had happened in the various geographic areas of Darwin...The decision to evacuate was canvassed, and subsequently confirmed at a second meeting held at 6 pm that day.

Beare says that the 'decision to evacuate was made not by show of hands but just by a general awareness amongst that group...It was almost self-evident...[Stretton] says he made the decision, but in fact it was a consensus that just was...was there.'

That evacuation was such a strong impulse says many things. In part it's just an adrenaline-fuelled reflex: not fight but flight. But it also says something about colonisers' tenuous connection to the lands of the Larrakia nation on which Darwin was built that the first thought when disaster hit was to bodily lift everyone out of the place. It also speaks to a frontier-town mentality, in which it was the role of working men to protect their women and children from the harsh conditions their jobs had compelled them to live in.

This is not to say there wasn't a serious basis for concern regarding the survivors' well-being. The decision was, in part, a response to Charles Gurd's advice that disease was bound to break out, given the lack of fresh water and the large number of people jammed into evacuation centres. The centres weren't set up to house people long term and it would be a while before basic services like running water and sewerage would return. McHenry also mentions the widespread concerns that Tracy would double back and send all the debris flying about again. That prediction did not eventuate; nonetheless the possibility of Tracy returning, or a second cyclone hitting the city, needed to be taken into account.

Stretton's arrival that night unbalanced the delicate ecosystem of power and responsibility that had developed over the traumatic first day. It was Hitchins' job to meet Stretton at the airport (based next to the RAAF) at 11 pm. That first meeting did not go well:

> I was driving him along a dark airfield after I met him at the aeroplane, but he told me, or gave me to understand, that he had the full authority of the Australian Government to take charge of Darwin and everything there and he had total command of the place, including, I believe he told me that he had powers in excess of those held by the Administrator. If he didn't tell me that then, he certainly did tell me sometime later. I was a little concerned about my own position and I sought an assurance from my own Service that the normal chain of command would apply, and I was very promptly officially told that that was so and that I was certainly not under the command of anyone other than those I would normally be under the command of.

McHenry claims Stretton disputed the decision to evacuate at the first meeting held after his arrival (around midnight) but Stretton denies this:

> Although there were varying opinions expressed about the necessity for evacuation and other matters, no positive decisions were taken at these meetings except that they would all meet again at 9 am on Boxing Day. This 9 am conference on Boxing Day therefore provided the forum for me to take firm control and co-ordinate the rehabilitation of the city.

Stretton's control may have been firm but it was repeatedly questioned and always beset by tensions both complex and counter-intuitive. Darwin's public servants saw—and resented—it as a military incursion, even though Stretton himself was of the view that it was civilians who should manage the relief and rebuilding. He and Ray McHenry were in agreement over this one thing at least: there should be no suggestion that Darwin was under military rule. This was understandable, but it had the effect of cutting out of the relief effort people who were trained to deal with the situation—as Air Commodore Hitchins discovered.

Like Stretton, Hitchins had fought in World War Two and Korea and had flown into Vietnam. His nickname was Crazy Horse, and he was not a man to be messed with. In all his photos the man has sparkling eyes, a jaunty moustache and a warm smile, but the smile would not be so apparent in the days to come. Hitchins believed the military should have coordinated the relief operations. In his view they 'were probably better placed to cope with it than anyone else and therefore should be given a chance to get on with it.' He felt particularly strongly on this matter when it came to the evacuation itself. Indeed, he had begun organising it with Qantas when McHenry told him he hadn't the authority to arrange 'anything of the kind'. Hitchins says:

> I apologised to the gentleman with whom I'd been speaking and said, 'Well, I'm very sorry. If I haven't got any authority around here, which apparently I haven't, if you want to see me I will be back at the Airforce Base where I do have some authority.' So I packed myself up and left them to it.

He was aware of fears that 'the military jackboot' was about to descend 'upon the population'. But he believed that his 'relationship and that of the other military commanders in Darwin was such that we would not have a problem'.

'I really and honestly believe that we knew—we were residents of Darwin in the same way as anyone else was—I am confident that we could have dealt with the problem without that sort of objection arising.' He thought a more serious concern was the Darwin people reacting badly to orders from down south.

His authority denied, Hitchins began evacuating some of the hundreds of people who lived on the base and for whom he was responsible. He thought it was all he could do, given McHenry's directive, despite his concern this would look as if he was taking care of his own first. (Much more shamefully, the British High Commission flew its own people out while refusing to help more broadly with any rescue efforts. In retaliation they were advised they could not fly within Australia, and ended up flying their people to Singapore.)

Hitchins remained relatively diplomatic whenever he was interviewed, but a pilot involved in the evacuation of Darwin all those years ago still has a bit to say on the matter. 'I can assure you Dave (Crazy Horse) Hitchins hated Stretton with a passion…Just why they overlooked Hitchins I have no idea, he was an ideal military man, competent, smart and a great organiser, who never suffered fools wisely.'[1] That pilot believes Hitchins never recovered from being sidelined, and also notes that he went on to be a great supporter of pilots during the strike of 1989.

So, that left civilians to deal with the problem. Hedley Beare, a compassionate and constructive man, had been quick to ask himself on Christmas Day, 'What do you do, when the world has ruptured like this?…How do we rehabilitate it?' With McHenry's and Stretton's permission he went on to coordinate the largest evacuation that has ever taken place in Australia: it's said that as many as thirty-four thousand were evacuated by air and road over a five-day period. Those figures vary wildly, in part because it was hard to know how many people drove out of town on Christmas Day. That figure was later put at 2500.

Organising the evacuation was particularly difficult when communications were fraught. Hitchins describes the elaborate process: 'If you wanted to find out what was going on on the tarmac, you had to write a note on a piece of paper, give it to someone, get him to go and find the recipient, write the answer on the back of the thing, and bring it back to you.' Beare was up against the same problem.

> We had to find a way of communicating with the bus drivers...And so our telephone was a group of about ten to twelve men, who could either walk or ride bicycles...I'd say: 'Look, would you go out to the Casuarina High School and tell Geoff Hodgson such-and-such,' and give him a list of details. He'd be gone for the day!

Casuarina is eight kilometres out of town. It would have been a hot ride.

> For about two days we were getting several hundred people out to the airport. So one day at the co-ordinating meeting I said: 'What we need is the means to communicate by radio or something, particularly to Casuarina, Nightcliff and Darwin.' And the Army brought in one of those field stations, so they located one at the MLC building, one at Darwin, Casuarina and whatever. And I think we tripled the number of people we put on the aeroplanes that day, because we could talk to the other centres.

There was difficulty in keeping up the number of voluntary evacuees to the airfield. Communication issues were one reason that it was a struggle to evacuate people. Another was the sheer numbers that had been committed to. There was a mad rush to get the population down from the official figure of forty-seven thousand (in fact there were a few thousand fewer in town over Christmas) to ten thousand, in ten days. It seems almost compulsive, and Bill Wilson and others have commented that the figure seems to have been plucked out of the air. Why ten thousand rather than fifteen thousand? Or eight, or twenty? Stretton claimed that he:

> had already doubled their recommended figure and proposed to double it again on succeeding days...It was unacceptable to have aircraft waiting with no evacuees at the airport; it was equally unacceptable to have large numbers of evacuees waiting for long periods at the airport with no aircraft.

Two days in, on 27 December: 'Dr Hedley Beare, the chairman, looked incredibly drawn as I informed him I was proposing to fly out over 4000 today and there would be considerable increase tomorrow.' Stretton had still not arrived at a final figure for evacuation but thought 'another 20,000 had to be got out'. By 28 December it's estimated that five thousand had gone by road, and twelve thousand by air. And Stretton had settled on his final figure.

> Jim Cairns reassured me that I had the full support of the Government. He stressed that the relief operation was fully in my hands. He accepted my decision to reduce the population to 10,500 and agreed that at his conference he would emphasise that I was acting in a civil capacity and there was no suggestion of martial law.

That last point might well have been a reaction to people's feeling that they were being forced out of the city. By 29 December Stretton spoke of getting eight thousand out in a single day, 'which, of course, is another record'.

By this point it starts to sound like a competition. Hitchins later commented: 'If General Stretton says the evacuation was completed in five days, I think he's probably right but I don't think it would have mattered a damn if it had been done over ten or twelve days and done in a much more organised fashion.'

Beare was helped by schoolteacher Jim Gallacher and six volunteers, and they filled as many planes as they could. Priority was given to the sick, injured and pregnant. Second priority was women and children only (unless the father was deemed to be essential to the well-being of the group). Third was elderly couples, then married couples, and lastly single people. They were allowed fifty pounds of luggage each. A powerful force at work in this prioritisation was the recurring, seldom-challenged suggestion that women had less to offer the rebuilding process. Only five to ten per cent of Darwin's female population was left in the town come 31 December. Many women had been shipped out when they didn't want to go.

Sergeant Kevin Maley and his family were on the first plane out at four on Boxing Day morning. When their home disintegrated around them, both parents and the children had been thrown fifteen metres to the ground. Maley required two hundred stitches, his wife broke her back and his daughter, Fiona, had severe leg injuries. They were among the hundreds put on planes, often in the clothes (what was left of them) in which they'd weathered the cyclone and not much else. They had identification tags tied to them if they were injured. Some were still covered in dried blood. A baby was born during a stopover in Brisbane, while the passengers waited in the Ansett terminal. In Adelaide that Boxing Day, according to the *Advertiser*, 'more than 400 haggard survivors of the Darwin cyclone poured into the airport terminal...The evacuees were nearly all women and small children. Many of the women were pregnant...bare-footed and shivering and clutching plastic bags and small boxes holding their entire belongings.' One man I spoke to was fourteen during Tracy. He remembers he was separated from his family and flown out alone. When he got onto the plane he was given a newborn to nurse for several hours. He'd never held a baby before and had no idea what to do. He is more disturbed by that memory—the responsibility and his helplessness—than much of what went before.

Quite often the planes used were military planes that were not intended for passengers. They were uncomfortable, they had no catering and no toilets. People ended up urinating in their seats—if they had seats. Julia Church remembers being strapped to the floor of a Hercules with her legs stuck out in front of her. It was incredibly crowded and there were babies crying everywhere. Once they were tied in, the army blokes stood and threw fruit to them for the flight, as if, Julia said to me, they were monkeys. Some crews fell asleep while flying; in those days there was no such thing as fatigue management.

Pilot Terese Green provides a vivid description of landing in, then leaving, Darwin. She went:

> with the sole purpose of picking up the Ladies about to give birth from the DRW Hospital...We left at 13.24 with 40 last stage pregnant ladies (much to our horror) 2CC, 2 Nursing Sisters and one doctor, 2 cats in cages (they belonged to the hospital) and my memories are the total carnage, a DC3 firmly implanted in the Base Commander's house, and the fridge in the water tower (30MTRS up). It was all downhill from there. Two ladies were in labour, so we went straight to Isa, no joy there, they were already packed from those who went by car, so running out of hours and ideas, I called up Mackay, and pleaded (no, threatened) that we needed help, and finally got in there vastly relieved, as the noises up the back were becoming terrifying to say the least.

In the short term Green ended up at a pub in Mackay to recover. In the longer term she ended up with the cats that had been on the flight that 'both lived to a great age and cost a fortune in Vet bills'.[2]

Colleen D'Arcy was evacuated with her seven children and, like many others, she struggled with a lack of information. She eventually found herself in Alice Springs after travelling to both Sydney and Brisbane. Bernard Briec was sent out after three days, with his siblings and some family friends. His mother and father stayed behind for a bit longer. 'You had to wait in alphabetical order, till your names were called, and all this sort of stuff. The men who worked at the airport said: "Forget about that, it's not working like that, it's chaos, it's mayhem. It's basically whoever's there gets on the planes."' But he was cheerful once he was on the plane and was well looked after by the friends he was travelling with. His memories of that time are not painful. His family planned to stay in Adelaide permanently, though after a few months their love of Darwin compelled them to move north again.

Katrina Fong Lim, the daughter of Darwin legend Alec Fong Lim, is the current lord mayor. She was in Sydney during the cyclone and her father, concerned the Darwin schools wouldn't open within the year, enrolled her and one of her sisters into a high school in Sydney for 1975. They were called 'Darwin refugees'. She remembers the shock of having to wear school uniforms, as well as the fact that she and her sister were the only two Chinese girls enrolled in the school. It was here she experienced racism for the first time—in Darwin she was unaware of such matters. She also remembers that an older sister went to Adelaide to complete her education and never really returned home at all. Many families were fractured in this way.

With a teenager's keen eye for bullshit, Julia Church recognised the patronising attitude of people who came out to greet them when they landed. They talked slowly, explaining obvious things like how escalators worked. On the plus side, she remembers the Salvation Army gave them seventy dollars each—and there were trestle tables of free clothes to riffle through, which was fun.

After Janice Perrin's mother got to the hospital she was told she could be treated there, or evacuated. She chose evacuation. After that, Perrin remembers, 'We didn't see her again. None of us saw her again.' A few days later Perrin and her children were also evacuated. 'Warren drove to Nightcliff High and then we listed our names and they had just a big sign and wherever you wanted to go, you went to that sign. So if you wanted to go to Sydney you went to the sign that said: "Sydney".' The airport was crowded and Perrin ended up in a fight.

> I moved my feet, which upset the case and upset the bag on top and I bent down to pick up the bag that I'd upset and they all attacked me. They just all flew at me. And I had very long hair which was plaited and they pulled my hair and they kicked me—it was really quite frightening.

Things got so out of hand that some Commonwealth police came over. It turned out that the family thought that Perrin was trying to steal their bag.

> From then on it was very nice because the Commonwealth policeman then took me and the two children into a little room at the—behind the airport desks and he gave me a brandy and patted my arm and [*laughs*] I had a whole seat to myself and then when the plane came in, he took me out to the plane with the kids and put me on.

Getting a seat to herself was no mean feat—Perrin was on the jumbo that broke the world record for the number of people on board—715 people on a jet configured for 365. She'd wanted to go to Canberra because she had relatives there but ended up in Sydney. When she arrived she was greeted by a man from Rotary, given some money (eighty-four dollars) and taken to a room with clothes piled up on tables so she could dress herself and her children properly. The man then invited her family to stay. Soon after that Perrin called Adelaide Red Cross to see if they could help her trace her mother. By this stage she was becoming concerned that her mother's punctured lung had killed her. She was eventually found in hospital in Perth: alive but not well.

This happened time and time again. So frantic was the rush to get people out that they didn't necessarily end up in a state or town where they had relatives. And then it was hard to get messages back to family to let them know where they'd ended up. Those in Darwin who had access to phones were uncertain whom to call; those evacuated could only get through to Darwin on a few lines, and they would have to leave a message and hope it would be passed on. People hung out at the various interstate airports for days on end in the hope of spotting friends or relatives on incoming flights. There was no other way of knowing if someone you loved had made it out.

When Howard Truran was interviewed about his experience fourteen years after the event he still remembers that, although he wanted his wife and kids evacuated because he was so worried for them, the experience was extremely traumatic.

> I wanted to get 'em out because everything was new to us; we didn't know what was happening. And then there was rumours that there was typhoid around, and [there was] no power, no sewerage, no nothing...[Getting them on the bus] was very heart wrenching. Therese was very upset and I was upset, and the kids. You just piled them on the bus; you didn't know when you were going to see them again: [there was] all this devastation around, and women crying

> and people on the bus and everybody [was] upset, and then just see the bus disappear.

He remembers that:

> the evacuation points were shocking: there was all the toilets of the school—you can imagine—(they) were all backed up; the stink and the stench; screaming kids; people sitting around in shock; people injured, in bandages; no clothes, except what they could find or get from their houses. It was a shocking state.

Bill Wilson says, 'the evacuation of people from Darwin was handled extremely well' but then goes on to describe traumatic scenes such as the one that Truran endured.

> Certainly the police families that I took out, we had two twenty-one-seater buses full of people from the police barracks that we put on, took out. A lot of them, tears were streaming down their face, not knowing when they were coming back to Darwin, not knowing when they'd see their husbands again. It was really traumatic stuff, leaving everything they knew...It had an impact on those of us left behind because (a) you threw yourself into your work, which was a good thing, but (b) people were lonely. It was a very lonely existence...it was probably a week before I managed to get onto Pat.

Air Commodore Hitchins remembers that no proper records were kept on how many planes left each day or where they went. He was 'incensed at the pell mell, disorganised, chaotic manner in which it was evolving'. Hedley Beare takes responsibility for the fact that people were flown all over Australia, and often didn't end up in the city they hoped to land in.

> I was sitting with the chief of the Red Cross unit who had come up, and we had people typing out—we'd found a few typewriters by then—typing up the list of people who were going on the planes. I was getting very agitated, because I was saying: 'We can't do this, we're holding up loading people. If they're sitting for four hours in an aeroplane, why can't they make a list once they're in flight?...' We sort of unilaterally said: 'No more lists. If they're out at the airport we put them on a plane, and if a person wants to go to Sydney but they happen to be on a plane to Perth, the infrastructure of organisation in the south will arrange for that.' We just needed to have every seat filled.

Beare is being generous in taking the blame: his situation was impossible. Hitchins is just one of dozens to state that Beare was a 'hell of a nice bloke' and that, with Ray McHenry, he did 'a mighty job and a very difficult job'. Despite his admiration for Beare, however, Hitchins took it upon himself to intervene, telling Stretton he 'thought it was high time that somebody, some suitably qualified person, was placed in charge of this activity because it was becoming quite chaotic.'

Stretton's first response was, once again, that civilians should be left to sort it out; however by 27 December (or 28 December—accounts vary) Hitchins was asked to take 'immediate control of the destinations of outbound aircraft'. Things improved rapidly. People were flown to the right places. Injured people had medicos to look out for them, rather than being left in the care of other traumatised passengers.

The decision to evacuate is the single most controversial decision taken in the aftermath of Cyclone Tracy. Charles See Kee, the first man of Chinese descent to be employed in Darwin's public service and a survivor of the World War Two bombings, has commented that 'all the mistakes that they made during the bombing of Darwin they made them again after Cyclone Tracy...They panicked during the bombing of Darwin, they panicked during Cyclone Tracy. I know that people were evacuated but I think a lot of it was unnecessary.'[3] He found himself wondering, 'If we have another thing in Darwin will we do it again?' Beare, in contrast, suggests that the panic was a healthy thing. 'In fact, the adrenaline of getting the city going again was the thing actually that saved a lot of us.' But See Kee is right to draw a parallel with the evacuation of Darwin in 1942; certainly the way women were treated after Cyclone Tracy created a real sense of déjà vu for those who'd been forced out before.

In her book *No Man's Land* Barbara James describes the method of the wartime evacuation, in ramshackle boats without proper provisions, as 'crude and cruel in the extreme...women and children were the ones who suffered most and were least considered'. Her mother-in-law, Wendy James, was a child at that time and her stories are devastating: she remembers the rage of her own mother, Pearl, that women were being forced out of the town, and the threats that were used to get them to go. It was terrible to experience a version of the same thing all over again thirty years later. Nellie Flynn, one of longest-lived Territorians, a venerable old woman of pioneer and Aboriginal descent, defied the evacuation orders in World War Two and defied them again after Tracy. 'For three days after the cyclone the indomitable Nellie, then aged ninety-three, hid under scraps of canvas in her roofless Rapid Creek home to escape being forced to evacuate.'[4] She was finally discovered, and allowed to stay.

Ray McHenry remains a strong defender of the decision to evacuate. 'Beware of academics and the grandstand critics who want to ram the planning jargon down your throat and criticise the decisions such as evacuation. See the problems of the evacuation system through the eyes of those affected...' He argued that those critics, often academics, came from outside the Territory.

> Their judgments were ill-informed. It would have been better without true knowledge of the situation not to have ventured an opinion at all…it's been said that it's contributed to trauma and break-down and so on; well, to me that's a bit like counting the chickens after they're hatched. None of it would have occurred had there not been a cyclone. What one had to measure is whether the effect would have been worse if all those people had stayed in Darwin.

He did, however, believe that counsellors should have been provided and regrets that they weren't.

McHenry was certainly right to suggest that most people who lived through the cyclone supported the evacuation, even if they had reservations about how it was carried out. Ken Frey says, 'I can't understand anybody, whether they be sociologists or psychologists or what, saying that it was wrong that this was done in Darwin.' Even Senator Bob Collins, despite his own reservations, told the *7.30 Report*:

> I've seen a lot of crap delivered about how it shouldn't have happened, it was a panic reaction. It's bloody nonsense. The city had no clean water, had no sewerage supplies. There was no other decision that could have been taken, other than to evacuate the women and kids.

(It should be mentioned here that Collins' concern for 'kids' is fraught. He was a witty and articulate narrator of the story of Cyclone Tracy, and I found much to like in his archival interviews. He was also, in 2004, charged with multiple child sex offences and three years later committed suicide just before the cases went to court.)

Many of those who claim to support the evacuation go on to describe a situation they clearly feel ambivalent about. Even Hitchins acknowledges that 'with the benefit of hindsight one could say that some of the evacuation was unnecessary but I do believe that it was the right decision at the time.' Bill Wilson, over the years, became more critical of the evacuation and decided that it hadn't been necessary. While he acknowledged that reducing the population in this way did leave men free to work extreme hours, he believes concerns about disease and starvation were exaggerated.

> At the time I think I was supportive of the view that we should evacuate...I'm less convinced now that the idea for the rest of the population was good...I think it was bad for the morale of the city, as it turns out, and it's taken a lot longer for people to recover.

Concerns about typhoid and cholera outbreaks were understandable, but in the event these diseases were managed effectively by a prompt vaccination program. Tetanus shots were given as well. Charles Gurd, the first man to raise concerns about an epidemic, acknowledged that none eventuated. Even gastro was held at bay. It was due, in part, to Gurd's effective management of the situation that Darwin remained relatively disease free.

Twenty years after Tracy, Elizabeth Carroll describes landing in Sydney with nothing but a man's shirt on and 'feeling like a refugee'.

> This is nothing against the people. I mean, it was wonderful to get us all out and all that, but it was what made us feel like that. I mean, we hadn't bathed, we hadn't showered; I can't remember what our hair must have looked like; no make-up: we had nothing like that. We didn't have shoes. Did we have shoes by then? I can't remember.

Wendy James suggests something similar when she talks of experiencing 'the indignity and disruption of refugees'.[5] Carroll believes that she was given no choice but to leave. 'I really wish that we could have stayed because we would have got there, we would have made it. We would have rebuilt…It was so traumatic and so hard, splitting the families, and starting a new life again.' Her kids were traumatised for years. 'Leesa used to vomit if you talked about the cyclone; she never, ever mentioned the cyclone, ever, and she would get physically sick if you mentioned the cyclone.' Carroll herself has never felt able to return to Darwin and when you read her interview, the pain and distress she still felt years afterwards are palpable.

Janice Perrin ended up staying in Canberra for two years after she was evacuated there. Like many evacuees, she never returned to Darwin, and, like many evacuees, she saw her marriage end. 'Warren had a lot of trouble settling and a lot of trouble sticking with a decision. He would decide that he'd come back to Darwin and he actually came back and sort of got to Alice Springs, then decided he didn't want to come back and drove to Canberra.' The injury to his foot from flying glass never properly healed. Carroll acknowledges that there were many separations, divorces after the cyclone but says,

> It didn't affect John and I as a couple for a few years. John was absolutely wonderful for the first few years; not that he wasn't wonderful all the way through…Then I remember two years in John started to really sort of crack and feel it. It did affect our relationship because it was not an easy [time for] many years, really, and I really do wish we could have stayed.

Julia Church's experience is typical in some ways. The evacuation was a second, unwanted, emigration hot on the heels of the family's initial move from England. Moving to Canberra was incredibly hard, particularly for her parents. 'It was like going back right to the beginning, immigrating all over again, but they were middle aged, not young.' Now in her early fifties, Julia is a renowned printmaker who lived in Italy for many years. She still feels the loss of Darwin as a home. We meet in a cafe in Canberra that feels as far away from Darwin as it's possible to be, and we are both struck by how hard she's finding it to talk about Tracy and what happened after. Every detail seems significant and painful, each represents the moment her life changed irrevocably. Julia keeps apologising for this, and seems to have a sense she's making too much of how difficult things were. 'But you're not,' I tell her. 'The archives and newspapers are full of people with stories like yours. Everyone talks of a pain they find hard to define.'

People had different reasons for the sense of loss they experienced when they were forced to leave. For some, it was being evicted from a place they'd always lived in and felt connected to; for others it was having finally found a place that they could call home, a place that they had fallen in love with. The Churches' lives had blossomed in Darwin—Julia at fourteen was loving school and discovering boys—and Canberra was a backward step. Darwin, caught up in the political tumult of the seventies, had been changing rapidly. Then suddenly Julia found herself back to old-fashioned when-the-bell-goes assemblies. At her school in Darwin:

> there were school excursions to Timor and Indonesia. It was an unselfconscious place. We hung out with Indigenous kids and even the 'local' kids came from all over the world, Chinese Australians, Greeks, Dutch. The teachers came from around the world also. It was one of the first open school systems and at school there was a lot of work done on Indigenous issues. We were being shown the bush and introduced to it. I guess I felt more of a sense of belonging rather than being other. Teachers were out there. Well travelled, radical, well read. Lesbians, communists. They wore sarongs. They introduced ideas that were new to us.

In Canberra the kids were nasty to them and accused Julia and her sister of feeling 'special' because of what they'd been through. One teacher actually said that to them. 'You might feel you're really special but you're nothing.' Julia ended up wagging all the time, and in general remembers that she and her siblings were 'pretty mental' for quite a while.

The lack of autonomy that evacuees, particularly women and children, experienced meant that for many of them they were, for the first time, treated as Darwin's Indigenous residents long had been (and as most refugees everywhere are today). 'Whites complained at being administered by methods refined against Aborigines for decades. Told where they could live, separated from spouse or children, needing permits to enter the city, at the mercy of police, politicians and pen-pushers...'[6] Separated from their families and taken from their homes. Told where to go and what to do but given minimal information. Left to sit around and wonder, 'What happens next?' People didn't like it. Of course they didn't. No one would.

The reality was that nearly half of the population of Darwin ended up scattered around Australia. Despite the fact, as the St Vincent de Paul Association for Darwin evacuees in Brisbane noted, that 'the majority had very strong feelings about Darwin being their home and returning at the earliest possible time', fifteen thousand never did return. Some of the anger around the evacuation led to the formation of residential action groups whose aim was to stay abreast of information, such as compensation, that affected evacuees. But there was more to it than that. The key reason that it was so hard for the non-returning evacuees was the loss of community. It's much easier to recover if you're with a group of people who have been through the same thing. In Julia's memory, her parents finally began to feel more settled when they could put money down on a house and set up the Woden Valley Bridge Club as a kind of Darwin away from Darwin.

Harry Giese, who had been working with the evacuation centres in the days after the cyclone, established the Disaster Welfare Council (DDWC) on 4 January 1975.

> One of the things that Ella Stack and I did—together with Bishop O'Loughlin and Ian Barker, a local lawyer...we had started to move around the suburbs and town area of Darwin to talk to groups of the people that remained in those areas, to build up something of an *esprit de corps* among them to give them a bit of hope, to try and inform them as to what was happening both here and elsewhere...Also with the interstate groups, so that we...could act as a liaison between the people here and those members of their family that were interstate.

They also provided an ongoing coordination point for voluntary agencies during the recovery period, including those from other states. The DDWC presented a report in March 1976 which recommended that large-scale evacuation of people only 'proceed in the most extreme of cases and encouragement be given to the movement of families as a social unit'.[7]

The Red Cross is just one of several organisations to ask themselves why some communities are more prepared, and more resilient, than others. Why do some just get on with the job while others fracture? Much has been written about the different fates of two superficially similar neighbourhoods in Chicago during the heatwave of 1995, which killed more than seven hundred within a week. The largest cluster of deaths occurred in the locality of North Lawndale, and the smallest in Little Village. Both areas were home to vulnerable people—a number of poor, elderly Hispanic people living alone—but in North Lawndale the fatality rate was ten times higher. The difference? Little Village was a close-knit community and people took to visiting each other when things got tough. In North Lawndale there was a drug problem, which meant there was a lot of violent crime and, as a consequence, people didn't go out much. Older people living there had no one to look in on them. The lesson generally drawn from this example is that community saves lives. But of course a sense of community is not something that can be built overnight.

After Tracy, the permanently evacuated were more likely to suffer Post Traumatic Stress Disorder (PTSD), sleeping problems, issues with addiction, anxiety, depression and a range of other disorders. A report published in the *Australian Medical Journal* in 1975 studied 67 Darwinians who'd been evacuated to Sydney. Five to eight days after the cyclone, when they were tested, 58 per cent were assessed as 'probable psychiatric cases'. (The likelihood of psychological disturbance increased with age[8] and was more pronounced in women.) A report by the same author published in a psychiatric journal in 1977[9] found that the two main risk factors for people experiencing ongoing distress were: having believed they would die, and the stress of relocation. 'While psychological dysfunction was increased initially (58 per cent) and at ten weeks (41 per cent), it had returned to an Australian general population control level (22 per cent) at fourteen months.' However psychologist Gordon Milne later found that the rate of disturbance did not drop nearly as quickly among those evacuees who never returned. In 1981, 31 per cent still suffered emotional disorders. The rate for those who returned quickly, or never left at all, was 13 per cent.

History has not been kind to our understanding of the evacuation. There is no doubt that it caused far too much distress at the time, and continued to do so for decades to come. There is no way of being certain, of course, that there wouldn't have been mass fatalities from disease, exposure or shortage of food and water, as those who took charge so obviously feared. What *is* certain is that what happened after

Cyclone Tracy has become—according to John Richardson, a recovery specialist with experience both in government organisations and with the Red Cross—a blueprint on how not to respond to catastrophe. Lives for the survivors were bisected into Before Tracy and After Tracy. This was especially so for those who never found their way back, and many of them feel sadness still.

FAULT LINES

TRACY, YOU BITCH

THERE IS a photograph, taken soon after the cyclone, of a Holden with the words *Tracy, you bitch* spray-painted across the bonnet. It seemed to capture the mood of the times.

The trend of naming cyclones and hurricanes began in 1887 with the famed Australian-based meteorologist (and expert on all things spiritual) Clement Wragge. He used the names of anything that appealed to him—from mythological creatures to politicians who annoyed him. When Wragge retired in 1908 the practice was carried on informally and it was at this point that the tradition became gendered: tropical cyclones (or hurricanes) might be named after fishermen's mothers-in-law or naval officers' girlfriends and wives. When formal naming resumed in 1963, female names were used exclusively—but Tracy changed that, as she was to change so many things. Not only was Tracy herself such a significant weather system that her name was permanently retired from use for cyclones, she also changed the naming tradition itself. 'Reeling from the enormity of damage caused to Darwin by the "she-devil" Tracy, the then minister for science, Mr William Morrison, "suggested that women would not have to bear the odium associated with tropical cyclones".'[1] Since early 1975 cyclones have been named after both men and women. (And recent research seems to indicate that more needs to be done on that front. 'Female-named hurricanes kill more than male hurricanes because people don't respect them,' claimed a *Washington Post* headline of June 2014, citing a US study that suggested 'people neither consider them as risky nor take the same precautions'.[2])

Even if one puts aside any wrangling over the hidden—or not-so-hidden—meaning behind calling a cyclone Tracy and Tracy a bitch, most people concede that Darwin has not been a town that was friendly to women. According to one commentator, 'The dearth of women at Port Essington [an early NT outpost]...Reflects in exaggerated fashion an Australian colonial problem...A new culture [built] from the old, the small, artificial male societies which give rise to the Australian legends of sport, hard drinking and mateship.'[3] Indeed almost all the women who went to Darwin in its early colonial history ended up in early graves. By 1871 there were still only twelve adult European women compared with 172 European men. Even in the decade before World War Two, the white women of the Northern Territory were outnumbered three to one by the men. In 1941 all European women and children were compulsorily evacuated (while Aboriginal children who'd been removed from their families into the 'care' of the state or the church, were left behind by all but the nuns who stood by them). Ted D'Ambrosio worked as a civilian zone warden during the war, and remembers his biggest problem was 'coping with irate husbands who didn't want their wives to go and took it out on us. I had so many bruises by the end of the evacuation it wasn't funny.'[4] Old-timer Tom Baird says that 'war did break up a lot of families and things like that—friends are scattered everywhere; some went down to Perth, some went to Sydney, Melbourne, Adelaide, Brisbane; you know, a lot of them went away and never ever came back; some of the real Territorians.'

The *Northern Territory News* was not a supporter of women, then or now. 'Girls: You're Fat!' a headline from 11 February 1974, captures the general tenor. Things weren't much better after the cyclone when the paper rose with aplomb to its task of patronising the women, at the same time as providing some nifty disaster-inspired product placement. Articles like 'Undies for the girls' claimed that the women left in Darwin got ten thousand dollars' worth of underwear, cosmetics, sunglasses and hosiery provided by Kotex, Avon and Polaroid. 'The committee said yesterday that most of the women left behind were working in essential services, including nursing, often outdoors'; they had, apparently, requested these items. On 11 January the paper returned to its tradition of a page-three girl (a tradition which appears to have been dropped for a week or so) by including a bikini-clad girl from Miami. 'It's a sobering thought that when this lovely lass was horsing around at Miami Beach, Cyclone Tracy was at work in Darwin.'

Tom Pauling was a sympathetic man. A member of the Arts Council, he was particularly sad that the Cavenagh Theatre blew away in the cyclone. He would go on to become the youngest chief magistrate in Australia, and demonstrate a progressive approach to Indigenous rights. He worked with Dr Yunupingu in setting up the Garma Council. When he was interviewed in 1980, Pauling remembered how grim the Darwin of 1970 was for women:

> A place of absolutely dull, bare, grey, fibro imminences called houses that were occupied by government servants who were here for limited tenure of two years so they never took much interest at all in their gardens. The houses were

> surrounded by aralias and there might be the odd undernourished tree somewhere or other.

Richard Creswick's wife became intensely frustrated with Darwin when she arrived in the early seventies. 'The outlets, the social outlets for women were far fewer than they are today, the cultural life was more primitive.' When Vicki Harris moved there in 1972, she too was unimpressed.

> It appeared to me to be very much a man's town in those days. It was virtually a frontier type of place. There weren't very many shops; Woolworths was in town; there was no Casuarina at that time. The shopping centre out there only opened just before Christmas of '74...I found the facilities for women, particularly those that weren't working, to be very limited.

David McCann, whose marriage broke down shortly before the cyclone, says that the type of housing provided to public servants contributed to the problems many couples were experiencing, and that 'wives weren't coping'. Margaret Muirhead, wife of Supreme Court judge James Muirhead and Chairperson of International Women's Year in the NT, concurs. 'The northern suburbs had always been a bit notorious about being so remote and women were stuck out [there]. Their husbands went off to work, probably they only had one car...'[5]

Of course it was not just Darwin where women's rights were yet to be claimed, and while change was underway there was still the distinct hangover caused by the discriminatory legislation of decades (or centuries) standing. It was only eight years since the ban on married women working in the public service had been lifted. (Bill Wilson's wife Patricia had had to leave the police force when she married him.) Women in the 1960s were routinely expected to have their husband or a male guarantor sign for a loan, even if they earned a wage. After Cyclone Tracy, when the women started to trickle back under the new permit system, Darwin officials would go and ask a woman's husband if he wanted her back before she was approved.

Many senior figures, Hedley Beare and Ray McHenry included, insist that women were not forced to evacuate. But the women themselves found that the pressure they were under to get out of Darwin amounted to the same thing. This coercion took different forms. People were offered free fares back to Darwin to encourage them to leave, but this did not guarantee they would be given permission under the permit system that was introduced on 28 December. Dawn Lawrie, who worked with evacuees, recalls mothers asking her if they could return to Darwin soon. Her answer was 'Of course!' and Lawrie was devastated when she realised that was not, in fact, true.

McHenry introduced the permit system because 'the trickle of people wanting to get into Darwin had become a flood'. It didn't help that at the very point they were trying to empty the city, politicians, journalists and others were being let in, which intensified the pressure on those who actually lived there. People were told, bluntly, that they had no options. Bill Wilson described the general approach thus: 'We're closing this place tomorrow, you've got nowhere to go, so you better pack your bags and go.' Kass Hancock claims that a soldier pointed a gun at her for a joke and said, 'You know I'll use it.'[6] She didn't laugh. General Stretton, in his regular radio interviews, was encouraging but none the less forceful. 'I urge you all to do what I said last night. If you want to take advantage of the offer of the Government to come back here at their expense, register and get yourself on an aircraft today or tomorrow.' He did go on to acknowledge, however, that some people had to stay to clean up, and also that leaving was a personal decision.

Tom Baird's wife Evelyn told him, 'Well, I'm going to put my foot down and say I'm not going.'[7] She knew that a homeless existence for months on end down south would be distressing, and she didn't want to be separated from Tom. Like all the men he was working around the clock, but that didn't mean he wanted his wife gone.

> You all worked like hell; there was that much work involved. There was very few women around at the time—most of them all evacuated, but the few that were left behind, they had a lot of work to do. My wife, they said 'You'd have to evacuate her'...So I took her into town and I said, 'Is there any voluntary work that she can do.' They said, 'Try the hospital,' so she got a job at the hospital.

Evelyn worked, like the men, until she literally collapsed.

Having maintained that women were not forced out, Beare goes on to say that some 'people' had to be told to leave because they were too traumatised to make up their own mind. 'Bear in mind all of us have a reality coloured by the experience we'd gone through, so often times you couldn't have expected rational behaviour out of people...But it was true that some people wanted to stay...and had they stayed it would have put a stress on the infrastructure of the city.' This sense of pressure contributed to the fact that some people—men and women—refused to go to hospital to get serious injuries treated for fear of being evacuated. On the flip side, others were very keen to leave and there were near riots when people thought they would miss a bus to the airport and have to spend another twenty-four hours in Darwin as a consequence.

Forty years later the rush to get the women out is hard to understand. It was clearly driven by two things: a paternalistic sense of care, and the insulting belief that women were of no use to the clean-up and, unable to cope, would become a burden. McHenry: 'I can remember

[Hedley Beare], the education guy, coming and saying, "If I can get my family out of here I will be able to concentrate in a meaningful way."' He talks of wanting his (male) workers to be able to give 'their 100 per cent effort, without the difficulties of a family sitting around on their backsides somewhere or other getting all agitated with the fact that the husband wasn't available'.[8] The thinking behind the evacuation not only infantilised women; it also put men under intolerable pressures, for months and years to come.

In an interview given soon after the cyclone, newspaper man Jim Bowditch said, 'I do think it was a mistake to rush the women out. I go along with the view that far too many men who were left here were quite useless and contributed nothing.' Church of England Minister (and founding principal of Nungalinya College) Keith Cole was another who spoke out against the evacuation of the women—although the way that support was articulated is shocking to the modern ear. He thought staying on would give 'bored, middle-aged women…something to live for and do'. Grant Tambling, a Country Liberal Party (CLP) representative in the NT's first Legislative Assembly, was less mixed in his messages: 'I think that the choice should in future be given to the women themselves to choose whether they feel they have a role to play.'[9]

McHenry argues that those who felt they could cope with the situation got back to Darwin quickly:

> this question of people being able to cope with certain things [is] pertinent, both to the evacuation process and the come back process. People who wanted to retrieve their families did so progressively; they found accommodation from somewhere or other and said, 'we want you to come back'. Other people made a conscious judgment, 'I won't subject my family to this sort of living; they're better off

> down south.' Others...said, 'I've got to have them back', and they were the ones who went and found accommodation from somewhere or other or cleared their own houses under floorboards, got tarp and God knows what.

McHenry, it should be noted, often used the word 'people' when he meant 'women'. Dawn Lawrie argued that the focus on women's inability to cope with the rugged conditions was a beat up.

> There were tales in the southern newspapers of Darwin being no place for a woman or children...Lies and damned lies. There was no threat to the women left in the town... For a few weeks Darwin was virtually a town without children and I realised then just what a dreadful act the Pied Piper had perpetrated on Hamelin. A town without children is a dead town...[10]

Road blocks were set up—illegal, some argued—which screened everyone trying to return. If you didn't have a permit, you couldn't go home and you couldn't get a permit unless you could nominate 'reasonable' premises you could live in. Lawrie takes some pleasure in recalling that there was one particular house that had weathered Tracy pretty well. Subsequently a hundred people were nominated as living there, while of course most were simply sleeping under a tarp in the ruins of a mate's house. Lawrie, the independent member for Nightcliff at the time of Tracy, was to become a key figure in the battle for citizens' rights in the months after the cyclone. She cut a dramatic figure with her beehive and caftans, and of course the *Northern Territory News* loved her. Lawrie is one of the few women to get a regular run in that paper under headlines that didn't include the word 'girls'. Her daughter, Delia Lawrie, is a member of the Labor Party and the current leader of the opposition in the Northern Territory.

On 31 December Prime Minister Gough Whitlam said 'that the people of the city would probably not be allowed back into the city for about the week'. And indeed by 2 January conditions for entry into Darwin had been relaxed slightly when McHenry stated, 'that men or women with property, business interests or essential work would now be considered for an entry permit' though 'it was not intended to issue permits to other women or to children'. However, road blocks remained in place until 1 July 1975. McHenry plays down the impact of this.

> People made a fair amount of play of saying that, you know, the ruthless bureaucracy wouldn't let people come back; it wasn't that way at all. We did suggest that for people's own benefit that they ought to think twice about bringing their families back into the sort of circumstance that applied, and until normality started to prevail.

To support his claims that the permits system was used sympathetically, McHenry has pointed out that by the end of February some twenty-five thousand people were back in Darwin. What he doesn't say is that many of these were not residents of the town but outsiders helping with the clean-up. Strangers, Lawrie argued, were being allowed in while locals fought for their right to return home. Construction workers were welcomed as long as they had their own tools, food and shelter—indeed one of the reasons given for moving people out, given the lack of resources, was to let people in who had useful skills. Some locals argued that they could provide these skills themselves but it is hard, from this distance in time, to judge the truth of that. According to McHenry, 'those who came in from out of town, army, navy people etc to help with the clean up did a marvellous, compassionate job, without taking it totally personally'.

Lawrie and her political foe Mayor Tiger Brennan usually met head to head (or perhaps beehive to pith helmet) but they were in agreement on one point: people react to catastrophe in different ways.

> I don't think they should've kept people out who lived here, you know...In a disaster people will panic, and they'll go away and then they want to come back. They wouldn't allow people to come back to see what had happened to their blinking gear while it was being looted by all the bloody hippies around the bloody place.

Brennan had a pathological hatred of hippies but he also had a point. He was just one of many who mention that people jumped in their car and left the day after the cyclone only to find that by the time they'd calmed down a few days later they were trapped outside the town's boundaries.

On 4 January Lawrie declared she'd take court action to have the permit system declared illegal. Roger Ryan of the CLP was unimpressed. 'We have been subjected to a tirade...The main reason for getting the people out of Darwin is to clean up to make it a reasonable place for the women and children to live.' Ryan, like McHenry, uses the word 'people' interchangeably with the words 'women and children', in what I read as a tacit acknowledgment that the ways in which 'people' were being spoken about was offensive. Lawrie failed in her attempts to have the permit system outlawed.

By 7 January there were only 582 children still in Darwin, and the female population was down to 23 per cent. By 16 January the men were getting restless. As they had in World War Two, some started a campaign to allow their wives back in. Curly Nixon, who still had the luxury of a wife in Humpty Doo, says, 'Now, I was here when they started the "bring the wives back" campaign, and I reckoned that it was the most stupidest thing that they ever did.'

Howard Truran had to queue for hours to get a permit that would allow him to join his wife and children down south for two weeks then return with them. When he got to the front of the queue he was told he couldn't have one.

> I really did my lolly. I suppose it was a little bit of stress. I said: 'Listen'—I abused him. I said: 'I've lived in this town for twenty years. I've seen it built up from war ruins and blown out. I've got a roof on. I've got water, sewerage, electricity. My house is liveable and I want to bring my family back. Now you get my bloody entry permit!' All the people back in the queue [had] probably been through (it) and they all yelled out: 'Good on ya, mate! Bore it up him!'

Finally, with the help of his friend Alec Fong Lim, he got his permit.

Ray McHenry, largely oblivious to the ways in which he, and the evacuation in general, were patronising towards women, was very sensitive to the paternalism being directed towards Darwin locals by the Commonwealth. 'Beware of those who advocate the "shock syndrome". It smacks of paternalism and is offensive to those who are able to cope. It often becomes an excuse for unwarranted intrusion in matters best left to local authorities.' Indeed, McHenry argued that surviving the storm was one of the reasons he was such a good organiser after it. 'The personal experience of the cyclone and the problems of Christmas morning were invaluable to me in the co-ordination, directing and decision making roles that followed.' He argued that, 'future arrangements for welfare counselling should incorporate provision for rapid training of volunteers and preferably those who have been involved in the disaster situations themselves'. Despite this advocacy for the recognition of those who had been on the ground during a disaster, McHenry doesn't seem to recognise that this criterion clearly skilled up many women as well.

Some women still found a way to make a contribution. Those living outside Darwin, particularly in Alice Springs and Katherine, took charge of the relief effort. In Alice Springs 150,000 dollars was collected within a few hours of reports of the cyclone filtering through. Women who stayed on in Darwin took on a range of tasks, including cooking, administration and nursing. Charles Gurd remembers that 'one lady in particular' did a wonderful job of getting messages out. She stayed on her wireless for a couple of days. He describes her as a local hero, though he can't remember her name. A woman called Eileen Cossons set up the kitchen–mess hall in the grounds of the old police station, fed hundreds of people most days, and even took it upon herself to rescue the Supreme Court judges' wigs and gowns which 'hippies' had taken to wearing when they sheltered in the Supreme Court buildings after the cyclone. One woman was kept on as an essential worker because she was a hairdresser, and hairdressers were considered to be essential to the morale of the few women left in town. Ironically, she ended up giving short back and sides to blokes for some time afterwards. Air Commodore Hitchins remembers that, 'several of the ladies who stayed behind there, the ones that didn't have young children, they started communal laundries for the blokes…Mrs Brown, she scrounged around and found as many serviceable washing machines as she could, set them all up under a brick building…'

Liz Foster made the decision to stay on Christmas Day, after surveying the extent of the damage. This was despite the fact that her marriage was unhappy and Tracy would have given her the perfect cover for separation. But she decided she didn't 'want to run away under those circumstances' and instead sat on the switchboard at Darwin police station working, like everyone else, until she dropped.

She and her husband were offered a functioning flat by a policeman who was happy to move to a hotel—on the proviso she managed to get his puppies out safely.

> A lot of the calls that came through, of course, were individuals from down south inquiring about their family, and we were issued with lists. As people had to register that they were okay, the lists came in. So we were able to check the list and, of course, if they weren't on that list as being confirmed okay, well then they were [considered] missing. And that's when they would get emotional...

It's hard to argue that it wasn't an important job, or that it needed a man, not a woman, to do it. Foster claims she felt not official but social pressure to leave town. She was asked, 'What are you still doing here?' by some, in a manner she felt suggested she should get out. In general, though, she was treated with respect but none the less, she found living in a town devoid of women and children difficult. The policeman's flat was:

> on the corner of Daly and McKinn and I remember having underwear pinched off the line, and that frightened me a bit. I used to go over to the Territorian Hotel and do my washing, and then I'd take it up to the CIB room in the police headquarters and do my ironing. Then, after that, I think I got a bit anxious—there were a few rumours going around—like the underwear being pinched and, I don't know, [I just felt] insecure. So we moved into the hotel. I had more things pinched there—my watch. There was no glass in one of the windows; we were in a corner room and we used to get wet every night.

Once the wet season ended she and her husband Greg moved back to their roofless house. The Fosters' already-troubled marriage was one of those that did not survive.

In the wake of disasters, pecking orders get reinforced. The rich are in a stronger position to become invested in rebuilding. Race and gender lines become more rigid. While a sense of community can be intensified after a disaster, its fault lines become exaggerated. A report on Gender and Health by the World Health Organization, published in 2002, wrote: 'When compounded by a calamity, the comparatively lower value ascribed to girls in some societies may take on lethal manifestations.'[11] To this day women get a raw deal in times of disaster. For a start, women and children are certainly more likely to die: after the tsunami that swept through Southeast Asia on 26 December 2004, women died at four times the rate of men. Most of those who survived did so by climbing up palm trees. When I visited, not long after the tsunami, and found myself looking at palm trees, sheer, twisted, without so much as a foothold, it became clear why so many children, women and old people died.

This was not, in fact, the case after Cyclone Tracy. Of the initial list of fifty-one fatalities only sixteen were female. The names added to this list once those found or deemed lost at sea were included were also predominantly male. However, the likelihood of assault and rape increases in the aftermath of such events and this does seem to have been the case after Tracy. These assaults can occur both because of the number of strangers that move into an area after a disaster, and the close and stressed living conditions everyone ends up living in. It can be difficult to find details of such assaults—it is in non-disaster situations too—and we're often reliant on anecdotal reports. For example, one observer noted in the WHO report subsequent to the floods in Australia in 1990, 'women experiencing violence in the home, who were socially isolated, became even more isolated and there was an increase in domestic violence'. After Hurricane Katrina the official number of reported rapes was four. However when Judy Benitez, the executive director of the Louisiana Foundation Against Sexual Assault, created a national database to track sexual assaults in the wake of the hurricane she found a different story. Six weeks after the website was set up it had received a further forty-two reports of sexual assault. One advocate for the database was the singer Charmaine Neville, who was raped on the roof of a school. Another woman says she tried to report her assault, but: 'The police was stressed out themselves... they didn't have no food. They didn't have water. They didn't have communication. They didn't have ammunition. The National Guards didn't want to hear it.'[12]

In Darwin, there was, by 3 January 1975, only one case of reported rape. However in the year 1974–5 thirteen 'Offences of a sexual nature' were officially recorded. In 1975–6 that number dropped to nine.[13] That's quite a statistical variation, especially if you take into account how small the population was in the first six months of 1975. It does suggest there were more sexually violent crimes as a direct result of the stresses and strains caused by the cyclone; and it is always true that many rapes go unreported. According to a survey reported in the *Northern Territory News* in October 1975, only one rapist in twenty was ever convicted and an estimated seventy per cent of rapes were not reported. (Things haven't improved. Sexual assault continues to be one of the most under-reported of all crimes. The Australian Bureau of Statistics [ABS] Personal Safety Survey [2006] found that the nationwide rate of reporting rape to the police has increased from 15 per cent in 1996 to 19 per cent reported in 2005. Only a minority of reported rapes will result in criminal charges, let alone a conviction.)[14]

Curly Nixon's wife was living just south of Darwin, and when he became concerned for her well-being, he said, 'Old Snowy and I got the twenty-two out, and taught her how to shoot from the hip with a twenty-two, and so forth.' Richard Creswick recalls that there was 'an influx of construction workers, single for the most part. A lot of people were working on the restoration of the power system and I think the character [of the town] started to change a bit.' There were social problems on the *Patris*, a liner from the Greek-owned Chandris fleet that was docked in Darwin Harbour for some nine months after Tracy, and: 'A perception that in that post-cyclone period we started to get the nasty things, the more murders, rapes and those unsavoury types of crime, but, you know, that may be subjective.'

Some people argued the permit system should have been even tougher in an attempt to keep unsavoury types at bay. This particular issue was fraught, as Dawn Lawrie pointed out in Giese's DDWC report. 'They disguise it [the permit system] by saying that we can't cope with no hopers, hippies, drop outs etc., and you ask them to define them and it's more or less everyone with whom they disagree.'[15] McHenry writes, in the same report: 'There would be people in Darwin who say we shouldn't have hippies here and yet there are hippies in every other part of Australia.' He elaborates, slightly confusingly, 'There are those who would argue that prostitutes should be here because there are so many single men around the place. I don't know which is worse, prostitutes to satisfy the blokes, or fights over prostitutes.'

Studies done after Cyclone Tracy,[16] and others on the psychological impact of cyclones in general, show that women often suffer a greater amount of psychological trauma after a disaster. This could be seen to support the belief that women were inherently less able to cope. I would argue, however, that part of the explanation was the way women were denied the right to share in the satisfaction that came from rebuilding their community. Instead they had to deal with 'Cramped accommodation with distant and sometimes incompatible relatives, constantly changing addresses, doubt about who would pay for dental, optical, physical and emotional care, and loss of contact with other evacuees.'[17] Since the 1990s serious work has been done to consider the different experiences of women and men during, and after, a disaster. In the World Health Organization's Gender and Health Report it was observed that after Hurricane Andrew hit the US in 1992, 'while men would build roads and houses the role of putting lives back together was the women's'.

Women were denied that role in Cyclone Tracy and it's important to note that men, as well as women, suffered as a result.

Hedley Beare was one of several senior men who conducted himself with extraordinary commitment and grace, while being exposed to horrendous stress. After his family were evacuated he thought:

> 'That could be the last time I see those four', because there was no certainty we would survive the emergency, and we were very conscious of the lack of amenities...You could smell the panic in the northern suburbs—there was a sort of stench which began to rise. We got—I reckon it was about the third day you sense a sort of terror taking people over, because the food was rotting, and somehow their world was rotting, and they felt that they might die.

It's quite a shock to realise that Beare thought he might never see his family again: not because they'd come to harm, but because he would. It really did feel like the end of the world for many of the men left behind. Fear of death was just one of the stresses that tended to lead to emotional problems after the cyclone. Beare slept one and a half hours a night for ten days, and was in a state of collapse when he finally got onto the first commercial flight out. He remembers his enormous gratitude towards the men who supported him, men that 'did the little personal things...That were family like.' In particular he mentions Doug McKenzie, the man who took over the care of the Beare family's dog, Muffin. 'I mean, you've got no family there, you sort of put your affection on it.' Beare's daughter, who'd had glandular fever at the time of the cyclone and was evacuated to Canberra, had health problems for the rest of her relatively short life. She eventually died of leukaemia. Beare believes the cyclone contributed to that. For all these reasons, for many more still, Beare remained traumatised by the ten days of the emergency. When he was interviewed twenty years after the cyclone he still struggled to talk about what happened. 'It affects me too deeply. It's traumatic for me, and it's still in my system.'

He wasn't alone. Vicki Harris's husband turned yellow a few months after Tracy and the doctors diagnosed shock. There were cases of psychosomatic paralysis. Frank Thorogood recalls that all the skin on his hands peeled off when he got back to Canberra. Men who may already have had drinking problems found their consumption of alcohol escalated. There were early retirements in the years to follow. Cedric Patterson, who was fifty when Tracy hit, went on to have medical problems.

> I was faced with a lot of traumas of rebuilding, as well as working hard at a particular time. And I really think that's one of the reasons that I was retired out of the department early, because I had reached a point where I think I was sort of going up and down in the one spot.

Meteorologist Peter Harvey retired from the public service in 1987, at only fifty, having been on sick leave for two years. He had an anxiety condition and high blood pressure, and believed his experiences during the cyclone were partly responsible. Driving a woman in labour to hospital the day after the cyclone was just the start of it. The meteorology bureau where he worked started to run limited services on the Friday after the cyclone; it was up and running by the following Monday and Harvey had to keep things going there for months afterwards. He started getting chest pains in '75 and '76 as did several of his friends. 'In retrospect it is a classical stress symptom.'[18]

Anne Petterson, a former administrator with the Red Cross and then a Welfare Rights Officer with the Welfare Council, wrote in the Giese Report that 'there should have been some assessment as to people's capability of handling the situation. I don't know how but it would have been better if very stable women stayed behind to hold things together here.' Men were deprived of the social support their families could have offered. The refusal of women, and the emotional world they were seen to represent, is directly related to the intense distress many men suffered both at the time and in decades to come.

DARIBAH NUNGALINYA

ONE JUNE when I was visiting Darwin to work on this book, I drove down to Kakadu. The highway was lined with a willowy and delicate pale lavender bush, and another bush, stark and long-limbed, with large bright yellow flowers. There were lots of little fires spotted alongside the road—an alarming sight for a Victorian—but they were under control. Kakadu is home to one of the oldest continuous living cultures in the world and its rock art chronicles that span of history—including the ice age of fifteen thousand years ago and the time when the thylacine lived in the north, some six thousand years ago. And while I had heard about these paintings, nothing could quite prepare me for what it felt like, after two hours of sweaty walking, to come across an overhang and the two-hundred-year-old painting within it: of a ship with tall white sails. Such depth of history is a stark contrast to white people's recent arrival in the Top End, which feels like a wound ripped through the land and the culture. This wounding, many Indigenous people believe, was one of the causes of Cyclone Tracy and many disasters before and since.

The specific factors that Indigenous people believe caused the cyclone vary, depending where people came from. However they all touched on this notion of the desecration of the land, and an associated warning to Aboriginal people to reinvigorate their cultural practices. Cyclone Tracy was believed to have targeted Darwin because it was the centre of European culture up north. Some said Cyclone Tracy was brought on because the Mirrar people were unhappy about exploration taking place for the Jabiluka uranium mine. They didn't want vehicles getting in there during in the wet, so big storms were sung up. When Echo Cole was asked about this he was circumspect. He didn't know, he said, but he acknowledged: 'In past history that I know of, our people do sing up for rain.' A report on Indigenous experiences of Cyclone Tracy was finally written in 2011. It noted that, while cyclones are viewed as negative events by many,

> Australian Indigenous people positively view cyclones as creative entities that bring renewal but act negatively as a punishment when improper engagement with the natural or supernatural work had taken place. Other extreme climatic events such as flooding and lightning-induced bushfires are similarly viewed as elements of a breathing landscape.[1]

History is never just history. Weather is never just weather.

The Larrakia themselves believed that Tracy was created by the anger of Daribah Nungalinya or 'Old Man Rock' who sits in the sea, out from Casuarina Beach. He is the body of a powerful ancestor and as such must not be damaged in any way. Daribah Nungalinya is responsible for earthquakes, storms and cyclones and the monsoon that comes rolling in from the Timor Sea over the rocks before it reaches land at Darwin's northern suburbs.

Principal Keith Cole of Nungalinya College recalls that some Larrakia believed that the sixteen-ton granite boulder that stood in front of his college had been taken from 'Old Man Rock' though he insists that it was not. (He said that the rock had come from Mount Bundy mines and this explanation was accepted.) Cole had genuine sympathy with the Larrakia's way of seeing the world, comparing it with what he called Old Testament thinking.

> The whirlwind, or in our terms, the cyclone, can be a vehicle of God's judgment or indicative of His sovereign power… The cyclone said to me, and many others have told me that the cyclone said to them, 'There is a God. He is Almighty, He is all powerful, and His fury is seen in the storm.'

In the early seventies there was a steady improvement in and recognition of Aboriginal rights. Lionel Murphy, then federal attorney-general, was keen that Indigenous people, particularly elders and their councils, be encouraged to make decisions regarding their own communities. Indigenous justices of the peace were being trained in remote areas. It was also a time when protocols regarding the treatment of Aboriginal people in court were being revised and the right of communities to enforce their own system of law was being given serious consideration. Clem O'Sullivan, the crown law officer for the Northern Territory and its first director of law, remembers that this was a process that 'accelerated considerably under the Labor government and the change in 1972…It was an interest close to Lionel Murphy's heart.'[2] The Whitlam government had begun drafting the *Aboriginal Land Rights (Northern Territory) Act* though it would not be passed until 1976. This was also the era in which missionaries lost their power, and Indigenous people were allowed to speak their own language again (though of course many had been speaking it, secretly, all along).

Indigenous people today comment that there was less racism back then than there is today and that Darwin was a friendlier place. But there is no doubt that one of the fault lines that yawned wide after the cyclone was race. General Stretton was alert to problems of racism, though his commitment to evacuation as the way forward offset some of his good intentions: 'It did not take too long for racial problems to emerge. I was approached by some leading citizens of Darwin with the request that, because of their propensity to spread disease, all Aborigines should immediately be moved out of Darwin irrespective of their wishes in the matter.' Stretton refused, saying: 'The Aborigines would enjoy the same priority as every other person in Darwin.' They were given three options. They could be evacuated south, fly back to 'reservations', or could remain in Darwin. 'Those aboriginals evacuated by air to capital cities were moved in accordance within the overall priorities except the head of the household was allowed to move with his family...Other aboriginals in the city and certain fringe communities were also assisted.' As it turned out, Indigenous families often were separated, much as white families were, which suggests that Stretton meant that those who lived traditionally were allowed to stay together as a unit but others were to be treated like everyone else. Other than the general pronouncement above, Stretton notes that the community at Delissaville—on the Cox Peninsula near Mandorah—was looked in on. That community was not evacuated, but nor did it want to be.

It was the job of people like welfare officer Michael Ivory to work with local Aboriginal people. He remembers that the day after the cyclone many of them had got themselves to the shelter at Ludmilla and from there he organised for some to go to Melbourne and some to Sydney, even though: 'They were blackfellas who'd never been out of the Territory in their life.'[3] Serious efforts were made to house Indigenous people within the Territory rather than interstate, so as to avoid extreme dislocation. Ivory again: 'There was a lot of Aboriginal people that had to be catered for, who wanted to go home, so we had to organise transport for them, such as it was. Normally it was by road.' Clem O'Sullivan remembers that he flew in to Darwin on 29 December on a chartered DC3 that had been used earlier in the day to move people to a community on Elcho Island. In the very fine twentieth anniversary feature run by the *Northern Territory News*, Barry Medley remembers that his employer, Perkins Shipping, delivered essential supplies to coastal Aboriginal communities and Mr Medley said it was crucial the job was done. 'We had to feed all the people on the islands so I stayed to give people a hand.' Bill Wilson also remembers evacuating Indigenous people out a day or two after Tracy.

All the people interviewed for the Haynes Report on Indigenous experiences of Cyclone Tracy felt they were treated well in the days immediately following the cyclone and during evacuation. They were given food for free, and were not expected to pay for things and were generally treated as well as any non-Indigenous people.

> I remember standing up in the line [for a $200 payment]... And the guy that was standing in front of me was a well-known and quite wealthy businessman...I remember then thinking to myself, 'We're all equal. Everybody's equal, you know, we've all been hit with the same thing.'

In *Returning to Nothing*, Peter Read notes that:

> the Bagot and Kulaluk Aborigines seem temporarily to have benefited. They had few material possessions. They belonged to the Darwin region as did few others; most of the land precious to them was already inaccessible because of buildings and fences...The barracks which the army had built on the most sacred site of the Larrakia people was in ruins.

Which is not to say that things were good—they weren't for anyone, black or white. Severe dislocation was caused in the camps which, according to Bill Day, 'were bare and the people scattered'. People from One Mile, the camp closest to the centre of Darwin 'had moved into two old classrooms behind the Cavenagh Street Woolworths store. The bare concrete rooms were unserviced but drier than any of the precyclone shelters in the camps.'

There are claims that, once they were evacuated south, Aboriginal people didn't tend to be offered the level of support that white evacuees were given, and sometimes encountered a kind of prejudice. Bonds of community are strong in Darwin and at times like this that could offset problems caused by racism. Chips Mackinolty reported that one Aboriginal family flown to Far North Queensland was separated from non-Aboriginal evacuees and put on the back of a cattle truck to be sent to Yarrabah Reserve, after Queensland authorities refused them permission to stay with relatives.[4] According to Maria Tumarkin, Mr Doug Scott, then the director of the Foundation for Aboriginal Affairs, 'had so far only been able to house two families out of sixty stuck in Sydney. "Some real estate agents have been sending Aboriginal evacuees to uninhabitable houses. Most of the seven to eight hundred Darwin Aborigines originally evacuated to Sydney have already escaped the city."'[5]

However not everyone reports having a rough time. Stephanie Nganjmirra Thompson remembers that she and her siblings were sent to Melbourne and put in a hostel down there, before being flown up to Oenpelli in Arnhem Land where she stayed with her uncle. She has no memories of being treated badly. One couple expecting racism were happily surprised. They'd driven to Katherine and when they got to the relief centre and explained they were half-caste and quarter-caste (so that a white person didn't accidentally take in someone of colour) were treated with nothing but respect. While the population of Bagot

Reserve dropped from 518 to 63, demountables arrived quite quickly to replace the homes that had been destroyed, and they were connected to electricity before many other homes in Darwin.

How Indigenous people felt about being taken, once again, from their land was a different matter. Many of them had been displaced several times over, and to be removed once again was deeply traumatic. This was especially the case if they were Larrakia, and they were being removed from their traditional lands. 'This is our coast. And you've got to be back home on your home ground.'[6] *Bunji*, a land rights newsletter edited by Bill Day, stated in January: 'The people of the dreaming cannot be chased from their land by a cyclone...We need them back in Larrakia country as soon as possible.'[7]

Lorna Fejo found being evacuated very painful. 'Oh it was really devastating...We had no home; we had nothing, but we still was determined we wanted to stay in Darwin. But we were more or less ordered: "Get out of Darwin. Go!"'[8] Fejo was put on a bus to Mount Isa but ended up further south. She finally found a way to return to Darwin (illegally, and without a permit) despite being told in Adelaide that Darwin was 'finished'.

Indigenous people in general were much more likely to return after evacuation—or try to—and they were likely to return more quickly. Most wanted to be home within two months, whereas non-Indigenous families were often away for six months or more. Around half the general population returned after the evacuation, but most Indigenous families did, with the exception of a few families who stayed on in either Katherine or Alice Springs.

It seemed that Indigenous people were treated increasingly poorly in the months (rather than weeks) after Tracy. For starters the restoration of Aboriginal settlements dropped lower and lower down the list of priorities. In January a meeting of sixty-five homeless Aboriginal people was held outside the classrooms the One Mile community had moved into, and that meeting expressed concern that no Aboriginal representatives were on the Citizens Advisory Committee of the Reconstruction Commission. There was also a concern that politics were being played with some aspects of the emergency, in particular that the permit system was being used to keep Aboriginal people out of Darwin on a permanent basis. The checkpoint set up on the highway at Noonamah, sixteen kilometres beyond the large camp at Knuckeys Lagoon, was particularly contentious with people being told they could only return when they had decent accommodation—which was farcical given that many Knuckeys Lagoon residents hadn't ever had adequate housing. The community there had been engaged in a dispute over title for several years, and their tent dwellings were an interim measure indicating the undecided legal status of the land. On 28 January, the Gwalwa Daraniki Association (*gwalwa daraniki* means 'our land' in Larrakia), were reported as encouraging members to drive through the road blocks as a form of protest.[9] 'Blacks to Challenge Road Blocks' blared the headline in the *Northern Territory News*.

In answer to complaints about the living conditions in the camps, the Darwin Reconstruction Commission replied in September 1975: 'You will appreciate that the construction of permanent works on the site [at One Mile] has to await the deliberations of the judicial body that is examining the title to this portion of land.'[10] But, as Bill Day goes on to point out, the system could move fast enough when it came to, say, letting out contracts for 1600 new houses in the suburbs of Darwin. In response to this the Gwalwa Daraniki Association began its own appeal for emergency funds. This did not resolve their problems, however. A donation of forty thousand dollars from the Papua New Guinea government for a shelter for Aborigines at Knuckeys Lagoon 'joined other funds for fringe dweller reconstruction and emergency relief which were frozen by a bureaucracy worried about a lack of legal title. In addition, there were to be no grants of leases for Aboriginal town camps while the future plans for Darwin were being debated.' The community is now known as Belyuen, but the housing has not improved. Some thirty years later, the community still lived in the temporary structures built a few months after the cyclone.

There is some validity to the argument that Indigenous people might be less distressed by the aftermath of a cyclone—both because they were less beholden to material things and because what they did have to lose (land) had been taken from them already—but that argument can be taken too far. Indigenous people are no more resilient than anyone else when it comes to corrugated iron flying through the air. Bill Day: 'The Aboriginal people in the camps who had experienced the cyclone now had a wariness of using loose corrugated iron for self-made humpies and of building under trees.'

The situation of Aboriginal people during cyclones remains a vulnerable one. One Mile camp has been in operation since the early 1900s and was granted a special lease in 1978. In 2005 the area was described as 'Darwin's own little Soweto' by the camp's project officer, Mick Lambe. It comprises 'a crumbling toilet block; and what is literally a wire-netting walled cage, like a zoo cage, that is the women's refuge from drunks the police dump at the camp during the night'. There were only about twenty people there when Tony Clifton visited in 2004 because Aboriginal people are effectively kept out of town during the dry season so as not to upset the tourists. 'But there might be 200 or more once the tourists leave in the wet and Aboriginal money becomes good again.' When I visited the camp during the dry of 2011 there were even fewer people. This pattern of pushing people out in the dry season and allowing them back in the wet means they are more likely to be in residence during the cyclone season. Now, as in 1974, the ruined infrastructure which abounds in these camps can become deadly if whipped up into the air during a cyclone.

Many remote Indigenous communities in Australia are in areas at most risk of a 'natural' disaster but the Northern Territory—in fact Australia in general—is a long way away from having developed protocols around the evacuation of Aboriginal people. This is difficult, it must be acknowledged, because every Indigenous community is different, and a 'one size fits all' approach would not be much use. What is essential is having emergency services personnel who, if they are not actually from the community, know and work closely with them. A case in point was the evacuation undertaken before Cyclone Monica, a Category 5, hit the northern tip of Arnhem Land in 2005. Elders were invited to play an active role and, importantly, avoidance relationships were respected. These relationships are particularly important because they dictate who can be in close proximity to whom. If these aren't understood and worked around, people might simply refuse to get onto the transport being offered. In this case the liaison officers were Indigenous, which made a huge difference to the emergency evacuation work.[11]

On the other hand there are many examples of evacuations that have caused extreme stress. The Western Desert community of Kiwirrkurra, badly flooded in March 2001, was a dry community but was evacuated to a community where drinking was allowed. There was such 'severe disruption to the social fabric of the community'[12] that they decided to move themselves closer to home and just stayed wherever they could. It was eighteen months before they were able to return to their land.

Evacuation was also distressingly disruptive to the people of the Warmun community in Turkey Creek, home to the art move-ment that had been triggered by artistic response to Cyclone Tracy—particularly the Gurirr Gurirr paintings—and Rover Thomas's extraordinary oeuvre, which includes some of the most iconic visual images of the cyclone. (No other artists have painted the recent history of northern Australia in such an ambitious, or, indeed, historically significant fashion. Thomas's painting in the late seventies inspired those around him, including Queenie McKenzie, a Gija elder and stock-camp cook who is now as famous as Thomas. 'If he can do that so can I,' she said.[13] And so an art movement was born.)

In July 2010, it rained sixty-seven millimetres in a single day at Fitzroy Crossing, and, locals told me, closer to a hundred millimetres in other areas of Central Kimberley. It typically doesn't rain a drop in July. Six months later the people of Warmun began to dream that something was amiss. On Sunday 13 March 2011, after days of heavy rainfall caused by a cyclonic depression, floodwaters began swelling Turkey Creek. In the space of a few short hours that afternoon, the creek rose beyond measure and a torrent of water sweeping across the red plains engulfed the remote community, washing away walls and taking a thousand paintings. Nicolas Rothwell reported in the *Australian*: 'It was devastation: houses were wrecked, trailers and demountables were smashed and turned upside down, refrigerators lodged high in the branches of trees.' One local, Leanne Mosquito, later said that the loss of so many paintings was devastating because it meant a loss of knowledge: 'People paint about their country. They talk about country through painting.' Art centre manager Maggie Fletcher and her husband Gary were able to save three hundred or so works of the Warmun heritage collection, but the community had to be evacuated to Kununurra, where tension was experienced between the people of Warmun and the people whose country it was. There are many reasons for this but one was that no formal permission was asked of the Indigenous community in Kununurra. Welcome to Country, like other Indigenous protocols, is not just a politeness. It's essential if two communities are going to live together. The point is illustrated by Maggie Fletcher's account of what the three hundred people evacuated after the flood experienced:

> This was a traumatic time...In a state of shock, lobbed together in a workers' 'village' in Kununurra, the community members suddenly found themselves homeless evacuees in a foreign land. It was two weeks later that one of the most senior artists managed to ask, 'Where are we?'...What this man meant was: 'Whose country are we on? This is not our country—we shouldn't be here without their permission.' The people felt they couldn't paint there. It wasn't right. They didn't like the paint. 'That's gardiya paint—white fellas paint. It's no good. It's not from our country.'

As soon as she could, Maggie and Gary 'took Warmun ochres and as many familiar painting materials as we could up to Kununurra.'[14]

It was almost a year later that the community got back to Warmun to find there were positives to be taken from the disaster. Mary Thomas, painter and Gija elder, said at the time: 'The floodwater came and washed all those bad things, you know, problems we had.'

THE WILD NORTH

THERE WERE men in uniform and men in civvies. There were Hawaiian shirts and undies, bathers, police caps, and men wearing dresses. What you wore became a contentious question in the crazy days after Cyclone Tracy. Neville Barwick, who headed up the Darwin Reconstruction Study Group, arrived six days after Tracy to find a colleague who'd been left with nothing but his life and his underpants. He was still in his Y-fronts, helping out around the office. Air Commodore Hitchins ran into problems when he was getting about in the old shorts he'd been wearing on Christmas Day. 'I'd quite forgotten that I'd got into an airforce aeroplane looking like an out of work fisherman which I probably was, and here was this very keen young airforce wing commander, dead keen to get going and he couldn't understand why this scruffy character kept getting in his way.'

Major-General Stretton tended to dress down in what he thought was Darwin style. According to Frank Thorogood:

Rover Thomas [Joolama]
Kukatja/Wangkajunga peoples
c.1926 Australia – 1998

Cyclone Tracy 1991
natural earth pigments on canvas
168 × 180 cm
National Gallery of Australia, Canberra
Purchased 1991

Aerial view of damage

RICK STEVENS / FAIRFAX

Last can standing

ALBERT A. DIXON COLLECTION, NORTHERN TERRITORY LIBRARY

Armed police patrol the streets of Darwin to stop looters

NEWS LTD / NEWSPIX

Evacuation via TAA

FROM THE COLLECTION OF THE NATIONAL ARCHIVES OF AUSTRALIA: A6180, 7/1/75/54

Evacuees aboard a US Air Force Starlifter

NEWS LTD / NEWSPIX

> [Stretton] took the view, that had he turned up in his major-general's suit, that would not have created the image that he really wanted to have. So, I believe that the shorts, the Florida shirt and the floppy hat was entirely consistent with the role, because everybody else in Darwin was dressed pretty much the same. On the other hand, I was dressed in shoes, long socks, shorts, khaki shirt, badges of rank—medal ribbon—as a uniformed Army officer. And I really gave him, by that appearance, the prestige and the status that he needed...he always wanted to represent himself as the Civilian Director-General of the Natural Disasters Organisation. Now that's the term that he used often—the Civilian Director. He kept saying, 'it's under civilian control'.

Uniforms were tied up with authority, in a town that resented it—especially if it came from outsiders.

When the interstate cops began to arrive—232 police came from the Commonwealth and another 151 were provided by states around Australia—Bill Wilson remembers that: 'They had clean uniforms, pale blue uniforms...We were filthy, didn't have proper uniforms.' The interstaters' uniforms didn't stay clean for long, though, and some took to wearing shorts and singlets while keeping a gun on their hips. The local police were also casually dressed, though they had more excuse since in many cases their uniforms had literally blown away. Whatever the reasons, this all made it increasingly difficult to figure out who was a policeman and who was not.

One compelling reason for bringing in reinforcements, uniform or no, was a fear that the local police wouldn't cope given what they'd all gone through. Wilson has some sympathy for this view, having recognised the great shock that he and others were attempting to manage as they went about their business. As well, many had been trying to survive on little or no sleep for three or four days at a stretch. More than one man slept for close to twenty-four hours straight when finally given the chance to rest. There was also the concern that Darwin was going to become a looters' paradise. Wilson elaborates: 'There was some suggestion that there was a fear of lack of control in town; they needed more police than there were to keep order if things got out of hand.'

Cedric Patterson remembers a certain edginess: 'People with shotguns sitting in their shop windows and doorways.' There is a photo taken at the end of 1974 that illustrates his point: a man sitting outside the remains of his shop on the Stuart Highway in Darwin, holding a shotgun. This sense that their town was being descended upon was in part a response to the fact that people had lost almost everything they owned and feared for their few remaining belongings. The man with the gun was, in a sense, warding off his sense of devastation.

A journalist who joined police on looting patrol one night described the atmosphere, 'A man, smelling strongly of alcohol, staggered past in the lights. He clutched a high velocity .22 rifle…"I've shot four dogs tonight," he slurred. "I got thirty or forty of the bastards yesterday."' It's impossible to know of course whether this is true or just the ravings of a drunk, but it gives you a sense of the madness that had descended on some quarters of the city. Shortly after this the man waved his rifle at police and had to be disarmed.[1]

But many believed, like Colonel Thorogood, that the entire issue was exaggerated. 'There wasn't a lot of looting in Darwin and I don't think there was ever a law and order problem of any consequence.' It would seem he was right: two weeks after the cyclone only fifteen people had actually been arrested for larceny and possession of stolen property. Richard Creswick didn't 'think there was any concept of looting as such because everything became a shared facility'. Kate Cairns also talks of sharing rather than looting, of 'using something that worked'. But she continues, 'when the person whom it belonged to returned to Darwin...it was given back—perhaps not in all cases—but in lots of cases it was. So what's looting?—I don't know.' She was, however, nervous that not everyone would share her relaxed definition. She remembers that although her neighbours told her she could grab stuff from their place after they'd gone, she didn't do so because she was scared she might be arrested.

To be clear, it is absolutely the case that goods were stolen for resale. Lists presented to the Supreme Court in the wake of various arrests include multiple TV sets, cartons of pantihose and what now seems like an amusing surfeit of banana lounges. But definitions can blur. Is it looting if you break into a pharmacy in the centre of a ruined city, and take the asthma medication you need or some nappies for your child? Is it looting if you take food, which will perish anyway, from a grocery store? What if it isn't medication or food but beer that you are desperate for? What if you take furniture to put under the remaining floorboards of your house? At what point do you draw the line? As Bill Wilson asked, 'Where does looting start and finish, and survival start and finish? If you're walking along and you're cold and wet the morning after the cyclone, and you see a raincoat draped over a fence, do you take it, and is that looting?'

Police commandeering was considered legitimate. Wilson has vividly described his attempts to drive around the town to try and help, the morning after the cyclone, only to have tyre after tyre shred.

> We had four flat tyres because of the debris on the road. I think it took us fifteen or twenty minutes to drive from Mitchell Street to Daly Street...At that point, there was a garage on the corner...We broke into the service station there, and got whatever wheels and tyres we could find, and managed to replace all the tyres...In fact we left a note

> and said: The police have requisitioned…whatever number of tyres it was and left it on the counter in there, which we thought made it okay…Later on we were told in fact that this was quite legitimate; that you could do what you want, provided it was recorded.

In a later interview he acknowledged that:

> official commandeering…was a form, I suppose, of looting…A policy was made quite quickly that legitimised this, and recorded it for future reparation to the owners of these places…for example, if an evacuation centre needed a generator, and there was one somewhere, then it would get taken and put into use. It wasn't for people's personal gain. I think that if it was for community gain it was acceptable; if it was not for community gain then it was unacceptable.

After reading many hours of interviews with Wilson I decided I had to meet him. I was impressed by his ability to remember emotional detail, among other things, and found I liked the man—despite never having met him. I tried to track him down in Darwin but, like most of the people I ended up interviewing, he no longer lived there. These days he lives in, of all places, Beechworth, a hilly and sometimes cold Victorian town not many hours from where I live. Aged seventy-one when we met—he was thirty-three during Tracy—he was, despite his age, still a big man as coppers often are. He'd long stopped being a policeman and in his fifties became a historian, then a lecturer in history and politics at Charles Darwin University. After that he'd become a senior advisor in Support and Equity, and you can see all these things in his Tracy interviews with Francis Good if you look for them. An eye for historical detail combined with real compassion. I wondered about many things, including the perhaps incidental detail of whether people actually followed up on these reparation slips. He told me that quite a few businesses did. It was an honour system that, to all intents and purposes, worked.

These issues become more complex when you consider that the city, or what was left of it, became for ten days or so a cash-free economy. Kate Cairns again: 'It was a cashless society—I mean if you wanted something there was always some way of getting it, you know. It was quite strange really.' Colleen D'Arcy remembers going shopping on Christmas Day—the only person I've come across with such a recollection—at a little shop in Westralia Street. 'I thought that was rather wonderful to think that—business as usual, after the night before,' however she soon found that, 'except for going down to Westralia Street, and the supermarket being open, money was of no use whatsoever.' Local businesses got into the spirit of the occasion. Antonio Milhinhos, the owner of a small supermarket in Nightcliff, gave away his entire stock to cyclone victims. The owners of W. G. Chin's in Smith Street gave away most of their goods as well. These were pragmatic gestures, as so much stock was water damaged, but they were also heartfelt. It would be three weeks before shops were operating again. In the meantime food was provided at the still-standing schools, such as Darwin and Casuarina High.

You could survive on free beer alone until 3 January when local businesses began to object to the lack of opportunity to sell anything. More broadly speaking, some of the people who were evacuated around Australia were provided with free food and board for months afterwards. Not everyone was convinced all this free stuff was a good idea. Keith Cole believed that the time during which people were given things went on for longer than was useful. 'We were being conditioned into getting things for nothing, and the more we got, the more we expected and wanted.' Mayor Brennan, ever alert to hippy and communist activity, felt even more strongly on the subject. 'It was a hippy's delight, this whole darn thing. They got fed for nothing, they'd go round and get clothing and all of that.'

This question 'what is looting' was not just an abstract one—a man's life could turn on it. Robin Bullock thought the whole debate had 'an element of hysteria' to it and pointed out that 'there can be a fine line between someone needing something and someone not needing it, but the person needing something being caught up in the accusation is a terrible thing to happen'.

Malcolm McKenzie, who operated the Rapid Creek betting shop, remembers that his son's boss was out in Nightcliff out of curfew,

> down at the Seabreeze Hotel, which was a very nice place. For some reason we don't know, he was moving around when the curfew was supposed to be on, and someone thought he was a looter and allegedly fired a warning shot, but unfortunately the warning shot turned out to be a fatal shot, because they shot [him] dead.

I haven't been able to corroborate that statement. Police Commissioner McLaren certainly denies it. 'No person was ever shot, no looter was shot at...there wasn't even a shot fired in the direction of a looter.'[2] Deputy Mayor Ted D'Ambrosio does, however, remember firing a warning shot at someone.

The truth can be hard to get to. There were rumours of looters being lined up and shot, then pushed off the pier and, while I found no evidence to suggest that this actually happened, I was struck by the fact that the story is not dissimilar to images that were to emerge out of East Timor a few months later, during the Indonesian invasion: the way, for example, that journalist Roger East would meet his end. East was on the personal staff of the head of the interim Darwin Reconstruction Commission, Sir Leslie Thiess: he came to Darwin shortly after Tracy, then headed further north to Dili, to help Fretilin. He was shot and thrown off the pier at Dili Harbour after the invasion. A few months later the displaced people of East Timor started to land on Darwin's shores, and it's interesting to see the way in which stories and memories morph.

Another ongoing meme of the cyclone was that Greek men dressed as women in their desperate bid to be evacuated. This rumour flourished immediately after the cyclone (and was later reinforced by the TV miniseries *Cyclone Tracy*), though in the hundreds of interviews I read, only one man, Tom Pauling, actually claims to have seen a man dressed as a woman. Everyone else repeats variations, including a version, described as a 'wild rumour' by Peter Harvey, that the men dressed as women were Chinese not Greek. Whatever the race of the men it's a rumour which suggests that women were the lucky ones, and that only the weakest of men thought to emulate them. The humiliation and mockery that's embedded in such stories says something about the status not just of Greek men but of women in Darwin in 1974.

There was, however, one particularly persistent story that does seem to have been more than a rumour: that the interstate police weren't so much a solution as part of the problem. Most contentious of all were thirty-eight policemen who arrived from NSW, particularly a small group who were based in Kings Cross, who many described as heavy handed and inclined to violence. Tom Pauling:

> Some police from New South Wales arrived looking as though they were going into a battle zone in Vietnam. McLaren was the police commissioner up here at the time and he ordered that all interstate police be disarmed except to the extent of one sidearm. They had riot guns and almost bazookas and cannons—that's what they looked like.

McLaren, it should be mentioned here, has been described as one of the heroes of Cyclone Tracy. Bishop Ken Mason described him as 'a quiet, gentle man…whose calm nature gave such a quiet, confident and consistent leadership'.

Peter Talbot recalls that 'up at the Travelodge there was a big party every night, booze party, all the coppers…we used to watch the Commonwealth police get around with that big rifle just like the wild west'. Before the cyclone, police had not carried guns in Darwin so this was a real shock. Lorna Fejo: 'I guess, me, as an Aboriginal person, I was really terrified of the Commonwealth Police because they were walking around with guns on their hips, and it frightened me and my children.'

The Kings Cross policemen were accused of looting and drunkenness by Tiger Brennan, who described incidents in which police 'stood over several publicans for beer'. By 1 January Brennan was telling the press, 'It's time for the southern cops to go home. I have heard complaints about some of the southern police but I am not prepared to give details now.' Another senior official described them as 'a gang of cowboys'. NSW Deputy Commissioner Newman defended his force, while McLaren insisted that evidence of police looting was not found and that all complaints were investigated. Wilson: 'As regards stealing, I've heard allegations, but I've never seen any evidence, and I've never heard of any proved things that some of the interstate police looted.'

Off the record, though, several people told me that police looting absolutely occurred—and I didn't have to look far for corroboration. I found the following notes in hand-written police journals in the Territory's archives:

> Interstate police—obtained 80,000 cigarettes from S.C. Eyles this date—Yesterday 6 NSW police went to camera shops—Coles Casuarina bypassed C'wth police on duty and removed a number of camera & equipment. Same Crew travel about in private car. Armfuls of clothing have been

> seen carried into Travelodge by interstate police who openly boast of achievements.

These accusations made it as far as a typed 'complaints' book but then appear to peter out.

When Darwin was burned and looted in wake of the bombings of 1942 much of the destruction was caused not by the Japanese who made it to shore but by Australian and US soldiers. As journalist Mark Day wrote about those fraught days, 'There was panic, looting, cowardice, desertion and a stampede south to get out of harm's way.' Darwin's Chinese population back then were victimised by looters, as they have been throughout history. Because they weren't Australian citizens they had less recourse to justice when attacked. Furthermore, as Charles See Kee has commented, those in Darwin, 'were worse off than in any other parts of Australia because Darwin was isolated away from everywhere and nobody knew what was going on'. After 1956, changes to the law meant that many Chinese people in the Northern Territory became naturalised, but even then they were still banned from a range of sporting and social venues. Nor were they allowed to join the unions. Bill Wong remembers that they weren't allowed to serve on a jury either, until well into the 1970s. It wasn't until he mentioned this to Jock Nelson that the situation was quickly sorted out. (And the Chinese community were cranky at him because it was a task they didn't particularly want to perform.)

Alec Fong Lim lost his brother Arthur in Tracy, his aunt had both feet amputated and two other relatives were badly crushed by falling walls. His family owned the Vic Hotel in the city centre, and Lim's Hotel in Rapid Creek, which was famous for its caged bar ('rage in the cage'). Fong Lim went on to serve on the Cyclone Trust Fund Committee and became mayor of Darwin in 1984. That was all well in the future and quite unimaginable when his family first moved to

Darwin, in 1938. At that time the Chinese numbered three hundred out of a population of two thousand. He remembers that the anglos lived in Smith Street, Mitchell Street and The Esplanade. China Town was in Cavenagh Street and Indigenous people lived in compounds and police paddocks. His father bought a shop next to the Star Theatre in what's now the Smith Street Mall.

> Imagine the consternation amongst the Chinese community, whose businesses were exclusively in Cavenagh Street, when this country bumpkin bought a business in Smith Street—the white man's domain!! 'You will never succeed', they said. 'The whites will not trade with you and you must operate in Cavenagh Street.'

Their shop was looted during a riot with soldiers in 1941. 'I can still see them, as we all cowered in the back of the shop, ready to defend ourselves...The damages were all blamed on the soldiers, but I remember that a lot of civilians took the opportunity to ransack my beloved tobacconist shelves.'[3]

The first person to be sentenced for looting after Cyclone Tracy was Guildin Kelly (newspapers and other records also called him Goldin and Goldie). He was arrested on Sunday 29 December and went to court the next day. Kelly was an Aboriginal man, and he had taken whisky and brandy worth fourteen dollars. But that was not all he was charged with and, in an ironic twist on the problem of policemen wearing civvies, Kelly, who was not a member of the police force, was wearing a police cap, apparently to trick a man into handing over his grog. This meant he was also charged with impersonating a police officer. Magistrate David McCann sentenced Kelly to nine months (though McCann and many others remember Kelly's sentence as three to six months). McCann described the situation this way: 'I was rather disappointed that the first person they'd managed to arrest and charge with stealing, which was in the area of looting, was an Aborigine…it would have been a little more representative of what was actually going on had somebody other than an Aborigine been charged.' McCann's record shows him being in sympathy with the fair treatment of Indigenous people in the Territory. He was certainly in favour of the shifts in the legal system that were occurring in response to Lionel Murphy's and Crown Law Officer Clem O'Sullivan's push for change. This makes his harsh sentencing puzzling. In this case, he argued, it was on the secondary charge that Kelly had to be made an example of. Kelly's claim to be a police officer may have been malicious, but it was also a bit of a joke since there were no Indigenous members of the police force in the Northern Territory in 1974. For this reason Frank Thorogood questions the legitimacy of the 'Aboriginal man impersonating a police office charge'. The then-president of the NSW Council for Civil Liberties, Mr K. D. Buckley, described the sentence as 'unduly harsh…the sentence seemed so severe it almost gave the appearance of discrimination', though his further claims that Kelly had actually been carrying out valuable work cannot be sustained. Major-General Stretton felt so strongly that the severity of Kelly's sentence was motivated by racism that he ran up Darwin's courthouse steps to confront McCann. To onlookers it looked, for all the world, like a military intervention. The ensuing altercation made the front page of newspapers around the country on New Year's Eve and became the stuff of history books, highlighting the tensions between the Commonwealth and the Territory as much as between black and white.

McCann: 'My immediate view was I wasn't going to take orders from anybody, particularly orders relating in a courthouse situation… Stretton, I think he was in his full regalia, not in his best uniform but, you know, it was quite obviously a military presence…' This is not quite true. The photo of Stretton charging up the steps that was run in the *Northern Territory News* is dramatic, but he's certainly not wearing anything resembling full regalia. However Clem O'Sullivan also describes Stretton's visit to the magistrate's courts as an 'invasion attack'. In hindsight, both sides have a point. Stretton that the racial politics of the Territory were problematic and McCann that Cyclone Tracy, like many disasters since, was becoming the excuse for what felt like a military, and federal, intervention.

Stretton's sprint up the courtroom steps on 30 December captured in a symbolic, albeit unintentional, fashion the deep rift between the Territory and the rest of Australia. His radio speeches also captured a certain disconnect between Canberra and Darwin, one that seems relevant here. It predates Tracy and is arguably present today. Thorogood said he had to ask Stretton:

> to be careful of one phrase. He kept talking about 'the people back down in Australia'...I kept on: 'No, no, down south, but not down in Australia'. But it never seemed to offend anybody so I guess it didn't matter. I guess people in Darwin often did think that the rest of it was Australia anyway.

Managing Indigenous people's relationship to alcohol using the law continues to the present day as the contentious, and recently defunct, Banned Drinkers' Register shows. Even the term long grasser is, according to Ted Egan, based on the fact that Indigenous people liked to drink outside. 'The arrangement was that the supplier, quite often a taxi driver, purchased the liquor for them, and left the wine "In the long grass".'[4] A friend, self-described planning reform enthusiast and co-director of the National Live Music Office Dr Ianto Ware, has said to me that the Northern Territory's Liquor Act has 'an above average capacity to rule against people's use of intoxicants'. While this isn't directed just at Indigenous people, this approach is 'unusual but also very, very old fashioned. Usually when it comes to alcohol consumption and the social contexts that surround it, we regulate the places people drink, without specifically targeting the drinker.'[5]

Some people were upset about Guildin Kelly's treatment for another reason: they felt the Greeks were the ones who should have been punished. Accusations of looting became a significant flashpoint for the racial tensions that existed in Darwin between Greek families—many of whom had been there since the 1920s—and the rest of the population.

The source of this antagonism towards the Greeks is unclear, though Jack Haritos remembers they were always known as the 'Greasy Greeks'.[6] When I spoke to Greek people still living in Darwin they had little interest in dwelling on the racism they (or their parents) had been subjected to.

There were complaints in police reports about Greek evacuees not sharing. Other accounts phrase it in terms of different cultural responses to disaster. They discuss the fact that those who came from a place where they could not expect government help were more focused on saving themselves. Spiro Papas, on trial for larceny and possessing stolen goods, explained it this way:

> I put my family in the school and I go round and try and find some food because we got the wrong idea, so where we could find the food—just stole some food to live, because the Greeks don't believe in Salvation Army and Red Cross. We don't have experience—in our country they're poor and happen, something like this happen—you know—we don't get help.

Curly Nixon remembers,

> the *NT News* was the judge and jury of a mob of Greeks that [are] supposed to have got caught looting and taking

> stuff south. But when it got into the court later on—without any apologies—it was proven in course that all the stuff that they'd had in these trailers actually belonged to them, and had belonged to them for ten/twenty years—some of it. Some of it had only been just bought before Christmas, as presents and that...there were signs appearing: 'Keep Australia Beautiful—Kill a Greek a day'...And when the poor bastards were proven innocent, there was no apologies or any headlines on the front page about how they were proven innocent, and a mistake was made—no way in the world.

Peter Talbot also defends the Greeks' reputation. 'Another thing too, they reckon all the Greek was the biggest looter in Darwin, they wasn't.' Meanwhile his daughter, who worked in the court system producing summonses, told him that most of those arrested had been 'Australians'. McLaren believes the Greek situation was exaggerated. 'There was a group of Greeks who went to a shopping centre and they were going to help themselves to food and so forth, no doubt I suppose not knowing what the future held for them.'[7] Bill Wilson again: 'You shouldn't tar the whole community with the actions of a few people, but if the police were winners, reputation-wise, out of the cyclone, the Greek community were the losers.' Cedric Patterson, who was a supervising architect for the Commonwealth Department of Housing and Construction when Tracy struck, remembers that:

> These two Greek fellows—young chaps, very good workers—they'd finished the contract they were on and they were going south with their families. And the way it was relayed to me, was that they were stopped at a road block, accused of looting and stealing which they certainly had not. And one of the fellows was smashed in the mouth by

> one of the police, and finished up having his jaw completely shattered and had to come back and have it all wired.

It's possible Patterson's story may be a variant of the arrest and assault of Theo Rigas. Rigas, a postal line worker and bricklayer who'd been arrested for larceny and possessing stolen property, was brought into the watch house at eight at night on Friday 27 December. He was one of seven men (including Spiro Papas) and two teenage boys who'd been questioned after their homes and cars in Rapid Creek were found to contain a large number of clothes, bolts of cloth, furnishings, cassette stereos and the like. The court transcripts quote Constable Ian Doube as saying: 'I noticed that the vehicles in the yard, apart from the truck, were loaded with what appeared to be new goods in the way of lazy boy chairs [sic], great quantities of food, great quantities of clothing and linen. Some of the clothing and some of the linen was in new wrappers.'[8] The men said that these were their own goods and certainly there are many stories of people being arrested for putting their own goods in the back of their car, or, as happened to Patterson, being harassed when they were trying to get back into their own homes. The Greek men were formally arrested and the children sent home—though not till the next morning. 'Both prisoners fathers still in custody and they were therefore given permission to sleep in one of the cells.'

On Saturday 28 December a legal aid solicitor came in to see all prisoners. At 11.30 am all thirteen prisoners were released for a court appearance, then returned just after midday. It was some time after 5 pm that 'Sgt Blake advised that prisoner 4764 Rigas [was] complaining of a toothache.' From that time on Rigas was described, variously, as suffering: 'a toothache', a 'mouth injury' then, twenty-four hours later, 'facial injuries'. Different coloured pens in the watch house journal suggest that these descriptions were added retrospectively, once it became clear that Rigas' injuries were so serious they could not be covered up. After a visit from the Greek consulate, police were 'advised that prisoner 4764 Rigas has a mouth injury'. Rigas was eventually taken to hospital under prison officer escort, where he had to have his jaw wired together. On New Year's Day he was out of hospital and taken to court to arrange bail, before being returned to hospital late in the afternoon.

QC Ian Barker attempted to get a clear picture of what happened to Theo Rigas when a preliminary hearing was held on 2 January. The Supreme Court of the Northern Territory transcript in which Barker interviews Constable Griffith of NSW, who'd arrived in Darwin on 27 December 1974, reads:

> And if people present said they saw you punch Rigas on the jaw, you would say that they, perhaps were not telling the truth would you?
> —That's correct Sir.
> I put it to you you did punch him on the jaw?
> —No Sir.
> I suppose you would go on denying that if I asked you for the rest of your life?
> —Yes Sir.

It was found there was enough evidence for the defendants to stand trial, and the trial date was set for March. The Greek consulate put up the bond for each of the defendants and soon after two of the men, A. Magaulias and G. Fordaulis, were released with only a sixty dollar fine. By 27 March 1975 it was Rigas and Rigas alone who stood before Justice Muirhead, and pleaded guilty to two counts of receiving stolen goods. In his defence of Rigas, Barker argued that 'it was hard for people like that to see their town virtually disappear overnight'. Muirhead responded:

> I will take into account, as Mr Barker has urged, that your behaviour was in some way an unfortunate unplanned reaction inspired by the destruction you had observed...as I have said previously the courts will not be slow to impose sentences which may serve as a warning and perhaps as a deterrent to those who have in the past been tempted to profit by or may yet be tempted to take advantage of unusually exposed premises and property.

Rigas was imprisoned with hard labour for fifteen months. Constable Griffith was never charged. As for Guildin Kelly, he appealed his nine-month sentence without success.

A few days after Selma fizzled out and before Tracy hit, Peter Dermoudy was quoted as saying that many houses in Darwin would not stand up to a big wind. He was right. There was a lot less material damage after the cyclone of 1937. While the storm surge after that cyclone was bad, so bad that everything turned green with algae afterwards, the buildings did okay. In general older buildings were more likely to be standing after Tracy, while only five per cent of buildings built since the mid-fifties had survived. Grant Tambling's house was one of the few modern houses that made it, but it was architect designed, and tucked behind a hill.

It's unsurprising that one of the first questions people asked after they staggered out of their houses and saw the completeness of the town's destruction—a question they still ask some forty years later—was why the damage caused by Tracy was so extensive.

So, while it's been conjectured that the earthquake that hit a few days before Cyclone Tracy—about 400 kilometres out, in the Timor Sea—led to some structural damage, the real problem was the poor standards houses had been built to, particularly in the newer suburbs north of the city. Mayor Tiger Brennan:

> There have been millions spent on developing those bloody suburbs. Right. Now they were the ones that suffered most. The older buildings seemed to stand up, and if you look at the buildings there you'll see that the housing commission buildings didn't suffer as much as the blinking administration buildings...Most of them suffered because they blinking built the things on stilts that the whole top went, they landed on top of these blinking low-storey buildings.

He's right that housing commission buildings, with their double brick walls, did particularly well. 'Those early days houses were built on like a tank, you know. They were very heavy timbers and things like that, and most of them lost their roofs, but they stayed actually on their foundations.' Ken Frey, who joined the Department of Works and Housing in 1946, argued that, regardless of craftsmanship, age strengthens buildings. They settle and as they do so, dust solidifies their joints.

A Larrakia woman I spoke to told me she felt that the racism Greeks endured after the cyclone was because they were often builders, and it was builders who were in the line of fire as the community cast around for blame. Frey, among others, suggested that poor Greek construction work was the reason that houses broke up. The line was that builders were using green wood, cutting it instead of bending it, not using enough nails, and generally engaging in shonky building practices. Government architect Cedric Patterson does not accept these assessments and talks about the Greeks and Italians as being the original builders of Darwin.

> If it was not for these Greeks and Italians, the cost of building in Darwin would have been a hell of a lot higher and not so satisfactory. They worked extremely hard and they

> deserve every respect and thanks from the people, for what they did in Darwin over their lifetimes.

As Patterson points out, while many of the builders of Darwin's newer northern suburbs were Greek, they'd also been the builders of the older houses which had survived the cyclone of 1937.

What had changed was the rate of development. When Charles Gurd arrived in 1972 'there were houses being built by the hundreds all over the place. They looked pretty flimsy, and I remember my wife saying that if there was a cyclone all these houses would blow away.' And it's certainly true that once houses broke up, more debris flew around and that, in turn, damaged more houses. By 1974, Darwin was growing at the extraordinary rate of 13.5 per cent per annum. The rapid expansion meant that it was hard to get workers of a high standard, in the numbers needed. Nor were there enough building inspectors. Len Garton:

> We employed about four or five [of] what we considered competent building supervisors. And we used to meet each night and discuss, along with photos, the various jobs that they completed that day and put a price on what we estimated to be the cost for repairs and so on. And we all felt, along with myself, that many of these houses were very poorly constructed...We've seen many instances where the bond beam had lifted and the curtains had blown under the bond beam and the bond beam had come back down and jammed the curtain. Obviously the bond beam wasn't anchored to the bottom of the wall, or the top of the wall.

He was also concerned that galvanised iron roofs were not fixed properly to the rafters.

> In the course of cleaning up—you know, you were just

> wandering around and see there's a stack of iron and you just go and look at it out of interest. And you find it's got half a dozen nails in the bottom and half a dozen nails in the top and nothing in the centre, which to me was a bit frightening, particularly as you look at the number of nails in the iron as of today—every second flute's nailed.

A lot of the damage caused by the cyclone was caused by the way the roofs behaved—blowing off the top of houses, and ploughing into, or landing on, neighbours. And of course once a house lost its roof, it was much more likely to collapse.

Cedric Patterson, on the other hand, suggests the buildings were of reasonable standard—they simply weren't tough enough to stand up to a 'freak' like Cyclone Tracy. And he certainly didn't think the fact that the houses lifted up, then dropped down again, indicated anything other than normal construction.

As well as the rate at which houses went up, there was the issue of building codes. As a result of Cyclone Althea, which hit Townsville in 1971, James Cook University developed cyclone-proofing guidelines in 1973. However, George Redmond, director of construction for the Department of Works at the time of Tracy, has said those guidelines didn't help much in Tracy because nobody 'realised the vulnerability of the high-tensile steel roofing, and the holding down of the roof'.[9]

Either way there was a limit to the difference a few more nails would have made. Ken Frey:

> Roofs before—metal roofs, galvanised iron—had been nailed. But even where they'd been screwed these failed, because tests done by manufacturers—and by universities—all relied on what they call static tests. In other words, they'd put a static load on the thing. But of course, in a cyclone it's not static, you know, you've got flutter in your wind,

> you've got little vortices coming off, and there's a whole lot of flapping going on. And even where the screws held, the sheet material of the roof would fatigue over the screw, and just split across it, and the whole roof then would peel off.

After Cyclone Tracy new screws and washers were developed to better withstand horizontal pressures and the constant jigging they had to bear during a cyclone. I remember Neville Barwick's evocative word, his description of the way in which buildings rattled and rattled until they simply 'unzipped'.

By 1974 houses were deliberately of a lighter construction. This was as much to do with modern aesthetics as changes in mass manufacturing. The CSIRO had developed a light timber code for houses, which was generally very successful but not good in areas where there could be a lot of wind. This extended to the furniture. During Tracy some people scrambled under standard-issue kitchen tables only to find they were too flimsy to provide adequate protection. According to Frey some of these issues, such as the CSIRO's building codes, were especially problematic in Darwin because it was a territory, not a state, capital. This meant that designs were reviewed in offices in Canberra and Melbourne where, Frey claimed, changes would be made without an understanding of the implications for those who lived in Darwin.

These days national planning codes still compel architects to reduce the number of glazed windows in buildings they design for the tropics so as to make them more energy efficient. This makes sense if you are designing a building that is to be heated or cooled with air conditioners, but not otherwise. It is plentiful ventilation that makes some tropical houses, particularly the early Burnett houses, such a joy to behold and inhabit. And, despite the lightness of their appearance, Burnett houses did better than many buildings during Tracy.

Beni Burnett was the principal government architect in the Northern Territory in the late thirties and early forties. The child of Scottish missionaries, he grew up in Asia then, as a young architect, worked in China and Singapore, and you see the influence of Asian architecture in his work. His first projects were residential accommodation for the huge influx of public servants coming to Darwin as part of the defence build-up in the pre-war years. One of the last buildings Burnett designed in Darwin, in 1941, was a new post office but, because of the bombing of Darwin, that building was never completed. Burnett was evacuated to Alice Springs just before the air raids and never returned to Darwin; but the mark he'd made in his brief time there was permanent.

His buildings were simple and maximised airflow. They stood on stilts, had high ceilings, banks of louvres above partial external walls and few internal walls. You only have to stand in one and you yearn for a plantation chair and a gin and tonic. When I spent time in Darwin one of my friends lived in a Burnett house, one of the last still standing. The owner of the house loves it but is not overly romantic on the subject. Louvres and mosquito netting don't block the increasing noise of the city. There is little privacy. The boundary between outside and inside is blurred. However it is a cool and beautiful space to sit in, filled with the whirr of fans and the click of geckos. It's these ambient qualities that make Darwin such a delight to be in, and, of course, so vulnerable when the weather turns.

It wasn't just the built environment that suffered in the wake of Cyclone Tracy, but the natural one. Robin Bullock remembers that after Tracy he was allocated a place at Union Terrace.

> It was like a desert. There was not a blade of grass, from Lee Point Road down to where Walagi [Sanderson] High School is now...The houses at the bottom used to have dingoes and buffalo wandering around there. I remember that. We were half-way down to there. But they scraped everything clean.

> It was red-orange dirt all the way from Lee Point Road down to Patterson Street. You could stand in your yard, backyard, and see right up both ends. Just not a blade of grass. A lot of coffee rock, so digging holes was hard. Any decent soil there had been scraped off.

Keith Cole says something similar. 'The tragedy of Tracy was also seen in the environment. Darwin had been a lush, tropical city with beautiful gardens and fine eucalypt stands and a wide variety of birds. Tracy smashed the lot.'

Perhaps this is why, in the years after Tracy, gardens were tended with an enthusiasm the good folk of Darwin had not shown before. Something about living in a town stripped of all plant- and wildlife meant that people were keen to bring plants, birds and animals back into their lives. Green ants took four years to come back, and some people missed them so much they took nests from further inland and put them in their gardens. According to Margaret Muirhead, nurseries sprang up all over the place. 'I remember one man say[ing], "unless you have a garden or went through Tracy, you really have nothing to contribute to the conversation".'

Botanical Gardens director George Brown drove 'around Darwin streets issuing two plants to every home…"You'd see them hugging the bloody things, you know, and the kids'd come up and say 'Can I have one too?'"'[10] It's good to know that such a tree-loving man went onto become the lord mayor of Darwin, a position he held up until his sudden death in 2002. The Botanical Gardens are now named the George Brown Darwin Botanic Gardens.

But despite talk of the damage that Tracy did to Darwin's greenery, the deforestation of the town had begun long before. Ken Frey recalls battles in the decades before Tracy to get housing-estate engineers to leave some trees when they cleared; in some suburbs there was hardly any topsoil left, let alone a tree. Paula Dos Santos remembers the kind of place Darwin had been, in this description of Nightcliff in the forties and fifties:

> It was thick rainforest. Just across here in Clarke Crescent, there was about eight banyan trees there, and all these ferns and that. They were all bulldozed to build Housing Commission houses...when I first moved in here twenty-seven or twenty-eight years ago, we'd have trouble sleeping at night with the thousands of lorikeets, cockatiels, budgerigars that used to sleep in the trees around here. They'd keep us awake, chattering half the night.

She also used to see crocs and buffalo at Rapid Creek, as well as black cockatoos and Major Mitchells, and frill-necked lizards. While Nightcliff would change in the years to come, it didn't suffer the same level of depletion as the northern suburbs. Its trees offered some protection from Tracy; the mangroves that pushed up against Nightcliff's shoreline also helped.

The species that withstood the cyclone most effectively was the coastal Calophyllum, also known as beauty leaf. Unfortunately, because they are big and slow-growing, people didn't tend to plant them. Naturally flexible trees survive much better than those that are brittle and prone to cracking, which is why palms also fared pretty well. However, while Carpentaria palms produced new leaves and flowered after Tracy, another type of palm common to the area, *Livistona benthamii* disappeared. Milkwood trees, indigenous to the area, did better than some vegetation because they shed their leaves in high wind, which means there is less pressure on the branches. The milkwood trees in front of Brown's Mart Theatre in Smith Street were planted in the 1890s and have survived at least two cyclones and the bombing of Darwin. There is a milkwood tree on Foelsche Street that predates white settlement. Banyan trees also do okay because even if their crowns are damaged their roots tend to hold. Apparently after the cyclone a spontaneous noticeboard was installed near the Darwin City Council banyan. The banyan in State Square, over two hundred years old, used to be a ceremonial meeting point for the Larrakia. On several afternoons I went and sat under it after spending time in the library, enjoying the views across the park to the water and the respite from heat under the massive canopy. In recent years development has led to the destruction of many of Darwin's remaining banyans.

A report on 'Cyclone damage to natural vegetation in the Darwin area after Cyclone Tracy',[11] carried out seven weeks after Tracy, found that the area of moderate to severe cyclone damage was about 465 square kilometres. Monsoon forests fared badly and were left even more susceptible to bushfire. (These micro-climates are the dinosaur relics of a time when fire was less common. The more recent interaction between cyclones and fires has been responsible for a great, if gradual, reduction in monsoonal forests. Increasing temperatures also make it unlikely these remnant rain forests will last many more decades.)

That report recommended that areas near the coast should not be built up, in case of storm surges, and that trees that could withstand cyclones better should be planted, in part because they provided protection for buildings. These findings were ignored. George Brown recommended African mahoganies be planted after the cyclone because they're fast growing, but he specified that the holes dug to plant the seedlings needed to be particularly deep. That was the kind of technical detail that, inevitably, got lost as people replanted their gardens in the years that followed Tracy. In 2011, Cyclone Yasi ripped African mahoganies out of the waterlogged earth by the dozens because of their shallow root structure. Once a tree is pulled up by the roots it becomes just another deadly piece of debris. In her play *Dragged Kicking and Screaming to Paradise* Suzanne Spunner wrote:

> After Cyclone Tracy, common native and exotic trees in the Darwin area were assessed in terms of stability—numbers of trees standing, leaning and fallen—and the mahoganies and tulips were downgraded to Category C 'Unstable', hence their dubious reputation. Also in the same category are evergreen frangipanis…and mangoes…[12]

My interest in environmental matters led me to visit field naturalist Hip Strider, now over seventy. He lives on a platform shelter out at Humpty Doo. A keen observer of local conditions for some fifty years, he's been keeping notes on a range of the major effects of practices such as grazing and burning off, as well as storms. Strider attends to the city, its outskirts and the edge of the cyclone damage zone. He has a long beard, wears old shorts and not much else, and his dog moves with him, constant as a shadow.

We sat under a slow-moving but noisy fan (so noisy I couldn't tape the interview). A couple of times, to illustrate a point, he got up to take a book from his shelves, only for silverfish to scatter as the book disintegrated in his hands. Conditions were harsh to say the least, but they also meant that Strider was alert to minor changes in wind speed and temperature and to all the shifts in the seasons. (A chronicler of most things, he took a photo of me sitting there in the heat and dust and I was, as I was most of the time I spent in Darwin, sweaty and red-faced, a fish out of water, a southerner come north.) He told me how to pick a tree that had survived the cyclone by looking for its scars.

On his advice, I went to visit one not far from where he lived. Older than the rest of the trees, it towered above the other gums and had the tell-tale knots where limbs had been torn from the trunk. Strider knew of only half a dozen such gum trees. Given the ravages of cyclones, fires and development, older trees are increasingly rare.

Trees that date back to the time before white settlement, or those that grew soon after, provide mute witness to several hundred years of history. They are memorials, of a sort. Yet there is no legislation to protect significant or historic trees in the Territory, and no plans to change that any time soon.

THE SHOOTING OF THE DOGS

KUNBARLANJNJA IN west Arnhem Land is Dog Dreaming country. An elder described his people's relationships to the animals this way:

> We can only say this—dogs are our friends. The belief of the people here is that a dog is just like a child and no one can hit the dog. People used to give each other dogs. The pup and the child would grow up together. Puppies would be promised to each other. This created for both groups what you say in English, 'family'.[1]

Pets suffered alongside their owners during Tracy and, as with humans, there were stories of miraculous survival too. People describe the trauma of finding their beloved cats or dogs crushed under rubble, or the hilarity of their cockatoos surviving—but being stripped of feathers. The day after the cyclone, journalist Barbara James found her cat—alive—in the washing machine where it had taken refuge. Beth Harvey spent much of the cyclone worrying about her cockatoo and cat, both of whom had dashed out of her car at the height of the storm. She found them when she got back to her house, although the cat wasn't in great shape, having been rolled in iron and jammed into a letterbox. It 'was a very paranoid cat after that'.

In general, animals that lived through the cyclone tended to be scared of the wind after that experience—as, indeed, their owners usually were. Bernard Briec remembers a family friend's Afghan hound that couldn't eat or drink for several days. 'Dad said: "It's not going to survive, better put it out of its misery," so Dad took him round the back somewhere and killed him...I mean, the owners were a bit upset at it, at Dad putting the dog down. But it was the only thing he could do really, when I think back on it now.'

As well as companion animals, countless farm and wild animals died. In the opening sequence of her book *Darwin*, Tess Lea speaks of her experiences of the cyclone and writes vividly of the stench of rotting marine animals 'swept in by the stormy waters and crushed against rocks'. There were stories of devastated chook sheds and dozens of birds being found in a terrible state days after the cyclone. One of the compensation cases that followed Tracy, and dragged out until 1982, was a chicken farmer complaining that his birds had been put down. Colonel Thorogood tells the story of one man, a crocodile farmer, concerned for the lives of his reptiles: 'And I told him that the quicker he could turn them into effing handbags the better—and that was the end of that call.' I laughed when I first read that, then remembered that back then crocs had only been a protected species for three years, having been hunted close to extinction.

There are haunting photos taken by Barbara James of dead livestock draped over the backs of utes, dead donkeys and, in one surreal shot, of camels and horses trotting through the ruins and rubble—escapees, it turns out, from a circus that was camped somewhere in town. In *The Furious Days*, Major-General Stretton wrote of a conversation he had with a garbo who cornered him at a press conference. 'No bastard will help me,' the garbo said. 'Me truck's broken down up the road with a load of stinkin' animal corpses. No bastard will git it going.' It's not clear if the animals had died during the cyclone or after it.

Birds stayed away from Darwin for close to a year, with the strange exception of thousands of kites. 'Before Cyclone Tracy you'd spot maybe a dozen a dry season. Around 1500 turned up in May 1975 and no one really knows why. Might be because the trees were knocked down.'[2] It was (kites excepted) a terrible absence. Donna Quong described the eeriness. 'I mean, you don't appreciate the noise of the wind through the leaves until you don't have leaves. And you don't appreciate the sound of birds until you don't have birds.' Tom Pauling was delighted when someone brought a canary in a cage to his house, one that 'busily sung from time to time'. Cedric Patterson became very fond of the lorikeet that moved into his house, 'a straggler' that had lost its flock. It stayed with Patterson for quite a while, seeming to need the company.

A gulf emerged between people who treated their pets as an extension of the family and those that came to fear them in this new, chaotic world. Certainly many an animal lover had been injured, even risked death, in an attempt to protect their animals. Richard Creswick was unusual only in that he was a cat lover rather than a dog man. 'We had three cats...And they were our surrogate children so I went to some considerable lengths to protect them and ensure that they survived.' It was a shock, then, for people to realise they weren't allowed to bring their pets to the accommodation and evacuation centres that had sprung up in high schools, fire stations and police stations. Of course some ignored the rules and took their pets along. Ken Frey was one of many who were concerned about this. 'People, although they'd been asked not to, brought their pets and wouldn't let them go, and all this sort of thing.' Senator Collins—who acknowledges that roaming dogs were a health risk—took quite a few dogs down to the CSIRO labs so they could be cared for there.

Not only were pets not allowed at evacuation centres, they were difficult to evacuate. Once Thorogood realised that 'a lot of people didn't want to leave Darwin because they didn't want to abandon their pets', he changed the rules to allow them to take the animals on the aircraft when they were evacuated. This has led to many a story of people on already overloaded aircraft finding themselves with birds flying around the cabins and puppies stowed in baskets. This didn't necessarily lead to a happy ending for either the pets or the owners. One pilot recalls a 747 with:

> kittens, puppies, goldfish, rabbits, guinea pigs, and whatever else you could hide. The crew…turned a blind eye, the customs and officials did not…most of these pets somehow disappeared. How anyone could take a beloved pet from a traumatised child is beyond me, but as you know there are always the officious arseholes in every exercise.[3]

Another pilot got as many animals out as he could, flying them to safety. Les Liddell recalls seeing them out at Tennant Creek airport, row upon row of cats and dogs wearing labels and destination tags. 'And it was the greatest thing—a humane thing—I've ever seen, to see all these animals sitting quietly there in this aircraft.'[4] Dawn Lawrie did manage to get her puppy safely evacuated—it was flown out on the flight deck—and hid her female boxer. Pets, she reasoned, along with children, were important to rebuilding a society. Other people gave in to the inevitable and, before they evacuated, took their pets to the local police station to have them shot. Elizabeth Carroll was traumatised for years afterwards by the fact she put her cat down. 'It was just so terrible to think that he had actually survived the cyclone, and he'd come home, and we had him, and we had to leave him…'

One recent survey suggests that forty-nine per cent of people say they would not leave their home if they could not take their animals with them. The real numbers would probably be lower than that;[5] however, as the number of disasters—cyclone, floods, fire and earthquakes—increases, the issue of what happens to the animals that are also affected does become more pressing. World Society for the Protection of Animals Australia CEO Carmel Molloy has noted that 'Lives were lost during the Victorian bushfires because people wouldn't leave their premises as their animals weren't being catered for at evacuation points.'[6] In response to criticisms of the way these issues were handled on Black Saturday, the Victorian Emergency Animal Welfare Plan set out arrangements for emergency animal welfare management. It should also be noted that it's estimated that more than a million animals—including livestock, wild animals and pets—died in the fire.

When the people of Turkey Creek were evacuated from Warmun to Kununurra after the floods in March 2011, they couldn't take their dogs. This was a source of real grief. One woman interviewed just before evacuation commented, 'Some of us also leave our dogs. We're going to leave man's best friend. They never left us but we're going to leave them.' Wayne Mulga, also about to be evacuated, made a similar comment: '…our animals and that back there. No good you know. Sad.'[7] During Hurricane Katrina many people refused to leave their home if they couldn't take their animals with them. Around six hundred thousand pets are believed to have died or been left without shelter as a result of that event. As a result of the mismanagement of that disaster, the *Pets Evacuation and Transportation Standards Act* was passed by the House of Representatives in May 2006. This legislation requires that state and local authorities seeking funding from the Federal Emergency Management Agency must take into account pet owners, household pets and service animals when drawing up evacuation plans.

Some say that the stories of the brutal treatment of dogs after Cyclone Tracy, particularly by police from interstate, was a beat up. Another crazy rumour sweeping the town. But this rumour is substantiated by dozens of people who witnessed the casual slaughter. Because of fears that hungry and traumatised dogs would form packs, the order had gone out that all dogs, and indeed cats, were to be shot. Some police dreaded the task. Others became a bit too enthusiastic. Air Commodore Hitchins found:

> a police gentleman with two loaded revolvers sticking out of his belt patrolling around the RAAF tarmac on a motorbike and when I asked him who he was, he said that he was there to make sure that there was no civil trouble and what's more there were a lot of loose roaming packs of dogs...And he was there to shoot all these dogs on the RAAF Base.

Hitchins told the man to get on his bike and bugger off.

Police were told that to set an example they had to destroy their own dogs. This, after nights of no sleep and evacuated families and devastated houses. One policeman, a friend of Beth Harvey's, tried to finish off his six-year-old dachshund, but found himself unable to do it. 'I went to shoot her and she just licked my hand.' He ended up giving her to Harvey to care for alongside her labrador. People were given the option: take their pets to the police station or take the risk that police would shoot them from their cars without warning and in front of the owners.

Cats were better at eluding armed police, but you have to wonder if the Northern Territory's present day feral cat problem—responsible for the extinction and endangerment of several species of small marsupial—escalated dramatically after Tracy. Ray Wilkie says that in the weeks following the cyclone the cats were left to run around—sometimes he'd look up at night and see thirty or forty pairs of feline eyes looking down at him from the wreckage.

Interstate animal welfare agencies arrived in town immediately after the cyclone but by 2 January the RSPCA were lobbying to get more of their staff into Darwin. According to the *Northern Territory News*, 'the society's phones were being jammed by Darwin evacuees seeking information about their pets'. Increasingly women looked out for animals, on their own behalf, and also on behalf of men who feared for their pets if they left them alone. Kate Cairns was living in Jingili under the 'dance floor' of a house across the road from her ruined one. She moved in there for a few days, along with eleven other people, as many dogs and two cats.

> I was looking after something like eleven dogs at one stage, because they were being shot. And these were pets. And the men were going out every day helping the clean-up... In some cases it was the only thing they had left and they weren't game to leave the dog unattended. And so when all the women went and—there were very few of us women left in Darwin after the mass evacuation—the guys would say: 'Katie, would you look after my dog?'

George Brown, who'd been out of town when the cyclone hit, felt great affection for the nameless woman who hid his dogs for him. The woman was

> ...one of the ones that determined she wasn't going to be evacuated. She contacted me and said: 'Do you want your dogs?' And I said: 'Yeah, well thank you very much', and sort of took her in my arms and thanked her and comforted

> her, and she comforted me that she was all right and I was back again, and there were the two dogs—well the dog and the pup.[8]

Shooting pets was an extreme policy without a shred of nuance, like much that happened after Tracy. However, concerns about the dangers of packs were not unfounded. Bill Wilson, a dog lover himself, acknowledges that 'dog packs formed and some of them were getting quite violent and they were quite dangerous'. Ken Frey was one of a number of people going from house to house doing a survey on the state they were in, and, if necessary, recovering bodies. It wasn't long before he got himself into a fix. 'In one place I got in and found, when I got into a bedroom whose door was not locked but closed, that there was a pack of dogs in there and they were by this time extremely hungry, and I was lucky to get out the front alive.' As a result of such experiences he had no qualms about the orders given to shoot dogs—after several run-ins he was wishing he could shoot them himself. But it's a long way from those concerns to what actually happened.

Ray Wilkie remembers the way one dog was killed. 'One day an officer came around, and there was an old dog in our place—he was a nice old fellow—and the [policeman] said: "You got a dog there?" and I said "Yes. He's not hurting anyone"...Out he came and bang, that was it.' Events like this were an added trauma for people who had just been through a catastrophe. Wilson: 'all they had left was their animals; they had no house, and in some cases no husband, no wife, and for these people to come in and act the way they did I think was wrong...' In its twentieth anniversary special, the *Northern Territory News* describes Anne Taylor handing over her cat but begging them not to touch the dog. To no avail. They shot the dog right there at the door in front of her. Taylor remembers, 'I went insane with rage. I got into the car and tried to run them over.'

Vicki Harris's description is the most distressing of all.

> Phil and Bob had gone—they'd gone over to Bob's place and on their way they'd seen the policeman shooting at this labrador. And the labrador had blood coming out its ears and its nose and they were just shooting at it because they couldn't catch it and they just kept shooting at it...And Phil said: 'There's no way I can leave our dog and just, for her to be shot like that,' he said: 'I couldn't do it.' So he ended up taking her to the police station at Casuarina and he had her destroyed; they shot her. And that's actually what they sort of said to people, you know: 'Have your dog put down humanely'... But she was a lovely dog and it was really quite sad. Phil had to take her in there and make her sit and stay, and the guy tied her up with this lump of rope, and you know he was only a really young policeman. He must've only just been in rookies, and he was given the unenviable job of shooting everybody's pets. I just wonder really, today, how that guy fared through it all because that would've been—on top of what he'd no doubt seen, with the dead bodies and one thing and another—that would've been the [last] straw, I think. It would've been absolutely awful to have had to shoot people's dogs.

It's likely that young rookie was Robin Bullock, who, after he finished up at the morgue, was given the job of shooting dogs and other animals.

> I think there was some sort of over-reaction there. I really think the dogs probably could've survived quite well, truth be told...I know that we had requests from owners who were leaving, to put the dogs down, because they couldn't stand the idea of them just wandering and perhaps not being fed—'cause they were all domestic animals.

Bullock reckons he shot twenty or thirty dogs in all, but only at the police station, when their owners brought them in. This was often done when people were being evacuated and couldn't take their animals with them. Former Sergeant John Wolthers, who was in charge at Casuarina police station, 'acknowledged the pain the policy inflicted on pet owners. He said it was one of the saddest tasks the police had been forced to perform.'[9]

Jingili was a suburb I spent time in when researching this book and at one stage I minded a dog called Daisy. At sunset, if the tide was low, I'd take her down to the broad expanses of Casuarina Beach, which was covered with dogs and their owners bounding, jogging and generally milling around. One night I had dinner with neighbours and sat on their balcony, surrounded by a dense tropical garden. I mentioned my interest in the dogs and what had happened to them. 'The dogs?' my host asked. 'They buried them all up the road.' He gestured towards the end of the street, towards Jingili Primary School. So, it seems there were mass graves after all, though it wasn't humans who were put into them. I sat there wondering if the garbo who'd buttonholed Stretton during a press conference all those years ago had been on his way there, to dump his carcasses in a trench that now sits under a primary school sports oval. Certainly the landscaping at the Jingili water gardens, at the other end of the street, had been moulded over the wreckage of the houses from the northern suburbs. 'You didn't know?' one of the gardeners told me, as I was walking Daisy one night. 'They bulldozed the rubble to make these hills.' I hadn't known, but there was no doubting that the gardens had some high hillocks. Modern Darwin is full of these little moments. Reminders that you don't have to dig very deep to find the remnants of all that horror, some forty years ago.

WINDS OF CHANGE

I'VE GOT TO HAVE MY TRIPS

IT IS impossible to overstate the significance of the timing of Cyclone Tracy's arrival a week before 1975. That was the year of the *Racial Discrimination Act*. It was the year Gough Whitlam went to Wave Hill and granted partial title to the Gurindji people 'and through Vincent's fingers poured a handful of sand'.[1] It was the year the *Aboriginal Land Rights (NT) Bill* was introduced into parliament. It was International Women's Year. Gay rights were finally on the agenda and homosexuality was legalised in South Australia. The death penalty was abolished. The Vietnam War finally ended, following Australia's withdrawal in 1972. Legal Aid was introduced. The British honours system was replaced by the Australian one on, of course, Australia Day (though the LNP government in power at the time of writing has reintroduced it, on 25 March 2014). No-fault divorce was introduced. By the time Whitlam was dismissed on 11 November 1975 a record number of bills had been introduced and enacted. By Whitlam's own estimation, more than half his reform plan was implemented during his government's two short terms. A few days after Whitlam's dismissal, East Timor declared itself independent, only to be invaded by Indonesia. Refugees who fled the slaughter that ensued arrived in Darwin close to a year after Tracy, to find a town still in ruins.

Even as a nine-year-old child I felt the seismic shift caused by the Labor Party's win in 1972, and the energy and charisma radiated by our new prime minister, Gough Whitlam. I sometimes wonder if one of the reasons that Cyclone Tracy has so imprinted itself on me is because it unleashed its force at such an extraordinary moment in modern Australia's history. As we headed into 1975 the ride just got bumpier, or more exhilarating, depending on your point of view.

The Northern Territory was feeling it too. Margaret Muirhead: 'I think we forget how many changes were brought about in 1975. For instance, in the Territory, that was the year that women were allowed to sit on juries.' At that time 'they couldn't be bank tellers either'. The rationale was that the money was too heavy for them to carry, and they couldn't handle a gun.

While Whitlam himself was not a young man (he was fifty-six when he took office) the generational change his government represented permeated everything. Australia was finally embracing its younger people and their values, rather than rejecting them. I don't know what I expected when I interviewed Malcolm Fraser, one of the men who brought Whitlam's term in office to such an abrupt halt on 11 November 1975, but he spoke about his former foe with great warmth. Indeed the tone of our conversation was so conciliatory I had to go back to Whitlam's famous speech on the steps of parliament, after his dismissal by Governor-General Sir John Kerr, to remind myself of the temper of the times. Malcolm Fraser, Whitlam boomed, his face fierce with rage, 'will undoubtedly go down in Australian history from Remembrance Day 1975 as Kerr's cur'.

It was important to speak to Fraser because his government was in power from 1975–83, which is to say for the years of the rebuild. It was not possible to speak to Gough Whitlam because of his poor health; many other key political players, such as Jim Cairns, have died. Despite how recent such events seem to me, it is sobering to be reminded that they now sit firmly in the realm of history.

The only other time I'd seen Fraser in the flesh was at protest marches against his government's attempts to cut tertiary education funding in 1981. So I hadn't expected to find his imposing presence so moving. I was struck by how much I liked him and what a sincere honour it felt to meet him. His voice, patrician, deep, controlled, threw me back to those highly charged years, much as Whitlam's speeches, when you listen to them, are now evocative of that time. At eighty-three Fraser still speaks with great clarity. He was highly engaging and our conversation helped give me both a sense of the times and the differences between Canberra's perspective on Tracy, and the perspective of those who'd been through it. The main question I asked of him, indeed the reason I'd wanted to meet him, was to help me understand whether Cyclone Tracy was more than just a destructive storm. Had it acted as a catalyst for political events during the tumultuous mid-seventies? His answer, in short, was that I should resist ascribing too much political power to those massive winds.

Prime Minister Whitlam was in Europe when Cyclone Tracy hit, which was why the task of heading the rescue operation fell to his deputy, Jim Cairns. Dr Rex Patterson, the minister for the Northern Territory, was staying on a cattle station in Queensland over Christmas but did end up arriving in Darwin on the same flight as Stretton. The two men got on well, and in *The Furious Days* Stretton says Patterson gave him much-needed support over the next week or so. Cairns arrived in

Darwin on Boxing Day and was affected by what he saw. As a result he did all he could to smooth the way for a quick and efficient federal response. His wife Gwen, who accompanied him on the trip, was also deeply moved by Darwin's plight and worked on behalf of evacuees once she returned to Melbourne. It was Cairns who took a submission to the cabinet on 28 December, acknowledging that the disaster was unprecedented in Australia, and endorsing the evacuation, as well as providing for the immediate payment of special benefits. Opposition leader Bill Snedden believed, Colonel Thorogood remembers, 'that disaster was above politics, the government and the opposition had agreed to co-operate fully in the relief of Darwin'.

When I spoke to Fraser he returned to this theme several times—that not everything that happened in a country should be politicised and that neither Tracy nor any other disaster should be played for party politics. It's possible of course that a certain bipartisan idealism is easier to maintain when one is no longer an active player; but certainly it's hard to imagine such a coming-together of the parties in today's political climate.

It's been said that the days after the cyclone marked the high point of Cairns' political career. By February 1975 Cairns had declared 'a kind of love' for Junie Morosi and by July 1975 he'd been dismissed from the ministry—unfairly, many felt—for misleading parliament. Tracy improved Cairns' political standing, albeit briefly, but marked a downturn for Whitlam, who returned to Australia on 28 December only to resume his overseas tour three days later. John Menadue, the head of the Prime Minister's Department, tried to persuade Whitlam to stay. But 'he looked me in the eye and said: "Comrade, if I'm going to put up with the f—wits in the Labor Party, I've got to have my trips."'[2] Thus began a series of headlines in newspapers around Australia, riffing on the pun of a ruined Darwin versus the ruins of Crete. On 3 January the *Northern Territory News* quoted the opposition spokesman for foreign affairs, Andrew Peacock, as saying, 'Australians have been given proof that the prime minister, Mr Whitlam, has abandoned credibility in favour of selfish junketing.'

Despite Fraser's suggesting otherwise, Whitlam did, in a sense, attempt to play party politics after Tracy. So it's surprising that he got his PR so wrong, given how right his party got other aspects of the emergency. The Labor government was extraordinarily generous to Darwin's citizens. And of course, like all politicians, Whitlam was aware of the disaster's potential to increase his standing. He was even overheard saying that rebuilding Darwin would 'win them the next election', or so the story goes. Bill Wilson insists: 'That conversation was reported to me later, and I have no reason to disbelieve the person who told me.' Whatever the truth of the matter, Wilson's description of Whitlam's behaviour when he visited Darwin reflects the disconnect between Canberra and the Northern Territory and suggests why criticisms of Whitlam abounded.

> I will never ever forget this—nor forgive... Whitlam arrived in Darwin and came to the police headquarters, and was to visit us in the communications centre. I've already described how that room was very hot, very smelly, I suppose, that we were not still not getting adequate showers, clothing was a bit dirty and so on. Five minutes before Whitlam came in, one of his aides arrived with two cans of fly spray, one in each hand, and promptly proceeded to spray the room—but not only the room, each of us sat at a desk they'd walk up to with this can and spray us to make the place smell nice. That caused a great deal of discontent. Those of us that were humiliated like that never ever, I don't think, forgave Gough Whitlam for the incident. He probably didn't know himself but he copped our blame for it. He walked in, the great man, and shook hands with us all and said:—Oh, great

> job you're doing. Fine, blah blah blah, And walked out in about thirty seconds…

Thorogood also saw the brief tour as problematic.

> Did Mr Whitlam's visit to Darwin, coming from Europe, staying for a day, going back to Europe again—did it achieve the aim? Well, I don't know what his aim was, but I'm not sure that it contributed much at all. I think the government relationship that had worked, and was continuing to work, was this great relationship that had been forged between Stretton and Cairns.

Whitlam was one of many cabinet ministers to visit Darwin between 26 and 28 December. Snedden flew in with Cairns at 2.45 pm on Boxing Day. Five ministers flew in on 27 December and attended a conference, chaired by Lionel Murphy, at which it was decided that the Australian government would pay return fares to Darwin for all evacuees. Air Commodore Hitchins attended that meeting. 'I remember being very impressed with the alacrity with which Justice [sic] Murphy got that act together and declared the government's intention to provide substantial aid to the people of Darwin.'

Despite the positive results, it was a lot of elite personnel to manage for a city under such extreme strain, and Stretton wasn't shy about saying so.

> Politicians and people seemed to think that we were there to act as their secretaries and I, at one stage of the game, had to ask Mr McClelland and a whole lot of them for about the fourth time to please refrain from interfering with what our operations' staff were doing with limited facilities and possibly one telephone that was trying to serve twenty purposes.

At one point Stretton asked Doug McClelland to leave the room so he could take a call and McClelland stormed out, unimpressed.

A series of photos of Stretton and Whitlam in Darwin shows two men in spectacular shirts, engaged in very intense conversation. I like to think that one of these photos captured the moment when Stretton remonstrated with Whitlam about the ministerial visits. Thorogood tells the story this way:

> General Stretton said: 'Prime Minister, is there any way that you could keep these ministers out of my hair.' I'm not sure whether they were the exact words he said, perhaps he said: 'keep them out of Darwin'. But he certainly made the point that the Ministers were really not appreciated and were not contributing to the relief operation very much. Now Whitlam—because he's a big fellow, and General Stretton's a big fellow—so I think Whitlam being slightly bigger looked down, and he said…'I don't know what you're complaining about General, I've got to work with the bastards all the time.'

It's easy to sympathise with Stretton's frustration—can you imagine having to play host to minister after minister in the midst of such ruin and deprivation?—but these visits signalled to the people of Darwin that what had happened to them was being taken very seriously. That yes, the rest of Australia did know what had happened to them, and that they cared.

It has been suggested to me that John Howard was the first Australian prime minister who really understood how to handle a disaster, as his exemplary performances after both the Port Arthur Massacre and the Bali bombings of 2002 testify. Certainly Whitlam did not get it right, and ten months after he was mocked for leaving the ruins of Darwin for those of Crete he was dismissed from office. However

Fraser—while he concedes that Whitlam did not seem to understand how important it was that he stay in Australia rather than returning to Europe—believes Whitlam handled the disaster well enough. He certainly didn't think that Cyclone Tracy contributed significantly to Whitlam's failing popularity. The government was already in trouble, he argued (and the opinion polls suggested) and those 'wounds were caused by recession, inflation and the oil shock'. If Fraser's point is that disaster management was, and was seen as, essentially bipartisan, it is borne out by his own record. The new Fraser government continued with the program that had been put into place for Darwin in the final few months of Whitlam's term.

1975

THE REASONS behind, and details of, Major-General Stretton's abrupt departure from Darwin are fairly murky. There were some concerns in Canberra about his management of the situation—and his grumpiness towards various ministers and senior Canberra folk wasn't helping. He certainly seemed to arouse unusual antagonism and jealousy in public servants in both Canberra and Darwin. The unions, in contrast, were supportive of him. The judgment of the man closest to him, Colonel Frank Thorogood, is that Stretton's authority was accepted. 'Mr McHenry chaired the first meeting, but I think already the force of Alan Stretton's personality was starting to become apparent, and I think he was seen as the natural leader to whom they could turn.'

However it is true that Stretton barely slept for a week after Tracy and by 30 December the strain was starting to show, as he himself acknowledged. 'After making some notes and compiling some draft signals, I got to bed after 3 am, and with the aid of the sleeping pills prescribed by the good doctor, I went off into my first sound sleep for six days.' He was woken at 7.30 am by the secretary of the Department of Defence who wanted to discuss Governor-General Sir John Kerr's visit two days later. The conversation was terse, to say the least.

It's been suggested that Stretton became obsessed with the protocol surrounding Kerr's arrival. While Colonel Thorogood doesn't dispute the timing of the tension he gives the reason as precisely the opposite: he says that it was Canberra's obsession with protocol that drove Stretton to distraction. But whatever the reason, and however unfairly, people were becoming nervous about the man. At eleven in the morning on New Year's Eve Stretton made his charge up the courthouse steps to attack David McCann, an event the media made much of. Some time that afternoon Stretton did something that made him the butt of many a joke: he issued a directive that New Year's Eve be 'cancelled'. Air Commodore Hitchins remembers that Stretton:

> directed that all Service messes were to be closed and that there was to be no frivolity on Service establishments on the ground that he felt this would be unfair to the civil population…Fellows had been working pretty hard and by the time we got to New Year's Eve, a lot of us, rightly or wrongly, had decided that it was time to relax a trifle.

Hitchins says Stretton's message got to him too late for him to act, though you'd be forgiven for thinking he simply ignored it. Ken Frey heard talk of 'banning of New Year's Eve' but decided to throw a party at the sailing club anyway. The party 'actually got a bit hysterical and people went a bit mad'. As *Sydney Morning Herald* reporters wrote of Stretton: 'In trying to stop the celebrations he bore a marked resemblance to King Canute. The tide of liquor was irresistible. The order most commonly heard in Darwin on New Year's Eve was "Roll out the barrel".'[1] Many of the town's citizens saw out the year as they'd seen in the cyclone: pissed.

There was concern expressed when Stretton shed tears during one of his regular radio broadcasts, and then again on television. Stretton, to his credit, argued that it was perfectly reasonable for a man in his position to become emotional given the amount of devastation and trauma he dealt with over those few days. It's hard not to agree with him. However it is indicative of the extremity of what unfolded in Darwin that Stretton, a man who'd played VFL, fought in World War Two and the Korean War and served three tours of Vietnam, found the experience so shattering. Or was it something else? A friend pointed out the obvious—that the devastation of Darwin may have triggered memories of other wars, those he fought in the forties, the fifties, the sixties. And here he was, in another decade, with yet more ruin all around.

Channel 7 news footage aired around this time talks of the 'combat fatigue' that was descending on the population. A program of examining people, military staff and others, was put in place by Canberra to ensure that the right decisions were being made and that people weren't becoming 'too emotionally involved'. Stretton had been one of the first to volunteer for examination and was passed as fit to carry on. This didn't stop a news reporter prompting one interviewee: '[Stretton] crack[ed] up at one stage, didn't he?' The man being interviewed paused. Then he said, 'If you went to Darwin and didn't shed a tear you really needed psychiatric care.'

Colonel Thorogood's account of his and Stretton's six days in Darwin are perceptive and sometimes amusing, but they also give you a real insight into the antagonism that Major-General Stretton and the blow-ins from Canberra managed to generate in such a short period of time.

> Stretton always sat at the head of the table, and it was my wish and his too, that I sat next to him, because I'm the one that had to be able to write down the points of action and interest and whatever. And on a couple of occasions a rather pleasant little chap, a round little man, kept sitting in my chair, and I had to tell him, politely but firmly, to piss off. And he mostly did piss off, but a couple of times I'd come back and found he was there again, and this became a bit of a standing joke. It wasn't until New Year's Eve, when Alan Stretton and I sallied forth to Government House to say we were leaving, and to hand over to his Honour, the Administrator, that I found this gentleman in fact had been his Honour, the Administrator.

The 'little' man Thorogood was referring to was Jock Nelson, a Labor politician who had been in public life since 1949. (The position of administrator—equivalent to the governor of a state—held symbolic power, but in a practical sense there was little he could do in a crisis like this.)

New Year's Eve heralded a symbolic end to the emergency. Hedley Beare remembers 'sitting in our house…when the fleet came up the harbour. It was one of those—almost a transcendental moment. They were just grey silhouettes as they moved up the harbour in the early morning.' This sense that the navy could save Darwin was one that Major-General Stretton cultivated. 'I deliberately overplayed the importance of the arrival of the fleet in Darwin…I presented the arrival of the fleet as coinciding with the end of the emergency and the return to normal.'

The navy's main job was to help with the clean-up. They brought helicopters, which were useful for moving debris, and dozens of strong young men, who were set to work on the thankless task of cleaning rotting food from the fridges. Curly Nixon:

> They all should have got a medal—the whole lot of them should have got mentioned in dispatches if nothing else because the poor bastards were unacclimatised, they were just sent straight out of there into the street and after about three days, the town—you know, the fridges that they were cleaning out and the places they were cleaning up were just putrid. And those kids—they would spew, have a mouthful of beer—because I was carting beer to them—have a mouthful of beer and then did it again 'til they did another bad one. They'd have another spew and another half a stubby of beer and then do it again. But Jesus they worked, them poor bastards, they really worked.

(And when they weren't working, he wondered 'what they expected the navy boys to do—run around and rape the girls that were left or something like that'?)

Tess Lea reminds us that it wasn't just the 'navy boys' who were sickened by this assault on the senses: 'Survivors recall the smell of rotting things, dead flesh rotting in wet ground, food putrefying without electricity, sodden materials rotting, sewer pipes dribbling and everywhere the dank clotting of mildew...'

Richard Creswick chose New Year's Eve to track down his wife. She'd been in Bali on holidays during the cyclone and then been refused entry back into Darwin. She was waiting for him in Perth but it had taken her some time to establish he was still alive. He'd sent her several telegrams saying he was okay but she hadn't received them. Creswick's convoy was one of the last to leave Darwin during the evacuation. 'We decided that we would drive down to Perth in convoy, three of us in three cars...And I loaded up into the ute what I considered salvageable and we left.' They each took one of the cats. He, Eric (the friend he'd sat in the bath and sung 'Waltzing Matilda' to as the cyclone bore down) and another mate had been drinking for much of the afternoon and evening and it was eleven or so at night when they left. At the Thirteen Mile turnoff there is a 'nasty' set of curves. The ute was fully loaded and they had a head-on collision with another car but then 'we sorted out our little drama and we continued on down the track'. By Katherine, tyres had blown and the cats were suffering heat stress. They got some tranquillisers for the cats at Katherine hospital then kept on driving into Western Australia.

Every day was a big news day in Darwin at that time, and New Year's Eve marked the return of the *Northern Territory News*. Some have commented that it was as if Tracy had blown away the (relatively) reasonable version of the paper—as personified by Jim Bowditch who was the editor from 1954–73—and replaced it with a crazier tabloid determined to throw its weight around. This is not to say that Bowditch had been scared of a stoush. Historian David Carment remembers that Bowditch, 'was a great crusading editor. He took up particular causes. He was very interested in, for example, pushing for the Northern Territory to have greater powers of self-government.'[2] He also intervened when three Malay pearl divers faced deportation, to the extent of actually breaking the law and hiding a man from the authorities.

But, despite some form, after Tracy the paper leapt into the task of opposing the various government bodies that were vying for control over the town with more vigour than usual. Ben Eltham and Alex Burns, in their essay on disaster journalism, noted that newspapers tend to get bullish after disasters, glorifying the victims and getting stuck into decision makers. Frank Alcorta, a journalist at the *Northern Territory News* downplayed the extent to which the *News* did this. 'The paper took it as one of its causes to be involved in the rebuilding of Darwin, and in the rebuilding of a new society there as we saw it.'[3]

Suzanne Spunner's riff on *Northern Territory News* headlines from the late eighties rang as true in the mid-seventies as it does today. 'Minister Resigns/Feds Interfere/Croc Attack/Black Land Grab/Boom Around the Corner/ Wild Dog Attack/Travel Claims Rort/Journalist Attacked/Croc Sighted/Miners Clash/Mangrove Protest/Territory Tops/Sex Disease Survey/Railway Link Coming/Croc Caught/Cavalry Coming/Hotel Deals above Board/Feds Intervene/Boom Still Coming/ Sex Not the Issue.' All I'd add to that is: tits. The paper has always had, and always will have, a sense of sheer cheek that can be redeeming.

The *Northern Territory News*'s headline on 1 January was 'Stretton Calls it Quits'. This was a fair summary of the situation. Stretton, who'd been due to leave after Sir John Kerr's arrival on 2 January, left abruptly at 3 pm on New Year's Day. He did so on the grounds that he did not want to make a fuss or risk large crowds and endless farewells at the airport, a concern that Stretton himself later acknowledged was 'vain'. Before he left he made a final warm and jovial radio broadcast—'Thank you all. God bless you all. Good luck to you… When I come back I want to make sure that bloody garbage is cleaned up…otherwise I'll be saying a few words to you people.' Paternalistic, of course, but you can see why the general population warmed to him.

There weren't large crowds but Stretton was met at the airport by a journalist who asked him how it felt to hand back more power than any individual had held in the country since Governor Phillip. Slightly obscurely Stretton replied, 'Son, when you study the Darwin disaster, you will find that you have had just as much power as I have.' Nonetheless his public position remained consistent. He'd left, he wrote, because he had done all that had been required of him and it was time to leave the running of the place to locals.

> The water and power was back on. The streets were clear of debris, traffic was flowing freely, some shops were starting to

> open and the first unit of the first fleet had arrived...Darwin was again functioning as a city. It seemed unbelievable that all this had been achieved within six days and without any further loss of life. I realised that the crisis was over and that my task was complete.

Stretton got to Melbourne around midnight, spent the night at Jim Cairns's home, and returned to Canberra the next day.

On the Queen's Birthday 1975 Stretton would be presented with an Order of Australia for eminent services in duties during the days following Cyclone Tracy, but this is not to suggest that his battles were over. Indeed they escalated in 1976 when his book about the emergency, *The Furious Days*, was published. In that book Stretton was deeply critical both of particular individuals and of Darwin's response to Tracy in general. Stretton accused the army—in contrast to the navy and the airforce—of lack of initiative after the cyclone and said that those at the barracks had looked after themselves rather than supporting the community. At the time, defence minister Jim Killen and prime minister Malcolm Fraser accused Stretton of 'great impropriety' for speaking out. When I spoke to Fraser he said he was sorry he'd chastised Stretton publicly and that he wished he'd taken the time to get to know him better. He no longer stood by his criticisms and believed Stretton had done a difficult job well. While aware of Stretton's ability to rub people up the wrong way, Fraser noted somewhat wryly that these qualities are sometimes to a person's credit.

The Darwin International Women's Year committee reformed as soon as enough women made it back to town to keep the committee going. It became a force throughout 1975. According to Margaret Muirhead, the chairperson of International Women's Year in the NT,

> We said, 'Right now we have all the more reason to do things for women in this year' because of the devastation that they'd suffered and the extraordinary circumstances that they were living under and looked as if they were going to be living under, certainly for the rest of '75.

Margaret Muirhead had needed to be convinced to take on the role. 'I'd never been very interested in women's issues. In spite of being uncertain of my own value as a housewife and mother of four, I still hadn't seen that there were any changes necessary in women's life, or possible.' Her work radicalised her. 'I think a lot of them said, "Ho hum, so what! It will all be over at the end of '75 and we can forget about it all."' Objections men had to IWY included: 'that women were wanting more to take the jobs of men...What would happen to the children?'

At this stage only around 2500 of the ten thousand people left in Darwin were women. Curly Nixon, who in normal times would have been working the wharves and acting in his role as president of both the Waterside Workers' Federation and the Trades and Labor Council, moved into entertainment. This would be, he thought, a corrective for boredom, missing wives, and rape.

> See there was those that wanted their wives back, and those that knew—had enough brains not to want their wives back because the conditions just weren't the place where you took wives. And, of course, I had to shut my mouth because I had mine here, so couldn't really take sides...Anyway I said to Rex: Listen, Patto, what say we set up an entertainment committee? Will you pick up the fare for anyone I can get to come here?

His first choice, Rolf Harris, now seems ironic, given that at the time of writing Harris was being tried on sex abuse charges, but back then he was a major star. He played two concerts on 8 January using cyclone debris for a didgeridoo. That concert and others that followed were hugely successful and a real morale booster. Other entertainers to tour included Johnny O'Keefe and Bert and Patti Newton, but it was Harris who is remembered with greatest affection. 'When he lobbed here,' Nixon remembers, 'he fell into line quite well, actually, old Rolf.' This was code for the fact that Harris took a genuine interest in what had happened up there, and didn't complain about the rough conditions. Other celebrities, I was told more than once, were not so amenable.

Things were slowly starting to improve. Sure, there was no running water but one of the pluses of that—in the retelling anyway—was that as you drove down the Stuart Highway you'd see the flicker of naked people having showers under open fire hydrants. People were being well fed at the high schools and the Greek club was good for a feed, too. By 1 January there were two hundred emergency phone connections up around the city. On 2 January the rush south had declined to a trickle and film of the devastation in Darwin was released to cinemas. The footage was first screened in Darwin itself at a charity performance of Barry Humphries' *Bazza Holds His Own*. Most postal services were restored. On 4 January the weather bureau was up and running which, given people's anxieties about cyclones returning, was a good thing. By 6 January there were four hundred phones and beer was back on sale (though restricted to six cans at forty cents each, which could only be purchased between noon and 2 pm, or 5 and 8 pm). Road blocks moved further south and people had greater freedom of movement. Buses began to run. On 7 January Woolworths reopened, as did the Karen Lee Hair Salon. By 8 January there was free repair of television sets and fresh bread was available to people 'with authority'. From 9 January you could head to the Nightcliff or Parap pool for a swim. Electricity slowly came on over several days. Cedric Patterson recalls that at first the streets around him were 'pitch black' then, 'all of a sudden this pinpoint of light appeared and then a little while later another one appeared and then a small string of lights'.

On 10 January Ray McHenry was, to quote the *Northern Territory News*, appointed 'Supremo at Last'. This gave 'unprecedented peace-time powers to the director of emergency services. A 41-year-old career public servant is now the virtual dictator of Darwin.' McHenry has said, 'The legislation which purported to give almost "dictatorial-type" powers did not follow until some weeks later. The powers were necessarily wide to enable the validation of the many acts which had been taken pursuant to the post-disaster effort.' He also said, more pointedly, 'I couldn't understand what the hoo-ha was all about...I don't know what in the hell they felt I was.'[4]

Harry Giese did understand what the hoo-ha was about.

> There was a great deal to be learned from the Darwin disaster about the way in which the government should impose itself upon the community. That you could have [the] El Supremo sort of thing, that one man could determine whether you had the right to take your family down south, or whether you had the right to do this or that, or where you should look after yourself, how you should look after yourself: there was the feeling that government was intruding too much into the affairs of the community, and into the affairs of individuals in the community.

Other leaders had also emerged, though: men such as Police Commissioner McLaren, Charles Gurd, George Redmond from the Department of Works. But McHenry was the most rewarded of these and federal cabinet confirmed his role as director of emergency services and co-ordinator on 29 January. McHenry remembers many positive things the close relationship with the federal government enabled, such as social security payments, free phone calls, free transport of pets, free food and the non-payment of rent. All these things, he believed, helped with the recovery process. And perhaps one of the reasons the federal government worked well with him was because McHenry was from Canberra—certainly he wasn't always on the side of *local* government. Mayor Tiger Brennan remembers that McHenry wouldn't let the aldermen of the city council return, which meant they didn't have the quorum to hold a meeting. Brennan found it counterproductive to keep city leaders out of their home town, when they were most needed.

Instead of the council there were committees. McHenry's disaster plan had originally called for seven of them, but they ended up with twenty-four. These included Aboriginal support, communications, clean-up, animal welfare, food, health and women's activities. Brennan described this turn of events as 'the blinking communist way'. These committees were slowly phased out as the emergency abated—but not before Brennan declared them the end of him. And so it was that 1975 was the year that Darwin's mayor, the hippy-loathing, pith-helmet-wearing Tiger Brennan, threw in the towel after three years in the job. With his leaving, a little piece of old Darwin died. Brennan was explicit about the fact that Cyclone Tracy had ended his career and that he'd been driven to exhaustion by the bureaucracy and committees that had followed swift on the cyclone's heels. 'Another six months and I would have been in the rat house.' His departure heralded a Darwin in which women had more of a say. Brennan, the man who'd been heard to complain about the 'women's lib crowd', only resigned in May once he established that Ella Stack was able to take on the mantle of mayor. Increasingly, more women took public office and from 1977 to 1983 a fifth of the Northern Territory's parliament was female, the highest representation of women of any parliament in

Australia. It was in those years, too, that Dawn Lawrie became the Commissioner for Equal Opportunity.

Press releases went out saying that things in Darwin were 'beginning to return to normal' but in truth things did not return to normal for a very long time. Maria Donatelli's restaurant, the Capri, was the first to reopen after the cyclone and the night that it did people lined up down the street. She describes the weeks that followed as the 'busiest time of my life. I kept praying somebody else would open.' Donatelli remembers that the community spirit of Darwin was strong after the cyclone, and that that strength of spirit lasted about four months. After that, things started to go wrong.

Richard Creswick reunited with his wife in Perth and after a few weeks the two returned to Darwin, living under a tarp at their house in Jingili then squatting at some ABC flats in Stuart Park. They ate at the high schools. He, like Donatelli, remembers some real positives from that early time. 'Life went back to basics. If you didn't have a television then you didn't watch it, you sat outside and you yarned with your friends and there was for that brief period a terrific feeling of community.'

Neroli Withnall conveyed similar sentiments to the *7.30 Report*:

> We waited about six weeks and then we went back. It was lovely...That was probably one of the best years of my life. We lived under the house with a tarpaulin over the floorboards for most of it. One of the things I suppose I learnt most clearly was how very little you need to get by and have a good time.

Her husband John remembered it somewhat differently. 'My memory is it was definitely a hard slog. She didn't seem to enjoy it at the time, I might add. There's not much to be said for lying awake at night in the wet season and having the water dripping through the floor of the lounge room above…' They agreed on one thing though. Neroli: 'It was such a cataclysmic event that everything was dated according to whether it was "before" or "after". It was like BC and AD.' John:

> My own feeling is it's as if a line was drawn across our previous life…When that sort of thing happens, it's an obvious opportunity to start afresh for lots of people in lots of ways. We were divorced in 1978—I don't think it had much to do with the cyclone, but you never know, you never know.

Eight months after the cyclone *Women's Weekly* ran a report on the state of Darwin post-Tracy.[5] Photographer Keith Barlow, who had been there in the days after the cyclone, then returned, was horrified. 'What the hell have they been doing?' Part of the reason was the population was back up to thirty thousand for the dry season. 'We now have the problem of trying to rebuild the city over the heads of the people.' But of course many of these thirty thousand were temporary workers rather than returned evacuees.

Ray McHenry considered this chaos a vindication of his position that the numbers of people in Darwin had to be kept low and the number of people evacuated high. But by June 1975 McHenry had moved back to Canberra. From the outside it appears that he, like Stretton, had been driven out of Darwin by pressures that included the ongoing campaign run against him by the *Northern Territory News*, but it's less clear from this distance whether the real pressure was political or personal. Certainly his public position was—ironically, given his role in separating families during the evacuation—that he didn't want to be apart from his family any longer. By the time he returned to Darwin for a visit, in early 1976, 'the depression in the place was absolutely unreal' he said, arguing that if the entire population of

Darwin had been put back as early as February 1975, 'that depression would have started earlier'.

Things were getting crazy. 'There were squabbles, and punch-ups, between "old" Territorians and "those blow-ins from down south".' There were strikes, which the *Women's Weekly* claimed were workers' responses to the extra bonuses being given to the public servants—usually southerners—who had stayed on or recently arrived in Darwin. These kinds of reports need to be balanced against the knowledge that members of the federal building unions from around Australia gave up their annual leave to act as volunteers. But Air Commodore Hitchins concurs that 'too much money was splashed around' and says that public servants were flying off to Brisbane every weekend and demanding flashy accommodation. While this may be an exaggeration, there is no doubt it was hard to get people to work in Darwin over these months, or to encourage them to stay.

According to the chairman of the Reconstruction Commission, Anthony Powell, 'There was a lot of tension in the community, and people weren't "normal". They're anxious and deprived, and it's hard to achieve consensus. We can't get skilled staff. They won't come up here without their families, and we'd have to house their families and so it goes on.' Jim Bowditch believes people weren't facing the fact that the old town was over. 'It was always a bull dust town. We aren't pioneers and we never were. We're a spoiled community, a city community.' People became passive, or perhaps overwhelmed, in the face of what was happening to them.

'Tracy Village' was set up for construction workers and another 1700 demountable dwellings and caravans were brought to Darwin and located on house sites. The hotels and hostels were full and some people just slept under bits of canvas strung up over the ruin of their homes. Out on Darwin Harbour, the *Patris* was costing the government fifteen thousand dollars a day to house about nine hundred people at any one time. About 5500 people lived there in the few months it was moored. The *Northern Territory News* described it, with typical insouciance, as a 'luxury' liner but the living circumstances were, as Richard Creswick and others have commented, pretty grim. It's hard to imagine for whom the *Patris* 'was the best time I ever had'—as one mother was quoted as saying as she stood on Fort Wharf watching the ship leave that November. One of the people who moved to the *Patris* was Peter Dermoudy.

> A lot of relationships that were shaky broke up and things like that. It was a time for people to reassess everything. I sort of had a change of life, too, I suppose. I had a change of female companions. The companion I was with went off with a 21-year-old gambler, funny things like that, you know. It wasn't quite so funny at the time, but it's quite humorous now.[6]

Here's a waltz through police log books[7] at the time which give you a bit of an idea of what life on the *Patris* was like: a person 'discharged' a firearm on 28 February causing Constable Snoad to fire a shot. Snoad 'was relieved from duties' and a man was arrested for disorderly behaviour. On Saturday 1 March police had to contact a Bob Gillings to let him know his wife was dangerously ill in Brisbane. Later that day Gillings was reported as drunk and disorderly in the public lounge of the *Patris* and police had to escort him to his cabin. On 3 March they tried to locate a man (in fact a headmaster) who was living on the ship regarding a five-year-old missing child who was believed to be camped in his car. On 5 March police boarded to look for a missing girl, Elly Jones, who was fifteen and was believed to be with her friend Maria in room 623. 'Negative result.' On 8 March a message had to be given to Mr R. G. Pollen regarding the death of his daughter-in-law. He couldn't be found. That same day a person was asked to

The PM and the major-general:
Whitlam and Stretton in conversation

JOHN HART / FAIRFAX

Prime Minister Gough Whitlam is
taken on a tour of the wreckage
NEWS LTD / NEWSPIX

Police, armed against stray dogs, check houses in the Casuarina area

RICK STEVENS / FAIRFAX

Dead horse in a trailer being taken out of town along McMillans Road

NORTHERN TERRITORY ARCHIVES SERVICE, BARBARA JAMES, NTRS 1683

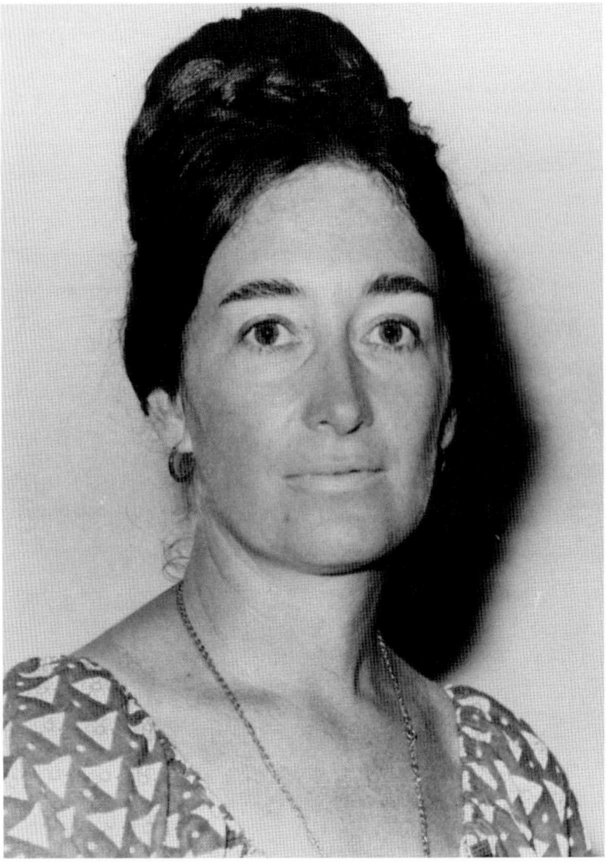

N. GLEESON COLLECTION

TSCHIRNER COLLECTION

ABC-TV COLLECTION

NORTHERN TERRITORY GOVERNMENT PHOTOGRAPHER COLLECTION

Clockwise from top left: Dawn Lawrie, 1977;
Hedley Beare (date unknown); Ray McHenry (date unknown);
Tiger Brennan shares the mayoral regalia with Ella Stack, 1975

ALL PHOTOS THIS PAGE FROM THE NORTHERN TERRITORY LIBRARY

remove their motorcycle from a restricted area but they refused. On 9 March an anonymous tip-off told police there was a game of two-up on 'Mediterranean' deck. 'It appears very likely that a game had been in progress but no evidence of same on arrival of police.' That same day there was also an incident in which two police were assaulted, 'outnumbered and withdrew'. They returned with more police and arrested two of the offenders. Complaints about noise in the lounge were made later that night. On Saturday 15 March two drunken men accused each other of assault and someone claimed that the *Patris* staff insulted them. On Sunday 16 March, several card games were reported. On 19 March an ambulance was called because a woman was ill. On Sunday 23 March police:

> received a complaint from a Mr Daltry of cabin no. 335 and a Mr Burns of cabin no. 298. Both men state they are disgusted with the behaviour in general on board the ship. They said they had their wives and children on board and that they could not use the lounge areas because of language, drinking and fighting. They further stated they were going to see their Member of Parliament.

An arrest was made at 9.20 pm that night. The captain, Kandinis, reported trouble on the gangway. Two men were ordered to be off the ship by noon the next day. On 24 March jewellery was nicked. On 27 March police had to look for the mother of a baby that was in hospital. She wasn't found. The search for Elly Jones continued and police were told that she might be found at the house of a man called Ralph. She was later located at a shopping centre and returned to her mother. That day a 'death message' also had to be delivered, in which a man was told his father had died. On 29 March there were reports of indecent assault. Police attended and spoke to a woman 'Who stated unknown person…caught hold of the lower half of her two-piece swimmers and pulled them down over her bottom, she stopped the person and left to seek help.' The man was later located and 'claimed he had had a few beers and it was only done as a joke.' The woman accepted the apology and didn't press charges then changed her mind soon after saying 'she had been made a laughing stock of the ship'. On the same night another man reported that two men had attempted to enter his daughter's cabin and wouldn't leave. The girl's mother tried to get them to leave and they still wouldn't go and only left once the father arrived. 'Persons believed to be members of visiting football teams. Unable to locate.' On 9 April a man became upset about the noise outside his cabin and confronted three Greek teenage girls. He 'obtained no satisfaction'. The brother of one of the girls approached the man, who punched him in the jaw. No charges were laid. In what is, perhaps, my favourite entry, a complaint was received on 16 April 'from a hippy type "gentleman" that Greeks fishing off wharf had their radio cassette up too loud…advised him that it would be better to retire to his cabin where he wouldn't be able to hear the noise'.

At this point the suicide attempts began. On 15 April a man took an overdose of tablets—Thiorodazine—and an ambulance had to be called. His girlfriend confirmed that he was depressed 'and they had been having domestic problems'. On 24 April there were reports that a woman had overdosed or was about to. Her main complaint was that her children couldn't sleep at night because of the noise aboard the ship. She was threatening to kill herself with a mixture of Valium, sleeping pills and Diagesics. When her husband was contacted he told them she'd had a breakdown. On 29 April another possible overdose was reported—this time it was a young woman.

On 26 April a woman who was four months pregnant collapsed on the dance floor. On 27 April a statement was given regarding a man who was drunk and disorderly, describing the man as 'pissed… Abusive and aggressive…He hates coppers. I don't blame the police for locking him up. He was in the wrong.' On 8 May a woman reported a man in her cabin 'who has her key'. On 9 June a man was spoken to about 'hitting and intimidating' an eight-year-old boy who was not his son. On Monday 9 June there was a disturbance when a man who was estranged from his wife became jealous of her alleged boyfriend. He also thought his daughter was having a sexual relationship with a crew member.

And on it goes, relentlessly, until the *Patris* left Darwin Harbour on 14 November 1975.

Thirteen of those on the *Patris* were refugees from East Timor, which was in the throes of the civil war that preceded the Indonesian invasion. Eric Rolls has described the following scene. After the invasion itself, in early December 1975:

> hundreds of frightened women and children got to Darwin in the clothes they stood up in, by whatever ships they could catch... The women, carrying babies and paper bags, came ashore to the shouts of wharfies telling them to go home. The atmosphere in Darwin was harsh; it was rebuilding...[8]

This contradicts many people's view that Darwin was, and continues to be, very passionate about the East Timorese cause and that many Darwinites were extremely welcoming. Either way, the Timorese had left a nation in ruins, to find a town not doing much better.

Recovery is a complex process and it takes a long time. The nature of the disaster will change communities forever: members are lost, services are disrupted, landscapes are changed, people's sense of safety is compromised. Even resilient communities can falter if the recovery period takes years. What happens to people is something akin to war weariness, a condition people in other circumstances have nicknamed 'bushfire brain'. Chemically speaking it's been described as the moment when people run 'out of adrenaline' and move 'into cortisole'.[9] This is one of the reasons it's said that the third year after a disaster is often the hardest. This is the case whether you've stayed in the place where disaster struck or whether you've attempted to get on with your life elsewhere.

But three years? Even getting that far looked like a long haul at the end of 1975.

I WASN'T WORRYING ABOUT BLOODY HISTORY. I WAS WORRYING ABOUT THE DAY

MONEY, AFTER those cashless days and weeks following Tracy, was beginning to dominate people's lives again: who got it, who deserved it, how it was spent.

In an address to the Melbourne Press Club on 9 November 1976, Major-General Stretton waxed sentimental for a moment: 'For a few glorious days the nation came together. We became one country with one purpose. If only we could recapture that unity, keep that spirit of Darwin going at all times.' Then he went on to express his concern about the ways in which millions of dollars in relief funds were being spent and call for a Royal Commission into the Cyclone Tracy Relief Trust Fund. 'I do not question the honesty of the trustees. However I do question the priorities.' Stretton felt that money should be spent on people, not on rebuilding churches, schools, cultural centres and the like. His point was that almost half of those evacuated never returned,

'So the cultural centre is not going to do them much good, is it?'

These days rebuilding such infrastructure would be seen as unequivocally essential to rebuilding a community after a disaster. But Stretton was not alone in his view and Ray McHenry expressed similar concerns about the uses the funds were put to. It's no surprise. These questions arise again and again after all disasters: the misallocation of funding, changes in land use that favour the rich, and the politics of exclusion of the poor and ordinary people from policy-making and decision-making.

The Cyclone Tracy Relief Trust Fund had been established at the beginning of 1975, when the federal cabinet decided that donations and offers of overseas assistance from the South Pacific, Europe and Africa needed to be formalised. As well, there were nationwide appeals encouraging Australians to donate money and goods. Minister Rex Patterson was the chairman of the fund, and its members included Jock Nelson, Mayor Tiger Brennan, Paul Everingham, Ella Stack and Alec Fong Lim. They received and distributed more than eight million dollars before being formally wound up in October 1976. As well as paying for various aspects of the rebuild, the fund gave out benefits that were allotted with blunt directness: women who had lost their husbands got a payout of ten thousand dollars, whereas a lost wife was only worth five thousand.

Regardless of the crassness of this kind of assessment, money was obviously extremely important at this time. While Les Garton remembers that some people tried to rip off the insurance companies after Tracy, in the great scheme of things this was not nearly as big a problem for the community as the opposite situation: people being woefully underinsured or not insured at all. In early 1975 the Department of Repatriation and Compensation surveyed 10,419 persons and 1830 businesses to try to assess damage. It was estimated that losses amounted to 187 million dollars, and of this amount 89 million was uninsured. Julia Church remembers that her parents weren't insured and the ramifications of that were enormous for them—as they were for many older people. Jim Bowditch, who was in his fifties, lost everything. Ken Frey, who had been about to retire, is just one of thousands who acknowledges 'financially of course, it was a bit of a disaster'. He, like many others who'd survived the cyclone, would struggle to get another mortgage. Certainly the cost—financial, emotional and physical—was simply too much for some people.

The reasons people weren't properly insured were various: lack of money, lack of care, lack of organisation, and a general reluctance to accept that a disaster might affect them directly. Not much has changed on that front. After Black Saturday insurance claims totalled more than a billion dollars but it was estimated that as many as thirteen per cent of the residential properties destroyed were not insured at all. And of course, as insurance premiums go up in response to the increasing number of disasters, it's likely that the percentage of people that remain uninsured will increase. Certainly the magnitude of claims that arose from the Brisbane floods in early '74 followed by Tracy at the end of that year led some insurance companies to 'withdraw from high-risk areas'. The insurance payout for Tracy was, at the time, the largest in Australian history at 200 million AUD (equivalent to 1.25 billion dollars today). Following Cyclone Tracy, the Insurance Council of Australia established the Insurance Emergency Service which developed into today's Insurance Disaster Response Organisation. More than fifty per cent of weather-related insurance payments in the last thirty years have been for tropical cyclone damage.[1]

On 31 May the federal government passed the *Darwin Cyclone Damage Compensation Act 1975* which was designed to compensate people for loss and damage on property up to fifty per cent of its value at the time of the cyclone, with an upper limit of twenty-five thousand dollars for houses and business premises and five thousand for personal belongings. Claims had to be lodged by 30 September 1975. More than twelve thousand household claims and almost six hundred business claims were processed. Just under twenty-six million dollars was paid in compensation and most claims were settled by June 1976.

The length of time it takes insurers to settle, or for compensation to come through, is always contentious. Two years after the series of earthquakes in Christchurch, most notably the big one of 22 February 2011, commentators were describing the insurance problems people were facing as 'a second earthquake'. Ninety per cent of people affected by the earthquake had made claims but two years later a massive sixty-nine per cent of them were waiting for a resolution. Some simply gave up and moved on, with no idea of whether they would ever receive any compensation.

On 31 December 1974 the federal government set up an interim Darwin Reconstruction Commission (DRC). According to the *NT News*, 'The commission will be asked to decide on the best use of Darwin's lands and remaining buildings. It will also be called on to make recommendations about the type of building that should go up in place of those torn down by Cyclone Tracy.' People assumed the worst when they read this, and by 3 January there were rumours that the Northern Territory's administrative capital was to be moved to Alice Springs. Such paranoia wasn't totally unreasonable—there *were* conversations taking place questioning whether Darwin should be rebuilt at all. Similar debate flares up after many a natural disaster. But as Dr Greg Holland, a meteorologist, a survivor of Cyclone Tracy and now an atmospheric scientist in the US, said on *Lateline* soon after the Black Saturday bushfires: 'Let's be honest: it's very hard to build in any area that's not dangerous to some extent.'[2] It is certainly unrealistic to expect that we won't build in areas where extreme weather occurs, in part because the population is growing exponentially, and in part because there is more extreme weather occurring all over the planet. More people live on flood plains and in surge zones, more people live in caravan parks in Tornado Alley, more people live in semi-rural areas bound to be affected by bushfire.

The DRC proper got going on 28 February 1975 when the *Darwin Reconstruction Act* was passed. It comprised eight members: Anthony Powell (chairman), Alan O'Brien (deputy chairman), Goff Letts, Ella Stack, Carl Allridge, Alan Reiher, P. L. Till and Martyn Finge. Their brief was to plan, coordinate and undertake the rebuild, with the CSIRO being called upon to advise new standards. Between 1975 and 1978 the DRC coordinated many construction projects including the building or repair of more than 2500 homes.

First up, though, they worked with the Cities Commission, a small Commonwealth agency established in 1973, to produce a town plan. There were many who felt, like Harry Giese, that the Cities Commission had made a mess of Canberra and now they planned to make a mess of Darwin. And it's true that when the DRC was established Darwin was compared to 'Canberra, Albury/Wodonga and other areas selected by the Whitlam government for "regional growth".'[3] Ten years later Suzanne Spunner would write that she 'was not prepared for the northern suburbs, flattened by the cyclone and rebuilt with miles and miles of kerbing, landscaped in wider and wider circles, courts, crescents and cul-de-sacs. Canberra with palms.' There was a strong feeling that people couldn't just come in from the outside, without understanding the psyche of Darwin, and tell them how to live. And there are clear echoes between Darwin residents' objections to having their land and autonomy taken from them, and the objections made by the area's original inhabitants, the Larrakia, to the same process.

Not long after the cyclone Jack Meaney was on his way to the council offices to see what needed doing (he ended up working as a cook at an evacuation centre), when he bumped into Bishop O'Loughlin. At the time Meaney was bemused by O'Loughlin's distress about Christ Church, which had been destroyed within an hour of midnight mass. The church had been built in 1917 and, 'He was really concerned about that old building, being a part of the history I suppose. I wasn't worrying about bloody history. I was worrying about the day.'

This fairly succinctly sums up the tensions in Darwin during the months and years of the rebuild. The cyclone made some residents more mindful of the importance of the city's heritage, while others just wanted to get their lives back on track as quickly as possible. So which side were those responsible for the rebuild on? Moving forward as quickly as possible, or hanging on to the bits of Darwin's history that could be salvaged from the wreckage? More contentiously still, should the rebuild take into account the possibility of future environmental traumas: more cyclones, higher storm surges?

Neville Barwick, who led the Darwin Reconstruction Study Group, arrived in town a few days after the cyclone and, among other work, began his survey of historical ruins with a view to assessing whether they could be saved. This was important work. But Meaney was right that in the immediate aftermath of Tracy, just surviving was as much as most people were up for.

At this time, when Darwin was often described as a giant rubbish tip, the fact there was no recycling of building materials became a cause of contention. Ken Frey remembers that so much timber was going to the tip he was worried there would be a termite problem, but he also believed it wasn't realistic to reuse the material under those conditions—it was too hard for the front-end loaders to clear the wreckage if you were also trying to sort as you went. Government architect Cedric Patterson concurs. 'There was a lot of good materials dumped but where do you stop?' The desire to do things quickly became, as so often before, the decisive factor. The Indigenous publication *Bunji* stated: 'The settlers are rushing about like ants, rebuilding. They are filling our land with their rotting garbage.'

Hip Strider's heart was broken by the authorities' refusal to recycle debris as building material. All these 'you-beaut building materials that would have been perfectly satisfactory to house the population were taken down to the dump'.[4] Bernard Briec and his family, who had planned to stay in Adelaide after their evacuation, missed Darwin so much they were back there by April. He remembers hanging out at Lee Point dump, which became a favourite scavenging spot—so at least the old building materials got to be reused by some.

The day Ella Stack was elected, the *Sydney Morning Herald* ran the story under the headline: 'After Tracy—Ella gets a louder voice'. Her first task after her election, she told the paper, 'would be to read up on the thousands of words that had been handled by the Darwin Reconstruction Commission'.[5] She was referring to the DRC's first report, which was delivered mid-year. That report recommended a balance between those who wanted the town rebuilt exactly as it had been, and those who wanted a thorough redesign. Some of the recommendations made real sense—anyone who has spent time in Darwin and experienced the way the airport carves the town in half would understand suggestions to resituate it. The airport was just one matter on which the city was recalcitrant.

Overall, the response to the report was extremely negative. It was felt that planners overlooked people's emotional investment in their own blocks of land.[6] For example, the entire suburb of Coconut Grove and some of Fannie Bay were to become parklands. That was obviously difficult for residents of those suburbs to take. Some 1200 objections were made to this first plan.

Discussions about whether rebuilding could take place within surge zones—and how those zones should be designated—became particularly fraught. Storm surges move from two to five metres above a normal tide and are often what kill people after a cyclone. It was the surge after Hurricane Katrina that caused such catastrophic damage, and that killed most of the eight thousand who died in Galveston in 1900.

The DRC wanted to play it safe and plan for a worst-case scenario but there wasn't much patience for long-term planning, particularly since the surge hadn't been a real problem after Tracy. Cedric Patterson, always the pragmatist, pointed out that if you took surge zones seriously 'it practically wipes out about a quarter of Darwin'. And, as is often the case, the surge zone included some of Darwin's finest real estate—including Mayor Ella Stack's house. Stack spoke for many Darwinites when she argued the surge line had not been high for some hundred years. Brave planners argued that there was no way of knowing what was to come. But when they eventually backed off it infuriated people even more. Spike Jones, a technician with the PMG who'd lived in Darwin for some twenty-four years, complained, 'All that stuff about buffer zones and green belts and the surge line, then they back off anyway. What a waste of time!'[7]

Ray McHenry felt strongly that the DRC should have stood its ground on this. 'It's only a matter of time—whether it's five, fifty or a hundred years, there will be a cyclone in Darwin, which will wipe out the people in that surge area; it's as plain as the nose on your face...' He's right. Global sea levels rose by about seventeen centimetres during the twentieth century, which certainly makes storm surges increasingly likely. But while McHenry agreed that issues like the surge zone and cyclone safety standards were relevant, he concurred with critics who believed the planning process was poorly handled and that 'delayed decisions about rebuilding basic accommodation were a worry to us all'. These delays had obvious consequences: people simply gave up waiting for formal permission and those who could afford it started to build houses on their blocks that did not adhere to any particular standard.

These days there are surge zones in place in Darwin and Lord Mayor Katrina Fong Lim insists that primary surge zones continue to be taken very seriously. Fong Lim has other concerns, though. She is worried that people still don't understand what it takes to prepare themselves for a disaster, or realise that if the worst happens they will need to be able to look after themselves for at least three days. The sturdy apartments they now live in pose another risk—that people become complacent. Survival isn't just about strong walls.

However in the early days of 1975 strong walls seemed to be the most important thing of all. Kay Brown, whose daughter Geraldine died in the cyclone, remembers being 'terrified about living in an elevated house again'. Her next house 'was besser block and filled with concrete'. She wasn't alone. After Tracy Darwin became a more boring-looking town, full of concrete bunkers that some called 'Tracy trauma houses'. Peter Dermoudy ended up abandoning his architecture practice in frustration at the trend towards housing like this. Architect and academic David Bridgman has pointed out that, while Tracy caused a radical rethink of building codes, the resulting houses:

> were predominantly of masonry or precast concrete construction, with small cellular spaces and small windows...these buildings were much stronger and more able to resist cyclonic winds, however, the small, poorly ventilated, interiors were often uncomfortable in the tropical climate and air conditioning became a necessity for comfort.[8]

Historian David Carment has said it took many Darwin residents less than a decade to realise that, while these houses might withstand a cyclone, they made life between cyclones 'feel like hell'.[9]

The extraordinary architecture firm Troppo responded to the prevalence of these bunkers by designing houses that were elevated, audacious, tropical—and safe. Their first houses were built in the early 1980s and you can see the influence of Burnett in their work. They have gone on to make a mark on both residential housing and public buildings in the decades since. If you wander through the back streets of Coconut Grove you can see them for yourself. They have an audacious quality—modern, on stilts, lots of louvres—that makes them stand out (if you can spy them behind their wild gardens, that is). Tragically two members of the Troppo practice, Greg McNamara and his wife Lena Yali, died in a car accident, alongside friend and landscape architect Kevin Taylor, while this book was being written. Shortly after their death Phil Harris wrote of the loss in the *Australian* as a blow for a form that was only beginning to express its 'Australian-ness'.

> Big Bill Neidjie ('Kakadu Man') would say we are yet to hold a real 'feeling' for country, one that reverberates with a sense of ecological connection between all creatures, the earth and landscape, and the seasons that check our progress through life.

The McNamaras were champions of such a connection.[10]

It's a connection that has been resisted by settlers since Darwin's earliest days. Captain Bloomfield Douglas was sent as government resident to the place then called Palmerston shortly after South Australian surveyor George Goyder had finished his work. Ianto Ware has vividly described what followed next: 'Douglas went up there, started building and then had a sort of Heart of Darkness experience; staff eaten by crocodiles, termites and ants ate everything, and when the dry season kicked in the heat drove everyone, particularly the resident, mad.' The land selection process was corrupted and one man,

William Henry Gray, snapped up most of the good land. He and his descendants refused to sell it, creating a lag in development that lasted right up until 1960. What sets Darwin apart is that while there is 'the usual disparity between the environment and land' the systems used to govern it are still 'overtly disconnected'. He also comments that 'looking through the laws it's not surprising the place didn't withstand a cyclone; it has a long history of having a legal system that doesn't adequately ensure the people living there can withstand the environmental extremes they're likely to be exposed to.'

Dr Slim Bauer was the first director of the ANU's North Australia Research Unit, which had been set up by Nugget Coombs to look into the problems of developing in the north. Keith Cole recalls sharing a meal with him not so long after Tracy, during which Bauer made a comment that resonates still. 'The white man in Darwin has not come to grips with life in the tropics and the environment,' he said. 'The disaster of Tracy will, sometime in the future, be overtaken by further disaster.'

Eighteen months after Cyclone Tracy there were forty-four thousand people in the city. This meant the numbers—if not the individuals themselves—were almost back to where they'd been before. Houses were being rebuilt according to new cyclone codes. In this way at least, Mayor Fong Lim can see the ways in which Tracy improved Darwin. 'It's a truly modern city.' Vicki Harris, who left after the cyclone then returned to live in 1980, concurs.

> There was a lot more civic pride than what there had ever been. Darwin had always been a frontier town and it was like a forgotten backwater, really, back in the early seventies. But in 1980 it was almost as if the cyclone had done it a favour by blowing it off the map, and they had to get

themselves reorganised and rebuild, and it had really blown out the cobwebs out of the place. And it had shaken the place out of its doldrums, too, I think. I mean, apart from the tragedy of human lives being lost, the fact was that Tracy really did this place a favour.

I MAKE THIS PLACE AS I GO

WHEN I began my research I was taken aback to find that one of the most striking images of the cyclone was not a photo but a painting, and that it had been painted not in Darwin, but a thousand kilometres southwest in the remote Kimberley community of Warmun.

It was 1991 when Rover Thomas painted the iconic *Cyclone Tracy*, in which a black gulf sweeps across the canvas eradicating everything in its path. The effect is not unlike one of NASA's images of a black hole collapsing in on itself, eating time and space and light.

But Thomas had been painting the cyclone for almost twenty years by then. He was still a stockman when, in early 1975, he received a visitation from a Gija woman he called auntie. She'd died as a result of injuries sustained when her car crashed on a flooded Kimberley road in the rains that followed Tracy. She was alive when she was picked up by a medical plane but died in the air above Broome. In Thomas's vision, the woman's spirit travelled with him across the Kimberley and across five different language groups. Finally, she showed him the Rainbow Serpent destroying Darwin. Thomas was known for his extraordinary visions but, to quote Wally Caruana, the former curator of Indigenous art at the National Gallery of Australia, it was the number of language groups this dreaming encountered, the breadth of the country it 'sang', that 'really knocked people out'.

The auntie's spirit showed Thomas aspects of country and taught him the Gija names for things. She taught him a song and a dance for this journey and showed him designs to paint on boards to be carried on the shoulders of men as they performed. This vision became the basis for the Gurirr Gurirr ceremony, described as 'synonymous with Rover Thomas and Cyclone Tracy',[1] which is still performed today. The Gurirr Gurirr, according to author Alexis Wright:

> demonstrates the continuing way Indigenous people have retained knowledge through a cultural sense of what the great ancestors in the environment are telling us. This is how the stories tie us to the land as guardians and caretakers, and the land to us as the most powerful source of law.[2]

The first Gurirr Gurirr storyboards were painted by Paddy Jaminji, a senior artist related to the woman whose spirit had visited Thomas. Thomas needed Jaminji's skills, as well as his relationship to the woman and her country, to provide the appropriate knowledge to create the song cycle. Thomas was born on the other side of the Great Sandy Desert at Yalda Soak, almost a thousand kilometres away. While Warmun was not his place of birth, it was his chosen home, and he was painting and singing his way into relationship. All Thomas's work, including the Gurirr Gurirr paintings, are an expression of the social and cultural dislocation that defined Indigenous experience last century and this. We hear this in auntie's voice as she passes over Mount Cockburn. That is when she cries out—according to the words of the song that accompanies the painting—'I'm leaving my country.' Further along in the cycle, she reaches Tablelands (represented by the distinctive silhouette of boab trees). There she says, 'This is my country now.'

To understand more about these paintings and the song cycle that they are a part of, I visited Kevin Kelly, who is both the curator of the Red Rock Art Gallery in Kununurra and the manager of Rover Thomas's estate. The Gurirr Gurirr storyboards he showed me had been painted by Tiger Moore, who briefly inherited the Gurirr Gurirr cycle during the nineties. The board representing Cyclone Tracy depicted the Rainbow Serpent for the Kimberley area, Wungul (also spelt Wungurr). In Moore's words: 'This is the same snake that killed mother [auntie] and caused Tracy. That's the song of that snake there now.' Wungul is also the name of the cyclone. A series of boards followed, including one of a truck that the snake grabs and pulls down the embankment—the accident that caused auntie's death.

I also travelled to Canberra to see the original storyboards, those used in the mid-eighties. These had been painted, by Paddy Jaminji and Rover Thomas, on masonite. That way dancers could create a wobble-board effect when they held them aloft. The images were slightly sketchy, having been produced in the knowledge that they were not standalone works but would be supplemented by the performance of the ceremony. They were scuffed with use and wear. As with all the Gurirr Gurirr images, animals were also places, weather and events. A serpent was a cyclone. A crocodile was a mountain. A person was a kangaroo. Time operated differently.

Thomas believed it was important the Gurirr Gurirr ceremony be performed for Europeans, and so it has been. His chronicling of contemporary events for both a black and a white audience continued after the Gurirr Gurirr series and included works on the Ruby Plains and Texas Downs massacres, as well as depictions of the impact on the landscape that occurred after the damming of the Ord River. No other artists have painted the recent history of northern Australia in such an ambitious fashion.

After the Warmun floods and evacuation of 2011, the source of the water that devastated the community was the subject of much discussion. The insurance company initially attributed the damage to the rise of Turkey Creek, which meant no payout. To provide evidence that water had also washed down directly from the plains, Maggie Fletcher took the question to the people.

'We had lots of conversations about the flood and where the water had come from,' says Fletcher. There was real concern about why the bad weather had occurred, about what was being communicated, rather than a focus on what might have been lost. 'This got people thinking and talking and after a while, people started to make paintings about the flood...These flood paintings are history in the making.' But, of course, these are different kinds of history from the ones white society, and law, rests on.

The ways in which Indigenous people maintain culture—through storytelling, dancing and painting—are poorly understood in the Australian mainstream. They are important for many reasons, not least to satisfy the laws requiring land rights claimants to show that ancestral customs and traditions have been maintained, that a link to the land has been retained and that the land has cultural significance. But it has not been easy to align these Indigenous forms of history with white law.

When Tom Pauling moved to Darwin in 1970 he was one of many who recognised that the way in which white and black law were integrating was not working. Some people advocated for a system which did more to involve Indigenous people in the process of the courts, rather than simply subjecting them to a series of experiences that were both incomprehensible and, ultimately, often fatal. This led to several innovations, such as elders being present during court cases, both to offer advice and to learn more about the legal process, and the acknowledgment in some courts of customary Law. (Depressingly, despite many attempts over the last few decades to improve the situation it seems to be getting worse, not better, for Indigenous Territorians. Between 2008 and 2012 their rate of incarceration, already disproportionate, rose by 34 per cent. The Territory also has the highest rates of Aboriginal deaths in custody in the nation.)

Storytelling incorporates contemporary events into the narrative of the Dreamtime, which is one word for the fabric of knowledge, history, culture and law that lies across everything. But the romantic and slightly fairytale connotations of the word Dreamtime are misleading. Culture, knowledge and law are tough. They are a set of intractable understandings and rules that have very real consequences in the day-to-day world. Detail is important. Law is a form of ritualised memory, and memory is knowledge: the kind of knowledge that can help a people survive. To know the Law is to have access to millennia of ecological information, and it informs the day-to-day decisions of elders. Memory of the land, the animals, the plants, the location of water holes: in all this there is power.

The depth of these memories gives them a resonance that we'd call spiritual, and indeed they are. But they are also real and relevant to the here, the now. Time and time again Dreamtime stories have been shown to be based on what we white people would call historical 'facts'—now proven through archaeological evidence. For Indigenous people culture is life but perhaps one of the things I am trying to convey, one of the reasons I have written this book, is that it's not just life for Australia's oldest inhabitants: it is for us newcomers, also.

*

Captain Cook law—white law—on the other hand, took a while to settle in the Northern Territory. The area was governed by South Australia for its first fifty years but after that it became the responsibility of the Commonwealth, and when Tracy hit Darwin it had been under federal administration since 1911. Tom Pauling says, 'It wasn't until about 1975 that we saw party politics as such operating in the Northern Territory. In those days, just about everyone was independent although it was well known that Dick Ward was either a communist or socialist.' The first fully elected Legislative Assembly of the Northern Territory was created by an act of the Commonwealth Parliament in October 1974. That's only a couple of months before Tracy. However the assembly had few significant powers and, according to Bill Wilson, even those powers were dismissed by Canberra. 'The federal government hardly recognised them, and they saw this [Tracy] as an opportunity to flex their muscles.' Wilson was not the only one to argue that Canberra bureaucrats used the cyclone to try and consolidate control over a town that was beginning to slip from their grasp. At the time of the disaster eighteen federal government ministers had special responsibilities in the Northern Territory.

Harry Giese, like many of Darwin's senior figures, believes the tensions after the cyclone further motivated the drive for self-government. There was a powerful sense that Territorians:

> should have the same rights and the same privileges, exercise the same powers and responsibilities, as any of the states. That feeling was very, very strong. I think Cyclone Tracy and its aftermath led to a strengthening of that attitude. Certainly, I think it brought forward some of the changes in government, in the powers and responsibilities of the Legislative Council, and of course, led to the '78 setting up of a Northern Territory Legislative Assembly.

Margaret Muirhead remembers 1978, and the declaration of self-government, as 'the highest pinnacle'. She too believed that it was a 'direct outcome' of the cyclone.

Paul Everingham, the Northern Territory's first chief minister after self-government, said these moves had been underway long before Cyclone Tracy. Malcolm Fraser insists that greater self-determination would have happened regardless of the cyclone—'the time had come'. He laid claim to being an advocate for statehood during the 1975 federal election campaign, when he announced that the Territory would be granted 'statehood in five years'. He 'also promised an immediate transfer of executive responsibilities to the Legislative Assembly if the coalition parties are elected on December 13'.

When I spoke to him, Fraser said the Territory itself resisted full statehood when it was offered, perhaps out of concern that it would be financially disadvantaged. He made this particular point in response to my suggestion that the granting of statehood for the Territory could be seen as a way of defraying the massive rebuilding costs that the Commonwealth Government (estimated to be between eight hundred million and a billion dollars, when all was done and dusted) undertook after Tracy. While he acknowledged that was a lot of money, he argued that the rebuild generated significant economic activity, so it was wrong to simply see it as a drain. Either way, in 1977 an agreement was reached that self-government would be achieved, through a gradual transfer of responsibilities, by mid-1979.

It was not just political will that was tempered by the cyclone. Residents' personal passion for the place had also become more steely. Peter Dermoudy has said that the cyclone made him and others 'commit themselves to the place or leave forever'.[3] Maria Tumarkin writes that in the aftermath of the cyclone 'people who had little consciousness of land rights and so on, all of a sudden discovered their own attachment to place'.[4] Barbara James concurs:

> Individuals made a real choice to come back to Darwin. The city had been destroyed, most people had lost their homes, most of their belongings. So the choice to actually come and stay here or move here was a very deliberate one and a commitment and I think it has stabilised Darwin's population to a large extent. It's a lot less transient than it was. But as a nation, I also think it was really important for the country to feel that it was part of rebuilding Darwin.[5]

James and others talk about the renewed heritage push that resulted from this increased engagement and 'sees the "town hall ruins", the crumbled remains of a former town hall that now stands in the heart of Darwin's business district, as a reminder of the power and influence the residents' groups came to yield'.[6] There was also a greater valuing of the few Burnett bungalows left on Myilly Point, and a hard-fought battle saved the remaining bungalows (including the Giese house) in 1983.

This change of heart set Darwin's newer residents on a direct collision course with its oldest. The parallels between white and black experiences may seem obvious to us now, but Dawn Lawrie appeared unaware of them when she criticised the impact of the permit system, then the DRC, on Darwin's residents, writing in her contribution to Giese's DDWC report: 'After your survival instinct and your need for love the third most basic thing is your territorial imperative, that's your bit of land. We are not very far removed from our ancestors in caves.'

The Larrakia have been fighting for their own land rights since being inspired by the walk-off at Wave Hill of 1966. In October 1972 they'd presented the 'Larrakia Petition' to Princess Margaret when she was visiting Darwin. The petition had more than a thousand signatures and was 3.3 metres long. 'The British Settlers took our land,' it stated.

'Today we are REFUGEES. Refugees in the country of our ancestors.' In the fight that broke out as they attempted to break through police barriers to get to the princess, the petition was torn. Bill Day eventually posted a copy of it to the Queen, who returned it to the Australian Governor-General, Sir Paul Hasluck, in early 1973.[7]

Malcolm Fraser believes that, given this momentum, and between Whitlam's government and his own, land rights would have gone ahead cyclone or no. But despite Fraser's reservations about reading too much into Tracy, there is no doubt that the cyclone was seen as a call to arms for Larrakia culture. In May 1978 *Bunji* was explicit on this point:

> The invaders came across the sea to Larrakia land (Port Darwin) in 1869. The invaders built a town on the Larrakia hunting grounds…The town of Darwin was destroyed on Christmas Day 1974, by a wild cyclone…Six months later Judge Ward recommended that Kulaluk and Goondal be returned to the Larrakia.[8]

The *Aboriginal Land Rights Act* of 1976 was proclaimed in January 1977. The Northern Land Council and Central Land Council were created. In 1978 the Kulaluk Aboriginal land claims over forty-seven acres were officially recognised. Eight years after Tracy, Daribah Nungalinya was registered as sacred with the Aboriginal Areas Protection Authority.[9] There were seven hundred members of the urban community in 1974. Today the figure is about two thousand. This came about, in part, because definitions of what it means to be Larrakia were challenged.

> The Larrakia tribe has had to make many changes to survive. For example they never make a distinction between those who are initiated and those who are not. It is not even

> necessary to speak the language to be a Larrakia...It is not land rights to almost wipe out a tribe and then judge them by anthropology books.[10]

However those anthropology books, and the laws that extend from them, still have a lot of power. In April 2006 a Larrakia native title claim over areas of metropolitan Darwin was rejected by the Federal Court. Justice Mansfield found:

> that the current laws and customs of the Larrakia people were not 'traditional'...because a combination of historical circumstances interrupted and changed the laws and customs of the present day Larrakia people from those which existed at the time of sovereignty.[11]

Ongoing tensions between Larrakia and non-Larrakia are also an issue. One respondent to the Haynes Report said, 'There's unrestrained development in our lands; there's people misrepresenting themselves as Larrakia...I think we need another big one [cyclone] to wake a few people up.'

Floods and cyclones are a reminder to stay connected to country, kin and spirit. As a senior Larrakia man Robert Mills put it to me, 'Your people think of cyclones as bad things, but we don't see it that way.' Some non-Indigenous people shared this sense that the cyclone could bring good things. There were ways in which Tracy was a liberating experience for many, in which normal rules no longer applied. One white man now in his late fifties described to me the exhilaration of being a young man staying on, alone, after his family were evacuated. There was a kind of freedom and wildness to that experience, a rapid coming into manhood that he found exciting. Peter Dermoudy, who took shelter in the World War Two armament structures down on East Point, says of the cyclone: 'It cleansed me.' He wouldn't have missed it for the world. After the Christchurch earthquake of 2011 and during the thousands of smaller quakes that followed, it was noted that there can be exhilaration in disaster. We're reminded that we're 'temporary inhabitants of a volatile earth…change is the only constant'.[12] We ask, 'How can we mark these places in our mind before they disappear?'

The stories we tell about ourselves and the manner of the telling are a way of singing ourselves into being. I think again of the Yolngu saying, 'I make this place as I go.' And it's true, we are remaking this place: we are ravaging it, and we are paying the price.

Climate change science has a long history though the urgency of the message is only a few decades old, as Tom Griffiths illustrates in his essay 'Prosper or Perish' when he describes the research of Swiss-born Professor Louis Agassiz.

> In the late 1830s Agassiz proposed not only that glaciers had moved rocks around and later retreated—hence explaining the puzzling presence of isolated boulders in Swiss valleys—but that whole countries had once been covered under miles of ice…His friend and mentor, Alexander von Humboldt, warned him against the ambition of his theory: 'Your ice frightens me.'[13]

And yes, we should be frightened. Climate change scientists have predicted in hundreds of reports over dozens of years that the number of extreme weather events is going to increase, and these events will become more severe. In Australia that means more flooding and cyclones up north, and more drought, extreme storms and bushfires down south. While no particular weather event can be laid neatly at the door of climate change—extreme weather has existed since the dawn of time—there is little doubt that the growing prevalence and severity of these weather events is in line with what scientists have predicted. In the last three decades the number of cyclones and hurricanes has remained constant, but the number of Category 4 and 5 cyclones has increased. We've ignored scientists' findings on climate change for decades but we've been ignoring Indigenous knowledge about weather since the moment we set foot on this land. In 2011 Alexis Wright asked:

> Are we not curious to know something about the deeply rooted beliefs of this country and why they were kept in place over many thousands of years? Why are we not hearing about any of these stories and trying to understand what they might mean?

She exhorted us to listen to 'the ancient stories of this country—that knowledge that goes back thousands of years. This is where you will find the weather charts, the records about the climate and how Indigenous people learnt to survive on this continent.'[14]

An increasing number of western scientific partnership projects documenting indigenous observations of environmental change have been initiated around the world.[15] There is a range of traditional signs Indigenous people used to read these things, which differ slightly from area to area. Aboriginal elders interviewed at New Mapoon in Cape York know, for example, that a period of continuous hot and still conditions can be the prelude to monsoonal rains or a cyclone. If the Manahawk, a large black ocean-going bird, is seen in large numbers about the coast, there is a 'big blow coming' within two to three days. Crocodiles building their nests higher than usual above the high-tide mark and long stalks on the mango fruit indicate that a 'big Wet' is expected.[16] However these same elders were concerned that their knowledge of seasonal weather patterns, passed on from generation to generation, is becoming less reliable for season predictions. They, too, see that Australian weather patterns are changing.

In 1988 Len Garton, the man who first saw Tracy hanging from the sky like a black velvet curtain, said:

> I do feel some concern for the weather pattern that seems to have changed…I find that the dry seasons are not the dry seasons I used to recall where you had a blanket at night. We've never had a blanket at night for the last two or three or four years…I don't know whether it's the greenhouse effect or these alleged currents that are floating around creating problems. I know, in flying, the weather patterns are completely different. One time, going back five, six, perhaps seven years, I never used to mind flying in the wet season. You did see a weather front in front of you, a rainstorm, and it would be ten [or] fifteen miles wide and not very severe. And you could invariably see the tops at about twelve or fourteen thousand feet or something. But now, when you see them they're a hundred and fifty, two hundred miles wide and they seem to go up out of sight in twenty, thirty—thousand feet. And very dense. I have flown in them a couple of times and frightened myself. The old ones you'd get a bit of buffeting, but nowadays there seems to [be] a lot of turmoil in them. I've never seen any records that substantiate this or otherwise but talking to private pilots like myself they all say: 'Oh yes, it's different, we won't fly through a storm anymore.'

There have been countless disasters since Cyclone Tracy. In 2005 it was estimated that tropical cyclones have caused an estimated 1.9 million deaths worldwide in the last two hundred years. In 2012 there were 552 disasters costing just under 158 billion dollars. The most expensive of these was Hurricane Sandy, which cost fifty billion dollars. The deadliest was Typhoon Bopha in the Philippines, which killed 1901 people.

Closer to home one could cite Victoria's Black Saturday bushfires of February 2009, or Queensland's Big Wet of 2011, which led to three-quarters of the state being declared a disaster zone. After those floods Germaine Greer wrote in the *Guardian*:

> Six months ago the meteorologists thought it was worthwhile to warn people to 'get ready for a wet, late winter and a soaked spring and summer'. So what did the people do? Nothing. They said, 'She'll be right, mate.' She wasn't.[17]

Brisbane was built on a flood plain, as many cities are. The Indigenous people knew this and when Surveyor-General John Oxley entered the Brisbane River to found Moreton Bay in 1824, elders 'told these white explorers of floods that submerged today's West End'.[18] Brisbane flooded severely in 1893 but few people with memories of that flood were alive in 1974, and not many from 1974 were in Brisbane in 2011 when the whole thing happened again. Matthew Condon: 'We forget, especially in this restless place where history finds it hard to take root. And here, in the young city, we are at least two generations from 1974, and all of the city's new inhabitants, squinting into tomorrow, just wouldn't know about the floods of 1974.'

The disasters of 1974—the Brisbane Floods, Cyclone Tracy—and those of 2011—Cyclone Yasi, more floods in Brisbane—were both born of the same weather pattern, La Nina. 2011's La Nina was the strongest we've seen since 1917. You would have thought that the lessons of 1974 would have prepared people for 2011, but generations of knowledge and memory keep slipping away. At times the reluctance to tackle these issues head on is more wilful, as suggested by recent reports that Victoria's power companies did not act on promises regarding the management of power lines after the Ash Wednesday fires of 1983. A *Four Corners* report in late 2013 pointed out that yes, it would cost 750 million dollars or more to put power lines underground in parts of southeastern Australia that are at high risk of fires. But the fires themselves? They're costing us billions of dollars—and hundreds of lives. Similarly, doing nothing about climate change will cost the planet much more in economic terms than the cost of addressing it.

In 'Prosper or Perish' Tom Griffiths writes:

> a place of escalating fatal bushfire, and with a small and embattled agricultural economy, Australians might have been expected to rush to sign Kyoto a decade ago...for two hundred years, the European colonisers of Australia have struggled to come to terms with the extreme climatic variability of the continent. Australia has a boom-and-bust ecology. Settlers have had to learn, slowly and reluctantly, that 'drought' is not aberrant but natural; they have struggled to understand seasonal and non-annual climatic variation; they have had to accept a wilful nature that they cannot control or change. They are still learning. And now, suddenly, Australians are confronted by long-term, one-way climatic change for which they, in part, are held responsible.

Tess Lea, writing of our propensity for a shared amnesia, linked it to, among other things, what she describes as 'the killing times of settlement'.[19] That is, our reluctance to acknowledge the warfare and attempted genocide that underpin colonisation. She is right to remind us that forgetting is strategic and that it has, in this country, become a very bad habit. Certainly before we have come to grips with the first factor—that Australia *is* a sunburnt country, one of droughts and flooding rains, of cyclones and bushfires—a second factor is upon us.

Six of the hottest Australian summers on record have occurred in the last eleven years. The United Kingdom has had its five wettest years and seven warmest years since the year 2000. In 2013 Australia's weather broke every record since records began. The summer of 2012–13 recorded the warmest September–March on record, the hottest summer on record, the hottest month on record and the hottest day on record. A record was set for the longest national-scale heatwave. It was also the hottest summer on record for Australian sea-surface temperatures, thus increasing the chances of a cyclone. All this in a year that was neither El Nino nor La Nina, the other oscillating weather pattern associated with extreme weather. Records are breaking so fast that no doubt several more will have shattered by the time this book is published. The week before I sent the final version of this manuscript to the publishers, several public figures raised their voices to call for the cutting of carbon emissions. Some of these could be said to be predictable, such as Nicholas Stern, the author of a 2006 report on the economics of climate change. Less predictable was the statement by US Secretary of State John Kerry that man-made climate change was 'perhaps the world's most fearsome weapon of mass destruction'.[20] Christine Lagarde, a conservative and the head of the International Monetary Fund, urged the Australian government not to abandon its role as 'a pioneer' in the debate on climate change.[21]

Justice Stretton may have said, 'We have not lived long enough.' But some of us have. The problem is we haven't been listening.

When, during my research for this book, I was shown around Darwin by Robert Mills, I asked him what his thoughts were on climate change. 'Is it true that the wet is coming later? And that when it hits the rain is heavier?' Mills and I were spending the day together so he could give me a sense of what Darwin was like before white settlement, and since. We'd never met before so, in my ignorance, I figured the weather was as good a conversation starter as any. And besides, I was frustrated that I'd been to Darwin several times during the wet season, but it never seemed to rain. Mills sat in silence beside me. I barrelled on. 'Do you think the climate is changing?' After a while he turned and looked at me. 'My people don't really like to talk about the weather,' he said. Some time later, I asked him to elaborate on his reluctance and he laughed and quoted Dylan: 'You don't need a weather man to know which way the wind blows.'

THE SHAPE MEMORY TAKES

I FELL in love with Darwin over the weeks and months I spent there, but, like many who have made this protestation in the past, my life was elsewhere. Whilst the city is bigger than it was back in 1974—the population is now over a hundred and thirty thousand—it continues to have a complex demographic and a population that floats around a small but stable core of people who are there for the long haul. In 2011 about thirty per cent of the population was Aboriginal and the number of overseas residents was as high as fifteen per cent. As well, long-standing Greek, Chinese and Filipino families remain. Chips Mackinolty writes: 'The Territory is heading towards the non-Anglo demographic structure that so alarmed the good citizens of Palmerston in the 1880s.' He goes on:

> the only periods of population growth from interstate migration have been sharply aligned to developments in the Northern Territory economy: the 'empire building' following

> self-government in the early 1980s, the defence build-up of the mid-1990s, and government-led capital works projects between 2007–09. As those periods of economic growth tapered off, people left in their thousands.[1]

But now there are new projects underway. In 2011 Prime Minister Gillard signed a deal with President Obama to allow the stationing of up to 2500 US marines by 2017. The troops will be rotated on a six-monthly basis. As well, developments such as the Ichthys gas project continue to attract mining and gas workers, though they tend to be 'fly-in-fly-out' workers, put up in a purpose-built village just outside Darwin at Howard Springs.[2] The split between those who consider Darwin home and those who just fly in for work and a good time seems wider than ever before. And with all those marines, pilots and miners it's probably going to keep on feeling like a man's town.

One of the central theses of Tess Lea's book *Darwin* is that the city has never, in fact, stopped being a defence town. She cites the decision to maintain the airport and RAAF base's position, slap bang in the middle of Darwin, as indicative of that. When Lea flew over the city not so long ago, what she saw was a town in danger of drowning, both in a literal sense, and a cultural one.

> A thousand feet up and the tough, delicate topography of Darwin comes into view, a place of military zones, industrial sites and back-to-the-future incarceration compounds. There is the huge chunk of habitable land consumed by the airport; the mangroves as they hold the slow-drowning delta system in fragile check; the inlets of East and West arm, showing how close to inundation Darwin's harbour has become.

On my final visit, in late 2013, I stayed in an elevated house in Jingili. It was the beginning of the build-up, so very humid. I slept at night with all the louvres open and the fans on. It was hard to sleep with orange-footed scrubfowl scuffing around all night and bats shrieking. The moon hung bright in the sky. The experience was both fabulous and exhausting, like sleeping in a tent. But that's the thing about Darwin: nature is a raucous presence. It crowds in on you. Early most mornings I'd head for the Nightcliff pool, before the heat set in, and swim laps overlooking the Arafura Sea. Nights were spent outdoors, at pubs watching the sun set, and I found myself wondering if it did something to the brain (good? bad?) watching that golden red ball fall into the sea, night after glorious night. Suzanne Spunner's phrase, 'you stagger up from yet another sunset' resonated. I saw fights on the streets, and in the parks between whites and black. Most tellingly, down at East Point under a sign that said 'No Camping', I saw a white man emerge from a camper van and squirt a group of long grassers with a hose while shouting at them that they weren't allowed to be there. They laughed at him. I tried to imagine what it would have been like for those living out in the days, weeks and months after the cyclone and the one word that comes to mind is sweat. Some days you sweat so much it seems a miracle that the fifty per cent of us that's meant to be water doesn't end up in a puddle on the floor.

On one of my first trips to Darwin I'd caught the ferry to the Mandorah Hotel to have one of their famed counter teas (among other things, they refused to do chips). I'd sat under a faded striped umbrella looking past a Cyclone Tracy memorial made of twisted metal to the beach, then to Darwin across the harbour. That was when I met the publican, Nick Candilo. I told him what I was working on and he pointed to a navigation light that flashes all night every night and told me that he often looked at it to remind himself of his friend, the skipper of the *Mandorah Queen*. On my last trip the Mandorah pub closed its doors for the last time. Candilo said its position, right on the water, made the forty-six-year-old building impossible to maintain. 'I don't think it's repairable and it probably goes way back to the cyclone.

The metal is rusting and it's like an old ship at the end of its days.'[3] It's easy to be nostalgic for a place you barely know, but even I could see that Darwin was changing rapidly and Cyclone Tracy was a story from a long time ago. A story that people new to Darwin, living in reinforced (but untested) apartments felt didn't affect them.

The morning I left I went for a long walk along Casuarina Beach at low tide. Sea water snaked in channels across the expansive sand like half a dozen glistening serpents. Daribah Nungalinya emerged as the tide dropped, squat and strong. With its sturdy fortress-like air it's not hard to see why the rock formation was considered a custodian of the lands and the waters in the area.

Issues of memory were on my mind. In a coming-together of my personal and professional life, Darwin was the place that my father received treatment for dementia. The experience endeared me even more to the place because people treated Dad with such care and understanding. Some days I'd dash to and from the archives to where he was staying, or to take him to doctor's appointments. What people remember, and what they don't, took on an even greater significance. A friend who writes on such subjects told me that people with dementia often remember the quality of an experience even though they forget the detail. If something makes them sad they feel down without remembering why, and if it was a good experience the converse is true: they feel strangely uplifted. One night I took Dad to the sailing club in Fannie Bay for dinner so we could watch the sunset. I was convinced I'd spotted some crocs circling. Locals told me that couldn't be right, before standing next to me, looking at the series of tiny tail fins moving through the water and conceding maybe I had a point. Swimming in the sea was never on the agenda for me up there, but even less so after that night. Dad ate some potatoes with his meal and they triggered a memory of a particular meal he had as a child. He was beaming. On other occasions, flickers of moments barely remembered made him flinch as if pained. The body, it seems, remembers longer than the mind. The things that happen to us, they stay with us. Even if they slip from our memory, they live on in our bodies.

When I met with Lord Mayor Katrina Fong Lim in those final few days, I asked her how Darwin planned to commemorate the fortieth anniversary of the cyclone in late 2014. 'It's a tricky question,' she acknowledged. 'It's certainly not something to celebrate. As a city we still don't know what to do. We can't have a party on Christmas Eve because everyone has their own plans. And if you have an event on another day, what are you celebrating?'

In the days and months after the cyclone people wanted to talk about it. A lot. Margaret Muirhead remembers that 'most people who'd been through the cyclone needed to talk...because Jim and I were not traumatised by the cyclone, we were able to listen and every dinner, every night at dinner, the cyclone, the cyclone, the cyclone...' In her interview with Richard Fidler in 2013, Wendy James recalled that this need to talk about the cyclone endlessly became almost debilitating, and finally, in an effort to move on, she instituted a system of fines at any dinner parties she held—if you mentioned the cyclone you were fined a bottle of wine or some beer. She also commented that she found the cyclone hard to talk about because it brings things back. Her breath shortens and goosebumps prickle along her skin. 'After all these years,' she said, 'it never leaves.'

Nowadays, in contrast, says Fong Lim, survivors 'don't want to talk about it'. She compared this to the commemoration of the World War Two bombings in 2012, when the seventieth anniversary fell. Those who were still alive were keen to talk about what had happened, indeed, memories were flooding back. She believed the survivors of Tracy aren't at that stage yet, despite the passing of forty years.

There is no doubt that the willingness to mark Cyclone Tracy has ebbed and flowed. My preferred memorial, the twisted iron in the Mandorah pub's beer garden, had been there since soon after Tracy. In August 1976 the foundation was laid of a new Christ Church to replace that old stone building Bishop O'Loughlin was so worried about. His concern for history rather than the day was given form through light, air and space: it's a beautiful church. The old stone porch was integrated into the back wall of a modern octagonal building, with massive arched windows. Inside is a Cyclone Tracy memorial window in hues of (mainly) purple and blue. Designed by artist George Chaloupka, it represents fishing nets and waves and is really quite something. The window was financed by a Gollin Kyokuyo Trust fund, and there is also a plaque to remember the seven men that company lost at sea. Almost ten years after the cyclone, another memorial was constructed using twisted girders from the home of Sergeant Kevin Maley, one of the first people flown out after Tracy. The girders had been bent by front-end loaders during the clean-up operations and a teacher from Casuarina High school had them set in concrete. The memorial was unveiled in June 1984. It's an affecting monument but there have also been criticisms that it was a reconstruction (bent out of shape by human forces) rather than indicative of the power of the storm itself. As well, it was the result of one man's initiative rather than the expression of a desire to commemorate victims led by any community organisation or form of government. Of course, despite government initiatives or lack thereof, individual survivors develop their own memorials. Bill Wilson and his wife continued their ritual of a scotch for Christmas breakfast for some twenty years.

People's relationship to the cyclone changed over time. At the time of the tenth anniversary, historian Mickey Dewar noted that there were:

> plenty of tangible reminders of the effects of the cyclone. Vacant lots, elevated houses with the upper storey gone and

> ubiquitous staircases that led to nowhere. Newcomers to Darwin were initiated in the stories of the cyclone in the same way that crocodile and box jellyfish stories are also told; accounts of hospital floors awash with blood, civilian looting, the hundreds of deaths that were concealed by the government. By ten years after the event, the historical event that was cyclone Tracy had become entrenched within the mythic folklore of Darwin.[4]

When Suzanne Spunner moved to Darwin those signs were still there: 'housing pylons left over from Tracy. "Cyclone ballrooms" they call them—freestanding polished wooden floors. Over time the wood rots and disappears leaving the steel and concrete bearers to support supple vines, where once they held up whole families, little worlds aloft in the air.'

Nowadays the vacant lots are gone and Ray McHenry's words from many years ago seem both more pertinent and increasingly remote. 'The best message, I think, is the visual impact of what happened in Tracy... What I have learned, I think, is that the further you get away from a disastrous experience, the more difficult it is to try and keep people interested in planning and in preparedness...'

In 1994, on Tracy's twentieth anniversary, Bernard Briec, like many Darwin residents, didn't want to accept that a cyclone like Tracy could ever hit again. 'I think one of the reasons that I don't feel that scared is, I don't think something like Tracy could happen again. I don't know if that's being complacent about it, or what, but I think Tracy was almost a one-off sort of event for Darwin.'

Francis Good asked him, 'You can't conceive that something like that could strike twice?'

'I pray to God it never will, something that bad,' Briec replied.

Mickey Dewar was responsible for developing the twentieth anniversary commemoration that is now a permanent exhibition at the

Northern Territory Gallery and Museum. Visitors to Darwin would know this exhibition, which was designed by Troppo, and includes a sound room that plays the recording made by Bishop Ted Collins in the early hours of Christmas Day 1974. A sign outside the room warns people who actually went through Cyclone Tracy that they may find it distressing to enter. When you step in it is dark except for occasional flashes. For me it was the strobing light representing lightning that was most agitating, but many can't bear the overwhelming noise of metal scraping the ground or the loud moaning of wind. Little kids who followed me in looked seriously freaked out, and who can blame them? About 300,000 people a year visit the Cyclone Tracy Gallery, which is considered a model for memorials after disaster.

Back then, though, Dewar found the mounting of the memorial a difficult task. Despite the fact that a similar exhibition had been housed at Fannie Bay Gaol for some years there were complaints that such a thing was even being contemplated. 'A commonly voiced fear concerning the commemorations,' Dewar wrote, 'was that by marking the anniversary we would be tempting fate and would bring another cyclone down upon the city.'

I think of Briec's hope that there will never be another Tracy, of Robert Mills telling me: 'My people don't really like to talk about the weather.' Of course when he said that, he meant the weather wasn't a subject for casual conversation. It was absolutely, as the Gurirr Gurirr cycle and many other paintings tell us, a powerful basis for ceremony. A Tiwi songman who composed a song about Tracy felt that the twentieth anniversary would be an appropriate occasion to choreograph a dance using men and women from Bathurst Island. This was performed at the exhibition's opening and I had the chance to listen to this rhythmic, haunting sequence in the National Film and Sound Archive.

Other events held back in 1994 were more lighthearted, and sometimes crass. They included cyclone-themed cocktail nights at the

Travelodge in 1994 (Menu, with original spelling: Rock Your Socks Off: ⅓ rockmelen, 60 ml coconut liquer, 30 ml rum, 4 strawberries, 100 ml pineapple juice. Christmas Breeze: 2 nips Gin, 1 nip strawberry liquer, 1 nip Pineapple Liquer, ½ cup cream, 1 cup pineapple juice, chopped strawberries, passionfruit juice.) I can't help thinking that simply chucking a couple of Holdens into the Travelodge pool so it looked the same as it did on Christmas Day 1974 would have made a stronger point.

In the *Northern Territory News* twentieth anniversary feature Sherylee Armstrong, whose mother died in the cyclone, was asked to given her account of that night. She replied, 'I think it's cruel, really I do. It digs up a lot of feelings a lot of people keep hidden…I don't know anywhere in the world where they celebrate a bloody tragedy.' It is significant that the paper reported her response because they deliberated long and hard about how best to approach the entire subject. The choices they made were good ones, I thought, and the result is some thirty pages of powerful journalism.

And while the reluctance of some to speak must be respected, we also need to acknowledge that people do remember tragedy, all the time, and all around the world. Ten thousand people attended the twenty-first anniversary of the Hillsborough disaster, in which close to a hundred people were crushed to death while watching a soccer match at Hillsborough Stadium in 1989. The entire site of the former Twin Towers is now a memorial to 9/11 and there are annual memorial events attended by thousands of people. After Black Saturday, hundreds of blacksmiths donated their time to forge a memorial tree out of copper and stainless steel, in which messages are carved onto the metal gum leaves, such as, 'In memory of the children who were denied the pleasure of gazing at this tree.' Many different people sponsored a leaf, dedicating it to communities, classmates, family and friends. The tree was installed in Strathewen in March 2014.

Katrina Fong Lim believes that people don't want governments organising their memorials for them and she may be right. The most successful memorials are those that grow out of a community groundswell, one where there is less chance that the event could be hijacked for any particular political purpose.

When I spoke to Bill Wilson in Beechworth he was concerned that the people he called the elders of Darwin—by which he meant those who'd been through Tracy—were dying. Jim Bowditch has died. Mayor Tiger Brennan died in 1979. Charles Gurd died in 1999. Ray McHenry died in 2000, as did Gwen Cairns. Jim Cairns died in 2003. George Brown died in 2002. Barbara James died of cancer in 2003. Senator Bob Collins was appointed an Officer of the Order of Australia (AO) for services to the Northern Territory and Indigenous rights in 2004 but he died of a deliberate overdose of prescription drugs three days before he was scheduled to face trial for multiple charges of child sex abuse in 2007. Hedley Beare received an Order of Australia, after an exemplary career as an educator, in 2009. He died a year later at the age of seventy-seven. Major-General Stretton died at the age of ninety in late 2012. Colonel Frank Thorogood continued to make a major contribution and ended up as the executive director of Red Cross in Victoria. He was active during the Ash Wednesday bushfires of 1983. He died only recently, on 27 December 2013. Gough Whitlam, at the age of ninety-seven, is extremely frail. Ray Wilkie became the weather man for Channel 10 Brisbane, and is still alive. Dawn Lawrie is now a marriage celebrant, and can still be spotted around Nightcliff's supermarkets wearing her trademark beehive and caftans. Dr Ella Stack is living in Canberra and recently published a book on her own memories of Tracy, *Is There Anyone Alive in There?*

Despite this, and despite the fact that about half the population changes every few years, Katrina Fong Lim believes that 'When it comes to Darwin as a community it still remains in people's subconscious. Cyclone Tracy is still a part of their consciousness.'

Two days after I returned to Melbourne, my relatively closed and hunkered down southern city had its own weather event. Winds of up to 150 km/h whipped through the city at around three in the morning. Trampolines were blown out of backyards and sailed through the sky. The noise was loud, too loud to sleep through. A kind of hollow, low whistle reverberated through the streets for an hour or two. I live in a solid brick house, in a built-up street. I suffered no damage to my house and was never in any danger, and still found it pretty scary. I lay there wondering what it would be like to experience winds that were two to three times as strong, and could not. And if the noise had been louder? Well, that was hard to imagine also. Perhaps the only thing I've experienced that comes close to it was the Sydney hailstorm of 1999 but that lasted minutes, not hours.

So why have I tried so hard to imagine these things? There are many reasons, not all of them clear to me. The clearest of all is that while many of us may not like talking about the weather, we have to. We certainly can't, as was suggested during the Blue Mountains bushfires of October 2013, avoid talking about disaster and climate change for fear of 'politicising' pain and suffering. At the time environment minister Greg Hunt said, 'I think we've all got to be very careful, in talking with the senior people at the Bureau of Meteorology, for example, they always emphasise, never trying to link any particular event to climate change.'[5] In fact, climate change scientists have been consistent in stating the difference between day-to-day weather, which can't be pinned on climate change, versus overall shifts in the climate, which can be. (Hunt's equivocation is almost as wilful as insisting if an extreme weather event is a cold one, it can't be the result of global warming. Warming of greenhouse gases causes extreme weather, but does not only mean that temperatures will rise.) But our children and grandchildren will judge us. History will judge us. Indeed we're already being judged by the international community and toyed with by the weather itself, like a mouse being batted around the room by a large cat.

It's not just crucial that we remember—it's important what we remember. The shape memory takes has something to teach us. It doesn't matter if we can't remember the exact order of events, or who said what to whom. It does matter what we learn. Memory is not a luxury: it is survival. I think of Slim Bauer's belief that the white man 'has not learned to come to grips with life in the tropics' and that Darwin 'will, sometime in the future, be overtaken by further disaster'. I think of the people of Sri Lanka who ran towards the tsunami because they did not know better. I think of the people of Darwin building a casino in the surge zone and over a Larrakia burial site. I think of Justice Leonard Stretton saying, after the Victorian bushfires of 1939, 'They had not lived long enough.' I think of Nick Candilo as he looked back across the harbour and told me that when he sees a light flickering he thinks of his friend. He does not let the light go out and nor can we.

But we can't just remember the strength and power of community spirit after Darwin, though that was beautiful to behold. We must remember all of it: those who were denied community, those who were shipped off in despair never to return. The policemen who had their children blown from their arms, saved them, then went on to find the bodies of other parents' tiny children in the ruins. Those who drowned at sea. We remember the missing and the elderly who died of heart attacks in the cyclone's wake. We remember those who panicked and didn't behave well. We remember the people whose lives were ruined and those who felt, suddenly, as if they'd just begun. We remember the woman Rover Thomas called auntie who died in the air above

Broome then showed him the Rainbow Serpent destroying Darwin. We remember her cry: 'I'm leaving my country.' We remember the Larrakia who were put onto planes and buses and taken, once again, to lands not their own, we remember the community at Knuckeys Lagoon and those at One Mile. We remember the distress and courage of a general, the teacher who did his best to save the women and children of the city then watched the navy come into harbour and hoped that he too was saved. We remember, as that teacher did, the eruptions of altruism and kindness. We remember a mayor who was forthright and distressed by what had happened to his town. We remember the nurses who worked till they dropped, those who cooked for and fed thousands, the women who protected the dogs, and those who gave birth in the eye of the storm. We remember the kids stuck down south in schools full of the uncomprehending and those who made it home and played in rubbish tips with bits of their old town. And yes, we remember the dogs that were shot, the mangled horses, the crocs turned into handbags, the devastated chooks, the cats that went crazy, the trees that were uprooted, the land flattened for years to come. We remember the palm flower that was about to bloom for the first time in a hundred years.

Time shifts and twists in difficult times, it expands and contracts. A week can draw out into infinity, a minute can last a century, a century can pass in the blink of an eye, but we need to understand what memory leaves us with: the lessons it has for us. This place, we make it as we go and all of it, the good the bad the ugly the glorious and the wild raging winds, the floods, the fires, the droughts, must be remembered if we are to survive the decades and centuries to come. Tracy was not a bitch, she was a warning. We should listen to her.

ACKNOWLEDGMENTS

THIS BOOK could not have been written without the support—and archives—of the Northern Territory Archives Service. At the archives, I would particularly like to thank Françoise Barr who worked with me closely on this project. She was amazing. Thank you also to the National Film and Sound Archive.

I would like to thank my readers for spending the time on and supporting the work: Ciannon Cazaly, Saul Cunningham, my agent Jenny Darling, Greg Hunt, Paul Kelly, Virginia Murdoch, Adrienne Nicotra, John Richardson and Sari Wawn.

To those who were so generous in sharing their knowledge with me and provided tips and contacts: Wally Caruana, Kate Cole-Adams, Mickey Dewar, Denise Goodfellow, Helen Hansen, Alan James, Kevin Kelly, Francis Good, Chips Mackinolty, Sarah Mathers, Shane Maloney, Robert Mills, John Richardson (again!), Suzanne Spunner and Ianto Ware.

To my friends and colleagues in Darwin: thank you most particularly to Megan Nevett for accommodating, feeding, listening to me and giving me beer; Kay Aldenhoven, Angus and Rose Cameron, Panos Couros, Robyn McLean, Sandra Thibodeaux and Rohan Wightman.

I am grateful to the editors and journals who published articles that went on to become chapters of this book, and their input into a work in progress: Julianne Schultz at *Griffith Review*, Jeff Sparrow at *Overland* and John Van Tiggelen at the *Monthly*. For allowing me to quote from their work, I thank Kevin Brophy, Paul Kelly and Adrian Hyland.

To my colleagues at Text: Mandy Brett, as ever, for terrifyingly forthright and excellent editing, Jane Novak both for organising publicity and her personal enthusiasm for the project, and my dear friend Chong Weng-Ho for the cover. I hope you all know how much I value you and the team at Text Publishing.

Words can't fully express my gratitude to those who, forty years ago, went through a wild storm and all that followed. I thank all those I interviewed (listed in sources), most particularly Bill Wilson. To all those who made their transcripts available to the general public through the archive service, please know what an invaluable gift that is.

NOTES

PROLOGUE

1 This inflation-adjusted cost of Cyclone Tracy in 2013 dollars is based on the national Consumer Price Index published on the Australian Bureau of Statistics website.

2 'Flood devastation as bad as Cyclone Tracy', Paul Lockyer, AM, ABC Radio, 11 January 2011.

3 Northern Territory Archives Service (NTAS), Commissioner of Police, NTRS 2999, reports by police officers of personal experiences relating to Cyclone Tracy 1974–5, Report by BAKER, Detective Sergeant Thomas.

4 *Kinglake-350*, Adrian Hyland, Text Publishing, 2011.

5 Dr Ella Stack also references this quote in her book *Is There Anyone Alive in There?*, Historical Society of the Northern Territory, Darwin, 2013. All quotes from Dr Stack from this source unless otherwise noted.

WARNING

1 NTAS, NTRS 226, typed transcripts of oral history interviews with 'TS' prefix, 1979–ct, WILKIE, W. R. (Ray), TS 675. All further quotes from Ray Wilkie come from this interview.

2 NTAS, NTRS 226, typed transcripts of oral history interviews with 'TS' prefix, 1979–ct, BRIEC, Bernard TS 830. All further quotes from Bernard Briec come from this interview.

3 Personal interview with Julia Church, Canberra, 20 June 2013. All further quotes from Julia Church come from this interview.

4 'Tracy—facing the storm', Genevieve Hussey, *7.30 Report*, 24 December 1999.

5 NTAS, NTRS 226, typed transcripts of oral history interviews with 'TS' prefix, 1979–ct, MCHENRY, Ray, TS 270. Attached to this transcript, at McHenry's request, was a paper he wrote called 'The role of a senior administrator in a disaster situation', for a welfare administrators seminar in 1980. All quotes come from one of these two archival sources unless otherwise indicated.

6 NTAS, NTRS 226, typed transcripts of oral history interviews with 'TS' prefix, 1979–ct, CRESWICK, Richard, TS 536. All further quotes from Richard Creswick come from this interview.

7 NTAS, NTRS 226, typed transcripts of oral history interviews with 'TS' prefix, 1979–ct, FREY, Ken, TS 630. All further quotes from Ken Frey come from this interview.

8 NTAS, NTRS 226, typed transcripts of oral history interviews with 'TS' prefix, 1979–ct, BAIRD, Tom, TS 155. All further quotes from Tom Baird come from this interview.

9 NTAS, NTRS 226, typed transcripts of oral history interviews with 'TS' prefix, 1979–ct, AH TOY, Lily, TS 1.

10 NTAS, NTRS 226, typed transcripts of oral history interviews with 'TS' prefix, 1979–ct, NIXON, Curly, TS 654. All further quotes from Curly Nixon come from this interview.

11 NTAS, NTRS 226, typed transcripts of oral history interviews with 'TS' prefix, 1988–ct, TRURAN, Howard, TS 511. All further quotes from Howard Truran come from this interview.

12 NTAS, NTRS 226, typed transcripts of oral history interviews with 'TS' prefix, 1979–ct, BISHOP, Ida, TS 773. All further quotes from Ida Bishop come from this interview.

13 NTAS, NTRS 226, typed transcripts of oral history interviews with 'TS' prefix, 1979–ct, HARRIS, Vicki, TS 585. All further quotes from Vicki Harris come from this interview.

14 NTAS, NTRS 226, typed transcripts of oral history interviews with 'TS' prefix, 1988–ct, GARTON, Len, TS 535. All further quotes from Len Garton come from this interview.

15 NTAS, NTRS 226, typed transcripts of oral history interviews with 'TS' prefix, 1979–ct, CAIRNS, Kate, TS 549. All further quotes from Kate Cairns come from this interview.

16 NTAS, NTRS 226, typed transcripts of oral history interviews with 'TS' prefix, 1979–ct, HARVEY, Beth, TS 490. All further quotes from Beth Harvey come from this interview.

17 'The experience of Cyclone Tracy', Chamberlain E. R., Doube L., Milne G., Rolls M. & Western J. S. Australian Government Publishing Service, 1981.

18 'In Praise of Characters', Erroll Simper, *Australian*, 30 September 2013.

19 NTAS, Steedman, Pete, NTRS 2366, transcripts of interviews relating to Cyclone Tracy, 1975–1975, BOWDITCH, Jim, TS 7902. All further quotes from Jim Bowditch come from this interview.

20 *The Furious Days*, Alan Stretton, William Collins, Sydney, 1976, p. 1. All further quotes from Stretton come from this source, unless otherwise stated.

21 NTAS, NTRS 226, typed transcripts of oral history interviews with 'TS' prefix, 1979–ct, HITCHINS, Air Commodore David, TS 458. All further quotes from Air Commodore David Hitchins come from this interview.

22 Bill Bunbury, *Cyclone Tracy: Picking Up the Pieces*, Fremantle Arts Centre Press, 1994, p. 116.

23 'Picking up the pieces after a big blow', by Chips Mackinolty, *Sydney Morning Herald*, 24 December 1994.

24 NTAS, NTRS 226, typed transcripts of oral history interviews with 'TS' prefix, 1979–ct, LIDDELL, Les, TS 781.

25 NTAS-NTRS 226, typed transcripts of oral history interviews with 'TS' prefix, 1979–ct, GIESE, Harry TS 755. All further quotes from Harry Giese come from this interview unless otherwise indicated.

26 NTAS, NTRS 226, typed transcripts of oral history interviews with 'TS' prefix, 1979–ct, McKENZIE Malcolm, TS 759.

27 '"Learned helplessness" leaves people in major cities unprepared to cope

in natural disasters', Margot O'Neill, *Lateline*, ABC News, 23 October 2013.

28 Aboriginal fringe dwellers in Darwin: cultural persistence or culture of resistance?, William Bartlett Day BA (Hons), Unpublished Thesis, Department of Anthropology, the University of Western Australia, 2001. All quotes from Bill Day from this thesis, unless otherwise noted.

29 Secret life of wounded spaces. Traumascapes in the contemporary Australia, Maria M. Tumarkin, PhD thesis, Department of History, University of Melbourne, 2002. All other quotes from, or attributed to, Tumarkin come from chapter two of this work.

30 NTAS, NTRS 226, typed transcripts of oral history interviews with 'TS' prefix, 1979–ct, FOSTER, Liz, TS 502. All further quotes from Liz Foster come from this interview.

DISAPPEARED

1 NTAS, NTRS 226, typed transcripts of oral history interviews with 'TS' prefix, 1979–ct, PERRIN, Janice, TS 537. All further quotes from Janice Perrin come from this interview.

2 Police Station, Darwin, F760, Watch House keeper's day journals, 1970–80, [before and after Cyclone Tracy from 1974 to 1979]. All other quotes from the watch house journals come from this source.

3 NTAS, NTRS 226, typed transcripts of oral history interviews with 'TS' prefix, 1979–ct, WILSON, Bill, TS 1119. All further quotes from Bill Wilson come from this interview unless otherwise indicated.

4 *Tracy: The Storm that Wiped Out Darwin on Christmas Day 1974* by Gary McKay, Allen & Unwin, Sydney, 2001, p. 69. All quotes from men out on the harbour come from McKay unless otherwise indicated.

5 NTAS, NTRS 226, typed transcripts of oral history interviews with 'TS' prefix, 1979–ct, WRIGHT, Patricia, TS 580. All further quotes from Pat Wright come from this interview.

6 NTAS, NTRS 226, typed transcripts of oral history interviews with 'TS' prefix, 1979–ct, CHRISTODOULOU, Savvas, TS 628. All further quotes from Savvas Christodoulou come from this interview.

7 Quoted in *Winds of Fury*, Keith Cole, Rigby, 1977, p. 16. All other quotes from Keith Cole come from this source.

8 NTAS, NTRS 226, typed transcripts of oral history interviews with 'TS' prefix, 1979–ct, SANDERS, Donald, TS 503. All further quotes from Donald Sanders come from this interview.

9 McKay, p. 140.

10 NTAS, NTRS 226, typed transcripts of oral history interviews with 'TS' prefix, 1979–ct, LAWRIE, Dawn, TS 505. All further quotes from Dawn Lawrie come from this interview unless otherwise indicated.

11 My description of Wendy James's experience comes from 'Wendy James' *ABC Conversations with Richard Fidler*, 3 October 2013. All quotes from Wendy come from this source unless otherwise indicated.

12 NTAS, Commissioner of Police, NTRS 2999, Report by BARRY, Constable Terence David.

13 NTAS, NTRS 226, typed transcripts of oral history interviews with 'TS' prefix, 1979–ct, DOS SANTOS, Paula, TS 573. All further quotes from Paula Dos Santos come from this interview.

14 Sister Anne Arthur quoted in Stack, pp. 14–15.

15 NTAS, NTRS 226, typed transcripts of oral history interviews with 'TS' prefix, 1979–ct, SPILLETT, Peter, TS 663. All further quotes from Peter Spillett come from this interview.

16 NTAS, NTRS 226, typed transcripts of oral history interviews with 'TS' prefix, 1979–ct, BARDEN, Roy TS 755. All further quotes from Roy Barden come from this interview.

17 NTAS, NTRS 226, typed transcripts of oral history interviews with 'TS' prefix, 1979–ct, COLLINS, Bob TS 831. All further quotes from Bob Collins come from this interview unless otherwise indicated.

18 NTAS, NTRS 226, typed transcripts of oral history interviews with 'TS' prefix, 1979–ct, D'AMBROSIO, Ted TS 555. All further quotes from Ted D'Ambrosio come from this interview unless otherwise indicated.

19 NTAS, NTRS 226, typed transcripts of oral history interviews with 'TS' prefix, 1979–ct, PATTERSON, Cedric TS 600. All further quotes from Cedric Patterson come from this interview.

20 NTAS, NTRS 226, typed transcripts of oral history interviews with 'TS' prefix, 1979–ct, BULLOCK, Robin (Pappy) TS 1058. All further quotes from Robin Bullock come from this interview.

21 McKay, p. 111.

22 Stack, p. 47.

23 NTAS, Commissioner of Police, NTRS 2999, Report by SIMPSON, Sergeant C.

24 NTAS, Commissioner of Police, NTRS 2999, Report by STEPHENSON, Constable. All further quotes from Constable Stephenson are from this report.

25 NTAS, NTRS 226, typed transcripts of oral history interviews with 'TS' prefix, 1979–ct, GURD, Charles, TS 678. All further quotes from Charles Gurd come from this interview unless otherwise indicated.

UNCERTAIN LIGHT OF DAWN

1 NTAS, NTRS 226, typed transcripts of oral history interviews with 'TS' prefix, 1979–ct, MEANEY, Jack, TS 558. All further quotes from Jack Meaney come from this interview.

2 NTAS, NTRS 226, typed transcripts of oral history interviews with 'TS' prefix, 1979–ct, BEARE, Hedley, TS 917. All further quotes from Hedley Beare come from this interview.

3 NTAS, NTRS 226, typed transcripts of oral history interviews with 'TS' prefix, 1979–ct, PAULING, Tom, TS 301. All further quotes from Tom Pauling come from this interview.

4 McKay, p. 141.

5 NTAS, Steedman, Pete, NTRS 2366, Transcripts of interviews relating to Cyclone Tracy, 1975–1975, BRENNAN, Harold (Tiger), TS 7901 All further quotes from Tiger Brennan come from this interview unless otherwise indicated.

6 NTAS, NTRS 226, typed transcripts of oral history interviews with 'TS' prefix, 1979–ct, CORMICK, Irene, TS 796. All further quotes from Irene Cormick come from this interview.

7 NTAS, NTRS 226, typed transcripts of oral history interviews with 'TS' prefix, 1979–ct, HAWKINS, Alan, TS 1088. All further quotes from Hawkins from this source.

8 'Institutional response and Indigenous experiences of Cyclone Tracy', Haynes K., Bird D. K., Carson D., Larkin S. & Mason M., National Climate Change Adaptation Research Facility, Gold Coast, 2011

(Referred to throughout the rest of this book as the Haynes Report.)

9 Gay Alcorn quoted in Tumarkin, p. 242.

10 Quoted in 'Darwin rebuilt', *Returning to Nothing: The Meaning of Lost Places*, Peter Read, Cambridge University Press, 1996.

11 NTAS, NTRS 226, typed transcripts of oral history interviews with 'TS' prefix, 1979–ct, BAUER, F. H. (Slim), TS 495. All further quotes from Dr Slim Bauer come from this interview.

12 NTAS, NTRS 226, typed transcripts of oral history interviews with 'TS' prefix, 1979–ct, CARROLL, Elizabeth, TS 762. All further quotes from Elizabeth Carroll come from this interview.

13 *Telling Stories: Indigenous History and Memory in Australia and New Zealand*, Bain Attwood and Fiona Magowan (eds), 'In the absence of vita as genre: the making of the Roy Kelly story', Basil Sansom, Allen & Unwin, 2001.

14 'The Year Zero and the North Australian frontier', *Tracking Knowledge in North Australian Landscapes*, by Deborah Rose and Anne Clarke, NARU, Darwin, 1997.

15 'How accurate are memories of 9/11?', Ingfei Chen, *Scientific American,* 6 September 2011.

16 NTAS, Commissioner of Police, NTRS 2999, report by TOWNSEND, Constable G.

17 *The Death of Luigi Trastulli and Other Stories*, Alessandro Portelli, State University of New York Press, 1991, p. 25.

18 'Oral history: facts and fiction', Patrick O'Farrell, *Quadrant,* vol. 23, no. 11, November 1979.

19 'Making disaster pay', Stephen Fraser, *Huffington Post*, 4 April 2013. All further quotes from Stephen Fraser come from this article.

THE MISSING AND THE DEAD

1 NTAS, Commissioner of Police, NTRS 2999, Report by BOURNE, Constable.

2 NTAS, Commissioner of Police, NTRS 3001, files relating to the identification of deceased persons after Cyclone Tracy, 1974–83, notebook, Robin Bullock.

3 Also spelled Leone in some records.

4 'Why Darwin must have something to say', Tess Lea, *Crikey*, 3 April 2014.

5 *Darwin*, Tess Lea, New South, 2014. All quotes from Lea come from this book unless otherwise indicated.

6 Paul Toohey, quoted in Tumarkin.

7 'Bombing toll could be five times higher', Conor Byrne, *Northern Territory News*, 19 January 2012.

8 Mickey Dewar, quoted in Tumarkin.

9 'Historian denies bombing toll was higher', Conor Byrne, *Northern Territory News*, 17 February 2012.

10 NTAS, Steedman, Pete, NTRS 2366, Transcripts of interviews relating to Cyclone Tracy, 1975-1975, MCLAREN, Bill, TS 7912.

11 NTAS, NTRS 226, typed transcripts of oral history interviews with 'TS' prefix, 1979–ct, TALBOT, Peter, TS 391. All further quotes from Peter Talbot come from this interview.

12 *Very Big Journey: My Life as I Remember It,* Hilda Jarman Muir, Aboriginal Studies Press, 2004.

13 NTAS, NTRS 226, typed transcripts of oral history interviews with 'TS' prefix, 1979–ct, MCLAREN, Bill, TS 7912.

14 NTAS, NTRS 226, typed transcripts of oral history interviews with 'TS' prefix, 1979–ct, HARMER Edna, TS 234. All further quotes from Edna Harmer come from this interview.

15 'Lilypad of the Arafura', Tony Clifton, *Monthly*, no. 8, 2005–06. All further quotes from Clifton come from this article.

16 Haynes Report.

17 NTAS, NTRS 226, typed transcripts of oral history interviews with 'TS' prefix, 1979–ct, COLE, Echo, TS 508. All further quotes from Echo Cole come from this interview.

18 Day quoted in Haynes Report.

19 'Volunteer divers piece together the mystery of the *Booya*', NT *Stateline*, Sarah Jaensch, 3 November 2006.

DOES ANYBODY KNOW THIS HAS HAPPENED TO US?

1 'Cyclone Tracy: A Story of Survival', a twentieth anniversary *Northern Territory News* special feature, December 1994.

2 'Tempests, thunderheads and trepidation', John Birmingham, *Brisbane Times*, 12 January 2011.

3 'Emergency 2.0: how social media proved itself in the Queensland floods', Emma Sykes, ABC Local Radio, 5 April 2011.

4 'Local people "need access to technology to survive disasters"', Mark Tran, *Guardian*, 17 October 2013.

5 Bushfires Royal Commission 2009: 155–72; Kissane 2010: 86–7, quoted in '"Catastrophic failure" theories and disaster journalism: evaluating media explanations of the Black Saturday bushfires', Burns, Alex and Eltham, Ben, *Media International Australia, Incorporating Culture And Policy*, 2010. All quotes from Burns and Eltham come from this source.

6 NTAS, NTRS 226, typed transcripts of oral history interviews with 'TS' prefix, 1979–ct, ROBERTS, Sally, TS 567.

7 NTAS, NTRS 266, typed transcripts of oral history interviews with 'TS' prefix, 1979–ct, THOROGOOD, Colonel Frank, TS 614. All further quotes from Colonel Thorogood are from this interview.

8 'Military man became Darwin's hero', Damien Murphy, *Sydney Morning Herald*, 31 October 2012.

WE WILL GET YOU ALL OUT

1 http://www.pprune.org/australia-new-zealand-pacific/473329-cyclone-tracy-1974-a.html

2 http://www.pprune.org/australia-new-zealand-pacific/473329-cyclone-tracy-1974-a.html

3 NTAS, NTRS 266, typed transcripts of oral history interviews with 'TS' prefix, 1979–ct, SEE KEE, Charles, TS 320. All further quotes from Charles See Kee come from this interview.

4 *No Man's Land: Women of the Northern Territory*, Barbara James, Collins Australia, 1989, p. 267.

5 Quoted in twentieth anniversary *Northern Territory News* special feature.

6 Bill Day, quoted in the Haynes Report.

7 'Final report of the Darwin Disaster Welfare Council' (later footnoted as the DDWC Report), Harry Giese (ed.), March 1976.

8 'Psychological disturbance in Darwin evacuees following Cyclone Tracy', G. Parker, *Medical Journal Australia,* 1975 May 24; 1(21):650–2.

9 'Cyclone Tracy and Darwin evacuees', G. Parker, *British Journal of Psychiatry,* 1977 June; 130:548–55.

TRACY, YOU BITCH

1 Quoted in Tumarkin.

2 'Female-named hurricanes kill more than male hurricanes because people don't respect them, study finds', Jason Samenow, *Washington Post*, 2 June 2014. (http://www.washingtonpost.com/blogs/capital-weather-gang/wp/2014/06/02/female-named-hurricanes-kill-more-than-male-because-people-dont-respect-them-study-finds//)

3 Quoted in Barbara James, 1989.

4 Quoted in Barbara James, 1989.

5 NTAS, NTRS 266, typed transcripts of oral history interviews with 'TS' prefix, 1979–ct, MUIRHEAD, Margaret TS 524. All further quotes from Margaret Muirhead come from this interview.

6 Read, p. 155.

7 NTAS, NTRS 2366, typed transcripts of oral history interviews with 'TS' prefix, 1979–ct, BAIRD, Evelyn TS 154. All further quotes from Evelyn Baird come from this interview.

8 Quoted in Barbara James, 1989.

9 Grant Tambling, DDWC report.

10 Quoted in Barbara James, 1989.

11 'Gender and Health', World Health Organization Report, 2002.

12 'More Stories Emerge of Rapes in Post-Katrina Chaos', John Burnett, NPR, 21 December 2005.

13 Northern Territory Annual Report 1975–6.

14 'What is the outcome of reporting rape to the police?' Study of reported rapes in Victoria 2000–03: Summary research report, Zoë Morrison, Australian Institute of Family Studies, ACSSA Newsletter no. 17, 2008.

15 Dawn Lawrie, DDWC Report.

16 'Psychological disturbance in Darwin evacuees following cyclone Tracy', G. Parker, *Medical Journal Australia*, 1975 May 24; 1(21):650–2.

17 Quoted in Read, p. 154.

18 NTAS, NTRS 226, typed transcripts of oral history interviews with

'TS' prefix, 1979–ct, HARVEY, Peter, TS 491. All further quotes from Peter Harvey come from this interview.

DARIBAH NUNGALINYA

1 Haynes Report.

2 NTAS, NTRS 266, typed transcripts of oral history interviews with 'TS' prefix, 1979–ct, O'SULLIVAN, Clement John, TS 447. All further quotes from Clem O'Sullivan come from this interview.

3 NTAS, NTRS 266, typed transcripts of oral history interviews with 'TS' prefix, 1979–ct, IVORY, Michael, TS 750. All further quotes from Michael Ivory come from this interview.

4 Mackinolty, 1994.

5 Quoted in Tumarkin.

6 Haynes Report.

7 *Bunji* was edited by Bill Day between 1971 and 1983. Chips Mackinolty has written of the magazine: 'Starting from wax stencil mimeographs, the 64 issues of *Bunji* chart the radicalisation of Aboriginal politics thousands of kilometres from better publicised events such as the Tent Embassy.'

8 NTAS, NTRS 266, typed transcripts of oral history interviews with 'TS' prefix, 1979–ct, FEJO, Lorna, TS 757. All further quotes from Lorna Fejo come from this interview.

9 *Northern Territory News*, 28 January 1975.

10 *Bunji*, September 1975.

11 Indigenous contexts of climate and change: narrating local realities within global discourses, Siri Veland, PhD thesis, Macquarie University, 2011, p. 198.

12 'Kiwirrkurra: the flood in the desert', *Australian Journal of Emergency Management,* Vol. 24 No. 1, February 2009.

13 'Immortal Ones: the road from Kununurra to Derby', *How to Make Gravy*, Paul Kelly, Penguin Books, Melbourne, 2010.

14 'Flood paintings are history in the making', Maggie Fletcher , Open ABC, 15 August 2011.

THE WILD NORTH

1 'Cyclone! Christmas in Darwin 1974', Peter Durish, Bob Howarth, Kenneth Stevens, *Sydney Morning Herald* Publications.

2 Bill McLaren, DDWC Report.

3 'Memories of pre-war Northern Territory towns', Alec Fong Lim, Occasional Papers no. 19, State Reference Library of the Northern Territory, 1990.

4 *Sitdown Up North*, Ted Egan, Kerr Books, 1977, p. 61.

5 Ianto Ware, email to the author, 20 September 2013. All quotes from Ware come from this email.

6 NTAS, NTRS 2366, typed transcripts of oral history interviews with 'TS' prefix, 1979–ct, HARITOS, Kyriakos (Jack), TS 578.

7 Bill McLaren, DDWC Report.

8 NTAS, Supreme Court of the Northern Territory, E100, Criminal dockets, annual single number series, 1955–79, file 17–30 of 1975.

9 NTAS, NTRS 226, typed transcripts of oral history interviews with 'TS' prefix, 1979–ct, REDMOND, George, TS 734.

10 Quoted in Read.

11 'Report on cyclone damage to natural vegetation in the Darwin area after Cyclone Tracy, 25 December, 1974', Stocker, G. C., Australian Government Publishing Service, 1976.

12 *Dragged Kicking and Screaming to Paradise* [second edition], Suzanne Spunner, Little Gem Productions, 1994. All further quotes from Suzanne Spunner are from this publication.

THE SHOOTING OF THE DOGS

1 Dog Dreaming, *Australian Screen*, 2001.

2 *Age*, 17 November 1977.

3 http://www.pprune.org/australia-new-zealand-pacific/473329-cyclone-tracy-1974-a.html

4 Quoted in *Darwin*, Tess Lea.

5 'Building Resilience: Animals and Communities Coping in Emergencies', Australian Animal Welfare Strategy (AAWS) and World Society for the Protection of Animals (WSPA), 2012.

6 'Animal welfare during natural disasters', Australian Animal Welfare Strategy (AAWS), 12 November 2012.

7 'The Warmun evacuation', Leanne Hodge, Open ABC, 7 December 2011.

8 NTAS, NTRS 226, typed transcripts of oral history interviews with 'TS' prefix, 1979–ct, BROWN, George, TS 572.

9 Quoted in twentieth anniversary *Northern Territory News* special feature.

I'VE GOT TO HAVE MY TRIPS

1 *Don't Start Me Talking: Lyrics 1984–2004* (2nd ed.), Paul Kelly, Allen & Unwin, 2004.

2 'Cyclone Tracy', *Sydney Morning Herald*, 1 January 2005.

1975

1 Quoted in Durish, Howarth and Stevens.

2 'Australia's most outrageous newspaper', *7.30 Report,* Susan Everingham, 15 February 2011.

3 *7.30 Report*, 2011.

4 Ray McHenry, DDWC Report.

5 'Darwin today: is there a future?', *Australian Women's Weekly*, Kay Keavney and Keith Barlow (photographer), 17 September 1975.

6 *7.30 Report*, 1999.

7 NTAS, NTRS 1504, Commissioner of Police sign-on book and journal 1975. Please note that names of the passengers on the *Patris* have been changed.

8 *Citizens: Flowers and the Wide Sea*, Eric Rolls, UQP, 1998.

9 'After the quakes', *360 documentaries*, ABC Radio National, Kirsti Melville (producer), 9 June 2013.

I WASN'T WORRYING ABOUT BLOODY HISTORY. I WAS WORRYING ABOUT THE DAY

1 'Cyclone Tracy', Greg Holland and John McBride, *Windows on Meteorology: Australian Perspective* edited by E. K. Webb, CSIRO, 1997, p. 20.

2 'Dr Greg Holland and Professor David Karoly join Lateline', *Lateline*, ABC News, 2 September 2009.

3 Quoted in Read, p. 159.

4 Quoted in Tumarkin.

5 *Sydney Morning Herald*, 7 May 1975.

6 'Financial relief and compensation', part 1, chapter 6: Cyclone Tracy 1974, National Archives of Australia.

7 *Women's Weekly*, 1975.

8 The Anglo-Asian bungalow: housing the Commonwealth in the northern tropics of Australia, David Bridgman, School of Architecture and Design, RMIT University, July 2006.

9 Quoted in Tumarkin.

10 'Architecture sector mourns a trio of its finest', Phil Harris, *Australian*, 19 August 2011.

I MAKE THIS PLACE AS I GO

1 'Gurirr Gurirr: the contemporary continuum', Chad Creighton, *Art & Australia*, vol 50, no. 3, Autumn 2013.

2 'Deep weather', Alexis Wright, *Meanjin*, 70.2 (Winter 2011).

3 NTAS, NTRS 226, typed transcripts of oral history interviews with 'TS' prefix, 1979–ct, DERMOUDY, Peter, TS 833. All quotes from this interview unless otherwise indicated.

4 Quoted in Tumarkin.

5 *7.30 Report*, 1999.

6 *Newcastle Herald*, 19 May 1999.

7 'The 1972 Larrakia Petition', Creative Spirits, website.

8 *Bunji*, May 1978.

9 *Bunji*, January 1982.

10 *Bunji*, May 1978.

11 'Larrakia native title claim over areas of metropolitan Darwin', *Risk v Northern Territory of Australia* (Unreported, FCA, 17 May 2006, Mansfield J), AIATSIS.

12 'After the quakes', 2013.

13 'Prosper or perish: a humanist on thin ice', Tom Griffiths, *Griffith Review* 29, August 2010.

14 Wright, 2011.

15 'Risks from climate change to Indigenous communities in the tropical north of Australia', Donna Green, Sue Jackson & Joe Morrison (eds), Department of Climate Change and Energy Efficiency, Australian Government, 2009.

16 'The experience of Cyclone Tracy', Chamberlain E. R., Doube L., Milne G., Rolls M. & Western J. S., Australian Government Publishing Service, 1981.

17 'Australian floods: why were we so surprised?' Germaine Greer, *Guardian*, 15 January 2011.

18 'The flood: history reclaims the chain of ponds', Matthew Condon, *Griffith Review*, 32, May 2011.

19 'Why Darwin must have something to say', Tess Lea, *Crikey*.

20 'John Kerry: climate change a "weapon of mass destruction"', Arshad Mohammed, *Sydney Morning Herald*, 17 February 2014.

21 'First among men', *Age*, 15 February 2014.

THE SHAPE MEMORY TAKES

1 'Triumph of the deluded', Chips Mackinolty, unpublished paper, 2011.

2 'Inpex gas project gathers pace as workers move in', Penny Timms, ABC News, 14 August 2013.

3 'Pub's closure a loss to Wagait residents, tourists and ferry', Clare Rawlinson, ABC Darwin, 1 May 2013.

4 'Marking time: individual memories, public commemorations and a sense of identity', Mickey Dewar, paper presented at the Australian Historical Association Conference, Melbourne, 14 July 1996.

5 'Greg Hunt uses Wikipedia research to dismiss links between climate change and bushfires', Esther Han, Judith Ireland, *Sydney Morning Herald*, 23 October 2013.

SOURCES

BOOKS

Carpentaria, Alexis Wright, Giramondo, 2006.

Citizens: Flowers and the Wide Sea, Eric Rolls, UQP, 1998.

Cyclone Tracy: Picking Up the Pieces, Bill Bunbury, Fremantle Arts Centre Press, 1994.

Darwin, Tess Lea, New South, 2014.

Don't Start Me Talking: Lyrics 1984–2004 [2nd ed.], Paul Kelly, Allen & Unwin, 2004.

Dragged Kicking and Screaming to Paradise [2nd ed.], Suzanne Spunner, Little Gem Productions, 1994.

How to Make Gravy, Paul Kelly, Penguin Books, 2010.

Is There Anyone Alive in There?, Dr Ella Stack, Historical Society of the Northern Territory, 2013.

Kinglake-350, Adrian Hyland, Text Publishing, 2011.

No Man's Land: Women of the Northern Territory, Barbara James, Collins Australia, 1989.

Returning to Nothing: The Meaning of Lost Places, Peter Read, Cambridge University Press, 1996.

Sitdown Up North, Ted Egan, Kerr Books, 1977.

Telling Stories: Indigenous History and Memory in Australia and New Zealand, Bain Attwood and Fiona Magowan (eds), 'In the absence of vita as genre: the making of the Roy Kelly story', Basil Sansom, Allen & Unwin, 2001.

The Death of Luigi Trastulli and Other Stories, Alessandro Portelli, State University of New York Press, 1991.

The Furious Days, Alan Stretton, William Collins, Sydney, 1976.

Tracking Knowledge in North Australian Landscapes, Deborah Rose and Anne Clarke, 'The Year Zero and the North Australian frontier', NARU, Darwin, 1997.

Tracy: The Storm That Wiped Out Darwin on Christmas Day 1974, Gary McKay, Allen & Unwin, 2001.

Very Big Journey: My Life as I Remember It, Hilda Jarman Muir, Aboriginal Studies Press, 2004.

Winds of Fury, Keith Cole, Rigby, 1977.

ARTICLES AND PUBLICATIONS

'Architecture sector mourns a trio of its finest', Phil Harris, *Australian*, 19 August 2011. (http://www.theaustralian.com.au/arts/architecture-sector-mourns-a-trio-of-its-finest/story-e6frg8n6-1226117688632)

'Australian floods: why were we so surprised?', Germaine Greer, *Guardian*, 15 January 2011. (http://www.theguardian.com/environment/2011/jan/15/australian-floods-queensland-germaine-greer)

'Bombing toll could be five times higher', Conor Byrne, *Northern Territory News*, 19 January 2012. (http://dev.video.ntnews.com.au/article/2012/01/19/284121_ntnews.html)

Bunji, William Day (editor). Issues appeared at regular intervals from 1971 until 1983.

'"Catastrophic failure" theories and disaster journalism: evaluating media explanations of the Black Saturday bushfires', Burns, Alex and Eltham, Ben, *Media International Australia, Incorporating Culture and Policy*, 2010.

'Cyclone Tracy and Darwin evacuees', G. Parker, *British Journal of Psychiatry,* 1977 June; 130:548–55.

'Cyclone Tracy: a story of survival', a twentieth anniversary *Northern Territory News* special feature, December 1994.

'Cyclone Tracy', *Sydney Morning Herald*, 1 January 2005. (http://www.smh.com.au/news/National/Cyclone-Tracy/2004/12/31/1104344989839.html)

'Cyclone! Christmas in Darwin 1974', Peter Durish, Bob Howarth, Kenneth Stevens, *Sydney Morning Herald* Publication.

'Darwin today: is there a future?', *Australian Women's Weekly*, Kay Keavney and Keith Barlow (photographer), 17 September 1975.

'Deep weather', Alexis Wright, *Meanjin*, 70.2 (Winter 2011).

'First among men', *Age*, 15 February 2014. (http://www.smh.com.au/world/first-among-men-20140210-32amz.html)

'Greg Hunt uses Wikipedia research to dismiss links between climate change and bushfires', Esther Han, Judith Ireland, *Sydney Morning Herald*, 23 October 2013. (http://www.smh.com.au/federal-politics/political-news/greg-hunt-uses-wikipedia-research-to-dismiss-links-between-climate-change-and-bushfires-20131023-2w1w5.html#ixzz31WRbaHft)

'Gurirr Gurirr: the contemporary continuum', Chad Creighton, *Art & Australia*, vol. 50, no. 3, Autumn 2013.

'Historian denies bombing toll was higher', Conor Byrne, *Northern Territory News*, 17 February 2012. (http://dev.video.ntnews.com.au/article/2012/02/17/289151_ntnews.html)

'How accurate are memories of 9/11?', Ingfei Chen, *Scientific American*, 6 September 2011. (http://www.scientificamerican.com/article/911-memory-accuracy/)

'In praise of characters', Erroll Simper, *Australian*, 30 September 2013. (http://www.theaustralian.com.au/media/opinion/in-praise-of-characters/story-e6frg9to-1226729469505)

'John Kerry: climate change a "weapon of mass destruction"', Arshad Mohammed, *Sydney Morning Herald*, 17 February 2014. (http://www.smh.com.au/world/john-kerry-climate-change-a-weapon-of-mass-destruction-20140217-hvcng.html#ixzz2teSURlqE)

'Lilypad of the Arafura', Tony Clifton, *Monthly*, no. 8, 2005–06. (http://

www.themonthly.com.au/monthly-essays-tony-clifton-lilypad-arafura-australia039s-last-frontier-society-long-gone-so-what039)

'Local people "need access to technology to survive disasters"', Mark Tran, *Guardian*, 17 October 2013. (http://www.theguardian.com/global-development/2013/oct/17/local-people-access-technology-survive-disasters)

'Making disaster pay', Stephen Fraser, *Huffington Post*, 4 April 2013. (http://www.huffingtonpost.com/steve-fraser/hurricane-sandy-recovery_b_3014342.html)

'Marking time: individual memories, public commemorations and a sense of identity', Mickey Dewar, paper presented at the Australian Historical Association Conference, Melbourne, 14 July 1996.

'Memories of pre-war Northern Territory towns', Alec Fong Lim, Occasional Papers no. 19, State Reference Library of the Northern Territory, 1990.

'Military man became Darwin's hero', Damien Murphy, *Sydney Morning Herald*, 31 October 2012. (http://www.smh.com.au/comment/obituaries/military-man-became-darwins-hero-20121030-28hht.html?skin=text-only)

'Oral history: facts and fiction', Patrick O'Farrell, *Quadrant,* vol. 23, no. 11, November 1979.

'Picking up the pieces after a big blow', Chips Mackinolty, *Sydney Morning Herald*, 24 December 1994.

'Prosper or perish: a humanist on thin ice', Tom Griffiths, *Griffith Review* 29, August 2010.

'Psychological disturbance in Darwin evacuees following Cyclone Tracy', G. Parker, *Medical Journal Australia,* 1975 May 24; 1(21):650–2.

'Pub's closure a loss to Wagait residents, tourists and ferry', Clare Rawlinson, ABC Darwin, 1 May 2013. (http://www.abc.net.au/local/stories/2013/05/01/3749366.htm)

'Tempests, thunderheads and trepidation', John Birmingham, *Brisbane Times*, 12 January 2011. (http://www.brisbanetimes.com.au/environment/weather/tempests-thunderheads-and-trepidation-20110111-19mue.html#ixzz2T9q0nf9G)

'The flood: history reclaims the chain of ponds', Matthew Condon, *Griffith Review* 32, May 2011.

'Triumph of the deluded', Chips Mackinolty, unpublished paper, 2011.

'Why Darwin must have something to say', Tess Lea, *Crikey*, 3 April 2014. (http://blogs.crikey.com.au/northern/2014/04/03/why-darwin-must-have-something-to-say/)

VISUAL

'Australia's most outrageous newspaper', *7.30 Report*, Susan Everingham, 15 February 2011. (http://www.abc.net.au/7.30/content/2011/s3139724.htm)

CTC 7 News Footage, 1974 [CYCLONE TRACY APPEAL AND INTERVIEWS], 1974.

Dog Dreaming, *Australian Screen*, 2001. (http://aso.gov.au/titles/documentaries/dog-dreaming/clip3/)

'Dr Greg Holland and Professor David Karoly join Lateline', *Lateline*, ABC News, 2 September 2009.

'"Learned helplessness" leaves people in major cities unprepared to cope in natural disasters', Margot O'Neill, *Lateline*, ABC News, 23 October 2013. (http://www.abc.net.au/news/2013-10-22/city-slickers-unable-to-cope-with-disasters/5038800)

'Tracy—facing the storm', Genevieve Hussey, *7.30 Report*, 24 December 1999. (http://www.abc.net.au/7.30/stories/s75061.htm)

REPORTS

'Animal welfare during natural disasters', Australian Animal Welfare Strategy (AAWS), 12 November 2012. (http://www.australiananimalwelfare.com.au/news-m/native-and-introduced-wildlife/animal-welfare-during-natural-disasters)

'Building resilience: animals and communities coping in emergencies', Australian Animal Welfare Strategy (AAWS) and World Society for the Protection of Animals (WSPA), 2012. (http://www.australiananimalwelfare.com.au/app/webroot/files/upload/files/Building_Resilience_Workshop_2012_Report.pdf)

Consumer Price Index, Australia, June 2013. (http://www.abs.gov.au/AUSSTATS/abs@.nsf/DetailsPage/6401.0Jun%202013?OpenDocument)

'Cyclone Tracy', Greg Holland and John McBride, *Windows on*

Meteorology: Australian Perspective edited by E. K. Webb, CSIRO, 1997.

'Disruptive weather warnings and weather knowledge in remote Australian Indigenous communities', Dr Douglas Goudie, Research Associate Centre for Disaster Studies, James Cook University, for Australian Bureau of Meteorology, May 2004. (http://www.jcu.edu.au/cds/public/groups/everyone/documents/technical_report/jcutst_056224.pdf)

'Final report of the Darwin Disaster Welfare Council', Harry Giese (ed.), March 1976.

'Gender and health', World Health Organization Report, 2002.

'Institutional response and Indigenous experiences of Cyclone Tracy', Haynes K., Bird D. K., Carson D., Larkin S. & Mason M., National Climate Change Adaptation Research Facility, Gold Coast, 2011. (http://www.nccarf.edu.au/sites/default/files/attached_files_publications/Haynes_2011_Indigenous_experiences_of_Cyclone_Tracy.pdf)

'Kiwirrkurra: the flood in the desert', *Australian Journal of Emergency Management*, vol. 24 no. 1, February 2009. (http://www.em.gov.au/Documents/Kiwirrkurra%20Report%20%20the%20flood%20in%20the%20desert_VOL24ISSUE1.pdf)

'Larrakia native title claim over areas of metropolitan Darwin', *Risk v Northern Territory of Australia* (Unreported, FCA, 17 May 2006, Mansfield J), AIATSIS. (http://www.aiatsis.gov.au/_files/ntru/resources/resourceissues/risk.pdf)

'Report on cyclone damage to natural vegetation in the Darwin area after Cyclone Tracy, 25 December 1974', Stocker, G. C., Australian Government Publishing Service, 1976.

'Risks from climate change to Indigenous communities in the tropical north of Australia', Donna Green, Sue Jackson & Joe Morrison (eds), Department of Climate Change and Energy Efficiency, Australian Government, 2009. (http://web.science.unsw.edu.au/~donnag/Risks%20from%20Climate%20Change%20to%20Indigenous%20%20%20Communities%20in%20the%20Tropical%20North%20of%20Australia.pdf)

'The experience of Cyclone Tracy', Chamberlain E. R., Doube L., Milne G., Rolls M. & Western J. S., Australian Government Publishing Service, 1981.

'The Warmun evacuation', Leanne Hodge, Open ABC, 7 December 2011. (https://open.abc.net.au/projects/aftermath-08vh8ac/contributions/the-warmun-evacuation-leanne-hodge-91ax5ln/in/places/warmun+wa)

'What is the outcome of reporting rape to the police?', Study of reported rapes in Victoria 2000–03: Summary research report, Zoë Morrison, Australian Institute of Family Studies, ACSSA Newsletter no. 17, 2008. (http://www.aifs.gov.au/acssa/pubs/newsletter/n17.html#What)

Northern Territory Annual Report 1975–6.

RADIO AND SOUND RECORDINGS

'After the quakes', *360 documentaries*, ABC Radio National, Kirsti Melville (producer), 9 June 2013. (http://www.abc.net.au/radionational/programs/360/after-the-quakes/4722828)

'Emergency 2.0: how social media proved itself in the Queensland floods', Emma Sykes, ABC Local Radio, 5 April 2011. (http://www.abc.net.au/local/audio/2011/04/05/3182906.htm?site=not-regionalised&source=rss)

'Flood devastation as bad as Cyclone Tracy', Paul Lockyer, AM, ABC Radio, 11 January 2011. (http://www.abc.net.au/am/content/2011/s3110187.htm)

'Flood paintings are history in the making', Maggie Fletcher, Open ABC, 15 August 2011. (https://open.abc.net.au/posts/-flood-paintings-are-history-in-the-making-59yp9aq)

'Inpex gas project gathers pace as workers move in', Penny Timms, ABC News, 14 August 2013. (http://www.abc.net.au/news/2013-08-14/inpex-gas-project-first-fifo-workers-arrive-at-village/4885974)

'More stories emerge of rapes in post-Katrina chaos', John Burnett, NPR, 21 December 2005 (http://www.npr.org/templates/story/story.php?storyId=5063796)

'Wendy James', *ABC Conversations with Richard Fidler*, 3 October 2013. (http://www.abc.net.au/local/stories/2013/10/03/3861510.htm)

WEBSITES

'Financial relief and compensation', part 1, chapter 6: Cyclone Tracy 1974, National Archives of Australia. (http://guides.naa.gov.au/records-about-northern-territory/part1/chapter6/6.5.aspx)

'The 1972 Larrakia Petition', Creative Spirits. (http://www.creativespirits.info/aboriginalculture/land/the-1972-larrakia-petition#ixzz2gQhkUbul)

http://www.pprune.org/australia-new-zealand-pacific/473329-cyclone-tracy-1974-a.html

THESES

The Anglo-Asian bungalow: housing the Commonwealth in the northern tropics of Australia, David Bridgman, School of Architecture and Design, RMIT University, July 2006.

Aboriginal fringe dwellers in Darwin: cultural persistence or culture of resistance?, William Bartlett Day BA (Hons), Unpublished thesis, Department of Anthropology, the University of Western Australia, 2001. (http://bill-day-bunji.tripod.com/Bill-Day-Thesis/Bill_Day_Thesis.c.htm)

Secret life of wounded spaces. Traumascapes in the contemporary Australia, Maria M. Tumarkin, PhD thesis, Department of History, University of Melbourne, 2002.

Indigenous contexts of climate and change: narrating local realities within global discourses, Siri Veland, PhD thesis, Macquarie University, 2011.

PERSONAL

Personal interviews with: Bill Wilson, Beechworth, 20 September 2012. Diane McLennan, Melbourne, 28 March 2011. Francis Good, Melbourne, 14 November 2012. Hip Strider, Humpty Doo, July, 2011. Julia Church, Canberra, 20 June 2013. Katrina Fong Lim, Darwin, 25 September 2013. Right Honorable Malcolm Fraser, Melbourne, 16 July 2013. Sir Neville Barwick, Melbourne, 27 April 2011. Stephanie Nganjmirra Thompson, Darwin, 19 January 2012.

Dr Ianto Ware, email to the author, 20 September 2013

NORTHERN TERRITORY ARCHIVES SERVICE

GENERAL COLLECTIONS—NORTHERN TERRITORY ARCHIVES SERVICE

Commissioner of Police, NTRS 2999, Reports by police officers of personal experiences relating to Cyclone Tracy 1974–5. Reports by:

BAKER, Detective Sergeant Thomas.

BARRY, Constable Terence David.

BOURNE, Constable.

SIMPSON, Sergeant C.

SMITH, Constable Dane.

STEPHENSON, Constable.

TOWNSEND, Constable G.

Commissioner of Police, NTRS 2978, Master indexes relating to the evacuation of Darwin after Cyclone Tracy, 1974–5.

Supreme Court of the Northern Territory, E100, Criminal dockets, annual single number series, 1955–79, file 17 to 30 of 1975.

Police Station, Darwin, F760, Watchhouse keeper's day journals, 1970–80, [before and after cyclone Tracy from 1974 to 1979].

Commissioner of Police, NTRS 3001, Files relating to the identification of deceased persons after Cyclone Tracy, 1974–83, notebook, Robin Bullock.

Commissioner of Police, NTRS 1504, Sign-on book and journal 1975.

ORAL HISTORIES—NORTHERN TERRITORY ARCHIVES SERVICE

NTAS, NTRS 226, typed transcripts of oral history interviews with interviews with 'TS' prefix, 1979–ct, AH TOY, Lily, TS 1.

NTAS, NTRS 226, typed transcripts of oral history interviews with 'TS' prefix, 1979–ct, BAIRD, Tom, TS 155.

NTAS, NTRS 226, typed transcripts of oral history interviews with 'TS' prefix, 1979–ct, BAIRD, Evelyn, TS 154.

NTAS, NTRS 226, typed transcripts of oral history interviews with 'TS' prefix, 1979–ct, BARDEN, Roy, TS 755.

NTAS, NTRS 226, typed transcripts of oral history interviews with 'TS' prefix, 1979–ct, BAUER, F. H. (Slim), TS 495.

NTAS, NTRS 226, typed transcripts of oral history interviews with 'TS' prefix, 1979–ct, BEARE, Hedley, TS 917.

NTAS, NTRS 226, typed transcripts of oral history interviews with 'TS' prefix, 1979–ct, BISHOP, Ida, TS 773.

NTAS, Steedman, Pete, NTRS 2366, Transcripts of interviews relating to Cyclone Tracy, 1975–1975, BOWDITCH, Jim, TS 7902.

NTAS, Steedman, Pete, NTRS 2366, Transcripts of interviews relating to Cyclone Tracy, 1975–1975, BRENNAN, Harold (Tiger), TS 7901.

NTAS- NTRS 226, typed transcripts of oral history interviews with 'TS' prefix, 1979–ct, BRIEC, Bernard, TS 830.

NTAS, NTRS 226, typed transcripts of oral history interviews with 'TS' prefix, 1979–ct, BROWN, George, TS 572.

NTAS, NTRS 226, typed transcripts of oral history interviews with 'TS' prefix, 1979–ct, BULLOCK, Robin (Pappy), TS 1058.

NTAS, NTRS 226, typed transcripts of oral history interviews with 'TS' prefix, 1979–ct, CAIRNS, Kate, TS 549.

NTAS, NTRS 226, typed transcripts of oral history interviews with 'TS' prefix, 1979–ct, CARROLL, Elizabeth, TS 762.

NTAS, NTRS 226, typed transcripts of oral history interviews with 'TS' prefix, 1979–ct, COLE, Echo, TS 508.

NTAS, NTRS 226, typed transcripts of oral history interviews with 'TS' prefix, 1979–ct, COLLINS, Bob, TS 831.

NTAS, NTRS 226, typed transcripts of oral history interviews with 'TS' prefix, 1979–ct, CORMICK, Irene, TS 796.

NTAS, NTRS 226, typed transcripts of oral history interviews with 'TS' prefix, 1979–ct, CRESWICK, Richard, TS 536.

NTAS, NTRS 226, typed transcripts of oral history interviews with 'TS' prefix, 1979–ct, CHRISTODOULOU, Savvas, TS 628.

NTAS, NTRS 226, typed transcripts of oral history interviews with 'TS' prefix, 1979–ct, DERMOUDY, Peter, TS 833.

NTAS, NTRS 226, typed transcripts of oral history interviews with 'TS' prefix, 1979–ct, DOS SANTOS, Paula, TS 573.

NTAS, NTRS 226, typed transcripts of oral history interviews with 'TS' prefix, 1979–ct, FEJO, Lorna, TS 757.

NTAS, NTRS 226, typed transcripts of oral history interviews with 'TS' prefix, 1979–ct, FOSTER, Liz, TS 502.

NTAS, NTRS 226, typed transcripts of oral history interviews with 'TS' prefix, 1979–ct, FREY, Ken, TS 630.

NTAS, NTRS 226, typed transcripts of oral history interviews with 'TS' prefix, 1988–ct, GARTON, Len, TS 535.

NTAS, NTRS 226, typed transcripts of oral history interviews with 'TS' prefix, 1979–ct, GIESE, Harry, TS 755.

NTAS, NTRS 226, typed transcripts of oral history interviews with 'TS' prefix, 1979–ct, GURD, Charles, TS 678.

NTAS, NTRS 226, typed transcripts of oral history interviews with 'TS' prefix, 1979–ct, HARITOS, Kyriakos (Jack), TS 578.

NTAS, NTRS 226, typed transcripts of oral history interviews with 'TS' prefix, 1979–ct, HARMER, Edna, TS 234.

NTAS, NTRS 226, typed transcripts of oral history interviews with 'TS' prefix, 1979–ct, HARRIS, Vicki, TS 585.

NTAS, NTRS 226, typed transcripts of oral history interviews with 'TS' prefix, 1979–ct, HARVEY, Beth, TS 490.

NTAS, NTRS 226, typed transcripts of oral history interviews with 'TS' prefix, 1979–ct, HARVEY, Peter, TS 491.

NTAS, NTRS 226, typed transcripts of oral history interviews with 'TS' prefix, 1979–ct, HITCHINS, Air Commodore David, TS 458.

NTAS, NTRS 226, typed transcripts of oral history interviews with 'TS' prefix, 1979–ct, IVORY, Michael, TS 750.

NTAS, NTRS 226, typed transcripts of oral history interviews with 'TS' prefix, 1979–ct, LAWRIE, Dawn, TS 505.

NTAS, NTRS 226, typed transcripts of oral history interviews with 'TS' prefix, 1979–ct, LIDDELL, Les, TS 781.

NTAS, NTRS 226, typed transcripts of oral history interviews with 'TS' prefix, 1979–ct, MCCANN, David, TS 451.

NTAS- NTRS 226, typed transcripts of oral history interviews with 'TS' prefix, 1979–ct, MCHENRY, Ray, TS 270.

NTAS, NTRS 226, typed transcripts of oral history interviews with 'TS' prefix, 1979–ct, MCKENZIE, Malcolm, TS 759.

NTAS, Steedman, Pete, NTRS 2366, Transcripts of interviews relating to Cyclone Tracy, 1975–1975, MCLAREN, Bill, TS 7912.

NTAS, NTRS 226, typed transcripts of oral history interviews with 'TS' prefix, 1979–ct, MCLAREN, Bill, TS 7912.

NTAS, NTRS 226, typed transcripts of oral history interviews with 'TS' prefix, 1979–ct, MEANEY, Jack, TS 558.

NTAS, NTRS 266, typed transcripts of oral history interviews with 'TS' prefix, 1979–ct, MUIRHEAD, Margaret, TS 524.

NTAS, NTRS 226, typed transcripts of oral history interviews with 'TS' prefix, 1979–ct, NIXON, Curly, TS 654.

NTAS, NTRS 226, typed transcripts of oral history interviews with 'TS' prefix, 1979–ct, O'SULLLIVAN, Clement John, TS 447.

NTAS, NTRS 226, typed transcripts of oral history interviews with 'TS' prefix, 1979–ct, PERRIN, Janice, TS 537.

NTAS, NTRS 226, typed transcripts of oral history interviews with 'TS' prefix, 1979–ct, ROBERTS, Sally, TS 567.

NTAS, NTRS 226, typed transcripts of oral history interviews with 'TS' prefix, 1979–ct, SANDERS, Donald, TS 503.

NTAS, NTRS 266, typed transcripts of oral history interviews with 'TS' prefix, 1979–ct, SEE KEE, Charles, TS 320.

NTAS, NTRS 226, typed transcripts of oral history interviews with 'TS' prefix, 1979–ct, SPILLETT, Peter, TS 663.

NTAS, NTRS 226, typed transcripts of oral history interviews with 'TS' prefix, 1979–ct, PATTERSON, Cedric, TS 600.

NTAS, NTRS 226, typed transcripts of oral history interviews with 'TS' prefix, 1979–ct, PAULING, Tom, TS 301.

NTAS, NTRS 226, typed transcripts of oral history interviews with 'TS' prefix, 1979–ct, REDMOND, George, TS 734.

NTAS, NTRS 226, typed transcripts of oral history interviews with 'TS' prefix, 1979–ct, TALBOT, Peter, TS 391.

NTAS, NTRS 226, typed transcripts of oral history interviews with 'TS' prefix, 1979–ct, THOROGOOD, Colonel Frank E., TS 614.

NTAS, NTRS 226, typed transcripts of oral history interviews with 'TS' prefix, 1988–ct, TRURAN, Howard, TS 511.

NTAS, NTRS 226, typed transcripts of oral history interviews with 'TS' prefix, 1979–ct, WILKIE, W. R. (Ray), TS 675.

NTAS, NTRS 226, typed transcripts of oral history interviews with 'TS' prefix, 1979–ct, WILSON, Bill, TS 1119.

NTAS, NTRS 226, typed transcripts of oral history interviews with 'TS' prefix, 1979–ct, WRIGHT, Patricia, TS 580.

INDEX